THE ESSENTIAL
SCRIPTURES

THE ESSENTIAL
SCRIPTURES

●

A Handbook of
the Biblical Texts for
Key Doctrines

KEVIN D. ZUBER

MOODY PUBLISHERS

CHICAGO

Scripture taken from the *NEW AMERICAN STANDARD BIBLE*®, © Copyright 1960, 1962, 1963, 1968, 1971, 1972, 1973, 1975, 1977, 1995 by The Lockman Foundation. Used by permission. www.Lockman.org

Edited by Kevin Mungons
Interior Design: Puckett Smartt
Cover Design: Charles Brock

All websites and phone numbers listed herein are accurate at the time of publication but may change in the future or cease to exist. The listing of website references and resources does not imply publisher endorsement of the site's entire contents. Groups and organizations are listed for informational purposes, and listing does not imply publisher endorsement of their activities.

Library of Congress Cataloging–in–Publication Data

Names: Zuber, Kevin D., author.
Title: The essential scriptures : a handbook of the biblical texts for key
   doctrines / Kevin D. Zuber.
Description: Chicago, IL : Moody Publishers, 2021. | Includes
   bibliographical references. | Summary: "In an easy-to-use handbook
   format, this reference work moves through the headings of systematic
   theology, offering quotations of the biblical verses that undergird
   various doctrines. Drawing from the literal and trustworthy New American
   Standard Bible, theologian Kevin Zuber gives you the biblical
   underpinnings for the doctrines you believe"-- Provided by publisher.
Identifiers: LCCN 2021003118 (print) | LCCN 2021003119 (ebook) | ISBN
   9780802420787 | ISBN 9780802499073 (ebook)
Subjects: LCSH: Theology, Doctrinal--Biblical teaching.
Classification: LCC BT75.3 .Z825 2021 (print) | LCC BT75.3 (ebook) | DDC
   230/.041--dc23
LC record available at https://lccn.loc.gov/2021003118
LC ebook record available at https://lccn.loc.gov/2021003119

Originally delivered by fleets of horse-drawn wagons, the affordable paperbacks from D. L. Moody's publishing house resourced the church and served everyday people. Now, after more than 125 years of publishing and ministry, Moody Publishers' mission remains the same—even if our delivery systems have changed a bit. For more information on other books (and resources) created from a biblical perspective, go to www.moodypublishers.com or write to:

Moody Publishers
820 N. LaSalle Boulevard
Chicago, IL 60610

1 3 5 7 9 10 8 6 4 2

Printed in the United States of America

For Beverly

CONTENTS

EXPANDED TABLE OF CONTENTS

3. GOD THE FATHER: THEOLOGY PROPER

6. MAN AND SIN: BIBLICAL ANTHROPOLOGY AND HAMARTIOLOGY

7. SALVATION: SOTERIOLOGY

8. ANGELS: ANGELOLOGY

9. THE CHURCH: ECCLESIOLOGY

10. Prophecy and End Times: Eschatology

FOREWORD

by John MacArthur

Understanding Christian doctrine is understanding what Scripture teaches. The word *doctrine* means just that—teaching. All true doctrine is drawn from an accurate interpretation of the Bible. The revelation of God in Scripture, rightly interpreted, is the only source of the truth that frames Christian theology. That means handling Scripture accurately is the means of acquiring divine truth.

Kevin Zuber has provided a fresh and dynamic book that shows us the essential connection between interpretation and its conclusion—theology. He does this in a very helpful way by identifying and presenting the relevant verses for each doctrine. With those verses he provides informative expositions to show how each text informs the doctrinal conclusion. The book is both a model for developing theological conviction as well as a tutorial on how to make the connection between the biblical text and the doctrine.

You hold in your hands an extraordinary tool by a gifted scholar who understands deeply the connection between exposition and doctrine. In this volume you will become a student learning from the master. Since nothing is more important than divine truth, this is the most important exercise a believer can commit to.

— John MacArthur | *Pastor-Teacher, Grace Community Church*

INTRODUCTION

The Essential Scriptures is a work *of* systematic theology but it is not a *complete* systematic theology. Readers will notice how the book follows the same *outline* one might find in a full volume of systematic theology—Bibliology, Theology Proper, Christology, and so on. This book, however, has a much more limited set of objectives. First, this is an attempt to provide the student of systematic theology, or actually anyone interested in the doctrines of the Bible, with succinct but informative expositions of the selected key texts in order to show how those texts relate to and inform the doctrine indicated in the headings under which they are found. Second, this is intended to show the way for students to discover how to "do theology"; that is, this book is full of examples of how it's done so that students and Bible readers can learn how to discern the key texts and relate them to the pertinent doctrines of systematic theology.

This handbook is intended to be a supplement to the study of systematic theology. It does not address and explain all points of doctrine as would a more complete systematic theology. Furthermore, this book cannot reproduce all the biblical texts, and does not attempt to provide a full exposition of the key (selected) biblical texts from which the biblical doctrines emerge.

A NOTE ON THE AUTHOR'S
THEOLOGICAL ORIENTATION

In a work such as this some authorial disclaimers are in order. First, this book is not intended to be exhaustive, nor does it claim to be definitive. As noted already, it does not contain every single one of the biblical texts that might be included. Other theologians will disagree with my selections, and they will think I missed some key texts. All I can say is, I will admit there are many texts I think are missing but these are the texts that I think are most essential. And as for the texts that are included, I can only say, the texts that *are* included are those *I* think are key. Actually, I look forward to those critiques and discussions. (Arguing over matters of doctrine is what professional theologians do!) This pertains to the doctrines selected as well. Some will think key doctrinal points are missing and others are over-represented. Again, all I can say is these are the doctrinal areas I have chosen. There may be more and other books following this format that can (I hope will) be written to cover the missing texts and doctrines.

Now, having spoken about the doctrines which I have chosen, perhaps some further information about me will shed some light on that selection. In matters of soteriology I describe myself as a Calvinist and reformed (the small "r" is important). In matters of soteriology I do not subscribe to all of the nomenclature of covenant theology but I do hold to such reformed doctrines as predestination, sovereign election, and particular redemption. (I have included the texts used by those who hold to general redemption in order to respond to them from the position of particular redemption.) I am also a premillennialist and I do not eschew the label of Dispensationalist (the capital "D" is important). Further, in matters of eschatology I am pre-tribulational and I believe in a literal, future millennial kingdom on the earth. (These positions will be made clear at the appropriate points in this volume.) Finally, I am a presuppositional theologian. Often the designation "presuppositional" is used to designate one's apologetics—and I am, indeed, presuppositional in my apologetics. However, I think "presuppositional theologian" is more descriptive of my actual practice, which the reader should be able to recognize in the several instances of "doing theology" in what follows.

A NOTE ON THE FORMAT

This handbook is divided by chapters, each of which is devoted to one theological *loci* or topics of systematic theology. In each chapter there are a series of subheadings that indicate the particular matters that one might find in a typical volume of systematic theology. (Again, this is not meant to be exhaustive and so the subheads do not necessarily cover every possible matter in that *loci* nor do they necessarily flow together.)

Under these subheadings the key texts (using the New American Standard Bible; NASB 95) are listed and reproduced. This is a key feature of this handbook. By reproducing these texts the student of theology is able to find the key texts printed in proximity to one another for easier reference and study. Also, this allows the reader to follow the exposition in the comments with immediate reference to the pertinent text.

After the text comes the comments and brief explanation of how that verse informs the doctrine under consideration. There are several types of comments. At times several texts are grouped together; this indicates that the comments will address all of them together, usually because these several texts are making the same or a similar point. At other times the comments on the text are brief. This may indicate that the way the text contributes to understanding the doctrine is fairly clear and needs little elaboration. Also, a text with a brief comment may indicate that the point to be made has been made already or will be made in other comments. The benefits of these first two types of comments are (1) they identify and bring together the key texts for comparison and study, and (2) they provide the student the most relevant ideas to look for in these texts. The third type of comments are much more extensive and are more detailed in terms of explanation and exposition. This type of commentary indicates that these texts are the most vital in articulating the doctrine being discussed. (Also, in the interest of full disclosure, the texts with extended comments indicate areas of particular interest to the author.)

Theology is for everyone. Indeed, everyone needs to be a theologian. In reality, everyone is a theologian—of one sort or another. And therein lies the problem. There is nothing wrong with being an amateur theologian or a professional theologian, but there is everything wrong with being an ignorant or sloppy theologian.[1]

---

1. Charles C. Ryrie, *Basic Theology: A Popular Systematic Guide to Understanding Biblical Truth* (Chicago: Moody Publishers, 1999), 9.

CHAPTER 1

PROLEGOMENA

Prolegomena, from the Greek words pro ("before") and legō ("word"), is a preliminary part of the study of systematic theology that answers questions such as "What is the nature of theology?" and "What are the objectives and purposes of theology?"

WHAT IS THEOLOGY?

Knowledge of God

Our wisdom, in so far as it ought to be deemed true and solid Wisdom, consists almost entirely of two parts: the knowledge of God and of ourselves.[1]

The knowledge of God must be the primary objective of life.

> **DEUTERONOMY 6:5**
> You shall love the LORD your God with all your heart and with all your soul and with all your might.

In Matthew 22:37–38 Jesus confirms that this is "the great and foremost commandment." This is not a commandment to seek an emotional attachment to Yahweh but it is a command to engage every facet of one's person—intellect, emotions and will—in one's commitment to God. The term for *heart* (Hebrew *lēb, lēbāb*) is not limited to one's emotions but includes all aspects of one's inner life. "[It] denotes the seat of emotion (1 Sam. 2:1), desire (Ps. 37:4), thought (Gen. 6:5), and decision (1 Chr. 12:38)."[2] Here the "soul" (Hebrew *nepeš*) is the inner man from which the deepest feelings often spring (see Isa. 26:9; Ps. 42:5, 11; 63:1; 103:1–2, 22). The term *might* (Hebrew *meʾōd*) has the notion "abundant force," so perhaps the idea there is that one will love God with "full intensity." The command here is to love God with a focused and intent mind, with the deepest intensity of one's being, and with maximum effort.

To gain the true knowledge of God, a person must earnestly engage the intellect to know God, must have a heartfelt desire to love God, and must make a sincere commitment to God that leads to earnest effort to obey and serve God.

> **PSALM 42:2**
>
> My soul thirsts for God, for the living God;
> When shall I come and appear before God?

> **PSALM 63:1**
>
> O God, You are my God; I shall seek You earnestly;
> My soul thirsts for You, my flesh yearns for You,
> In a dry and weary land where there is no water.

The psalmist's desire for a relationship with God is likened to a deep yearning for water, as when one finds himself in a desert and is extremely thirsty. The psalm title of Psalm 63 identifies the psalmist as David and adds the location as "in the wilderness of Judah." This is significant, for this part of the land was often extremely dry and at certain times of the year access to sources of water was difficult if not impossible. Life in such a location required constant attention to satisfying the physical need for food and water. This is the degree of devotion that is necessary for anyone who desires the knowledge of God. The terms *soul* and *flesh* refer to the inner and outer man.

The psalmist is saying his desire for God involves his whole being. The effort to gain the true knowledge of God requires this same level of yearning and desire.

> **PSALM 73:25**
> Whom have I in heaven *but You*?
> And besides You, I desire nothing on earth.

The terms *in heaven* and *on earth* are opposites that, when used together in the same context, indicate a totality. There is nothing in heaven or found on earth that the psalmist desires more than God Himself. The psalmist's desire for God is all-encompassing. The term *desire* (Hebrew *ḥāpēṣ*) often has the notion of delight. For the psalmist the greatest delight in heaven or on earth is the knowledge of God. The pursuit of the knowledge of God requires a singular focus that prioritizes the knowledge of the transcendent over the knowledge of the merely temporal.

WHY STUDY THEOLOGY?

To Know God

> **JEREMIAH 9:24**
> "But let him who boasts boast of this, that he understands and knows Me, that I am the LORD who exercises lovingkindness, justice and righteousness on earth; for I delight in these things," declares the LORD.

The primary pursuit of theology must be the knowledge of God—or better, a personal relationship with God. The goal of theology is not accomplished by merely accumulating more facts and information about God. The goal of theology is personal knowledge of God Himself and a close living relationship with Him. The term *understands* (Hebrew *śākal, haskêl*) has the connotation of "practical insight" and the term *know* (Hebrew *yādaʻ*) has the connotation of "intimate knowledge." The study of theology is meant to provide practical knowledge for one's life and for living in a personal relationship with God. Specifically, one must know God's lovingkindness (Hebrew *hesed*)—His "loyal love" (i.e., His commitment to His covenant promises) and His justice and righteousness (i.e., His quality of fairness and His external demonstration of rectitude). God is just and right (in Himself) and all that He does is just and right.

> **JOHN 17:3**
> This is eternal life, that they may know You, the only true God, and Jesus Christ whom You have sent.

The scriptural notion of "eternal life" is not merely unending life. It is the opposite of "eternal death," which is eternal separation from God (see **Personal Eschatology**). Eternal life is a quality of life—a full, joyful, blessed life. It is a manner of living life—with the rich experience of a relationship with God that gives life meaning and value and purpose. It is the life humans were meant to live and will live in the eternal presence of God. Believers have this life now in their relationship with Jesus Christ (see John 3:36). To know God is the highest goal; indeed it is the very purpose of human life (see Jer. 9:24).

Question 1: What is the chief end of man?
Answer: Man's chief end is to glorify God and to enjoy him forever.[3]

To Know Christ

> **JOHN 20:30–31**
> Therefore many other signs Jesus also performed in the presence of the disciples, which are not written in this book; [31] but these have been written so that you may believe that Jesus is the Christ, the Son of God; and that believing you may have life in His name.

This is the purpose statement or thesis of John's gospel. John is telling his readers that he wrote so as to convince them that Jesus of Nazareth was and is the Messiah and the Son of God. He wanted his readers to know not merely some of the stories and incidents of the life of Jesus, but to understand what those accounts revealed (and what the signs and miracles He performed verified)—namely, that Jesus was God (see John 1:1–3; 8:58) and that He came to reveal God (see John 1:18; 14:7–9). John is telling his readers that his gospel enables them to know Jesus Christ and through Him to know God. In principle this thesis may be applied to the whole of the Bible; the purpose of the Bible is to reveal God, His nature, His will, His eternal purposes, and His salvation to enable us to know Him (see John 17:3).

To Know God's Thoughts

> **DEUTERONOMY 29:29**
> The secret things belong to the LORD our God, but the things revealed belong to us and to our sons forever, that we may observe all the words of this law.

The knowledge of God is utterly dependent on His self-revelation. There are truths about Him—His nature (e.g., the Trinity), His attributes, His eternal decrees—that we, as finite (and even fallen) creatures, could never discover by ourselves (see Job 11:7 and the exchange between Job and the LORD in Job chapters 38–42). There is information that only He knows such as the truth about creation (since only He was present at creation) and the events of the future (since He is the sovereign God "who works all things after the counsel of His will" [Eph. 1:11b]; see Isa. 46:10). On the other hand, we can be sure that what God has revealed is true (see John 17:17) and that we can know and understand His revelation well enough to believe it and obey it (see 1 John 5:20).

> **JOB 11:7**
> Can you discover the depths of God?
> Can you discover the limits of the Almighty?

This is a rhetorical question that assumes the answer is negative. It is an admission that as mere men—finite creatures of God—on our own, we are not equipped (intellectually or morally) to ascertain fully the nature of the transcendent, infinite, eternal God.

> **ISAIAH 55:8–9**
>
> "For My thoughts are not your thoughts,
> Nor are your ways My ways," declares the LORD.
> ⁹ "For *as* the heavens are higher than the earth,
> So are My ways higher than your ways
> And My thoughts than your thoughts."

The context of Isaiah 55 reveals that Yahweh offers the sinful and rebellious nation of Israel (see Isa. 1:4ff; 46:12; 48:4) spiritual nourishment and life (Isa. 55:1–3) through the ministry of the Messiah (descendant of "David," Isa. 55:3; "leader and commander," Isa. 55:4; "Holy One of Israel," Isa. 55:5). The invitation to the nation to repent is urged (Isa. 55:6–7a) and the compassion of Yahweh is assured (Isa. 55:7b). But this mercy and grace is not something the nation had expected, nor is the work and compassion of the Messiah something human reason would have conceived of on its own. How could a righteous God offer such a sinful people not only the opportunity to repent ("forsake his way," "return to the LORD (Yahweh)," Isa. 55:7) but also send them a merciful and compassionate Messiah? Two clauses, which begin with the word "for" (Hebrew *ki*), explain the dilemma. First, Yahweh asserts that His thoughts and ways (intentions and plans) are not to be judged by how human beings reason and calculate. His greater knowledge and His superior ways cannot be assessed from the limited knowledge and narrow perspective of mere men. Second, His divine perspective is greater—"as the heavens are higher than the earth" (Isa. 55:9)—than is the perspective of man. Simply put, Yahweh knows more and sees further than we do. His perspective is morally superior to that of fallen humans. Human beings should not question the wisdom of God's mercy and grace but should embrace the Messiah in repentance and faith.

To Promote Sound Doctrine and Teaching, and to Refute False Teaching

> **2 TIMOTHY 4:2–3**
>
> Preach the word; be ready in season *and* out of season; reprove, rebuke,

exhort, with great patience and instruction. ³ For the time will come when they will not endure sound doctrine; but *wanting* to have their ears tickled, they will accumulate for themselves teachers in accordance to their own desires.

TITUS 1:9
Holding fast the faithful word which is in accordance with the teaching, so that he will be able both to exhort in sound doctrine and to refute those who contradict.

Paul exhorted Timothy and Titus to preach and teach the word (understood as the Scriptures) in accord with "sound doctrine." The term "sound doctrine" (Greek *hygiainousēs didaskalia*) is literally rendered "healthy teaching." Healthy teaching is the objective of good theology and is the opposite of false teaching, which is based on man's ideas rather than the revealed truth of God in His Word. "**Sound** translates *hugiainō*, from which we derive the English *hygienic*. It has the basic meaning of being healthy and wholesome, referring to that which protects and preserves life. In his preaching and teaching, it should be the pastor's sole objective to enlighten his congregation in **doctrine** that protects and preserves their spiritual health."[4]

To Test the Teaching of Others

1 JOHN 4:1
Beloved, do not believe every spirit, but test the spirits to see whether they are from God, because many false prophets have gone out into the world.

It is an unfortunate reality that there are false teachers and there have always been many of them. This requires that every truth claim be tested by the only standard of truth available—namely, the Word of God (see John 17:17, "Your word is truth"). The task of theology is not primarily to integrate other supposed avenues or sources of truth but to investigate them, test them, and in light of the truth divinely revealed in the Scriptures, to expose them and, if necessary, to reject them. That requires a thorough understanding of the theology contained in the Scriptures.

To Live a Life Approved and Be Equipped

> **2 TIMOTHY 3:17**
> So that the man of God may be adequate, equipped for every good work.

The study of theology requires diligence (see Prov. 2:1–5 under **Solomon on How to Study Theology**) so as to be "approved to God" (2 Tim. 2:15). To be "approved" (Greek *dokimos*) means to be tested and found genuine (e.g., as in testing and approving coins and paper currency). The opposite of approved is "ashamed," that is, embarrassingly exposed as unworthy, illegitimate, and false. The study of the Scriptures and theology is what qualifies and equips one to avoid this shameful exposure. The term "adequate" (Greek *artios*) indicates that one is capable and proficient. When one is proficient with the Word of God, then one is equipped, prepared, and supplied to live for, and to serve God.

To Be Filled with Wisdom and Knowledge

> **COLOSSIANS 1:9**
> For this reason also, since the day we heard *of it*, we have not ceased to pray for you and to ask that you may be filled with the knowledge of His will in all spiritual wisdom and understanding.

THE OBJECTIVES OF THEOLOGY

> **PROVERBS 1:1–7**
> The proverbs of Solomon the son of David, king of Israel:
> ² To know wisdom and instruction,
> To discern the sayings of understanding,
> ³ To receive instruction in wise behavior,
> Righteousness, justice and equity;
> ⁴ To give prudence to the naive,
> To the youth knowledge and discretion,
> ⁵ A wise man will hear and increase in learning,

And a man of understanding will acquire wise counsel,
⁶ To understand a proverb and a figure,
The words of the wise and their riddles.
⁷ The fear of the LORD is the beginning of knowledge;
Fools despise wisdom and instruction.

Solomon begins the book of Proverbs by listing several outcomes or objectives to be achieved by the study of his proverbs. These can reasonably be understood as also the outcomes or objectives to be achieved by the study of theology. "Wisdom" is often understood as "having a skill" (see Ex. 36:1–2 where the words translated "skillful," and "skill" are literally "wise of heart" and "wisdom.") Here the idea is that a person who knows the proverbs (and theology) will have "skill in living." A wise and knowledgeable person will be able to "discern," that is, will be able "to distinguish, divide, separate" between the good and bad, useful and worthless, profitable and wasteful. The wise person will keep gaining knowledge and increase in his or her ability to use it. This one will grow in the facility of applying knowledge in order to resolve difficult questions. The wise person understands that wisdom (as a skill applied) and knowledge (as information employed) depends on the "fear of the LORD"—which is honor in one's mind, reverence in one's heart, and submissive obedience of one's will.

> Systematic theology correlates the data of biblical revelation as a whole in order to exhibit systematically the total picture of God's self-revelation.⁵

THE KEY REQUIREMENTS OF
DOING THEOLOGY

Faith

HEBREWS 11:3, 6
By faith we understand that the worlds were prepared by the word of God, so that what is seen was not made out of things which are visible. . . .

> [6] And without faith it is impossible to please *Him*, for he who comes to God must believe that He is and *that* He is a rewarder of those who seek Him.

Doing theology requires "faith seeking understanding." This phrase was used by both Augustine and Anselm to emphasize the necessity of belief in, devotion for, and commitment to God as a requisite to right thinking about God. It is particularly important to start with faith in God when considering the matter of creation because only God was present at creation, only God has the power to create (*ex nihilo*), and only God can reveal the truth about creation—as He has done in Genesis 1 and 2. Furthermore, faith is required to "please God." In the context, it is clear that this refers to Enoch who "walked with God" (Gen. 5:24). Enoch's life of walking in faith, trust, and obedience was what "pleased God."

While many attempt to take up the task of theology in order to prove the existence of God (which would be philosophical, or theoretical theology), the biblical theologian must presuppose the existence of God. This is not a subjective "leap of faith" (i.e., "fideism") but a presupposition based on the objective truth that God has revealed Himself in the inspired Word of God— the Scriptures. In that Word it is revealed that God exists ("He is") and that He is involved in His creation.

> "I am not trying to scale your heights, Lord; my understanding is in no way equal to that. But I do long to understand your truth in some way, your truth which my heart believes and loves. For I do not seek to understand in order to believe; I believe in order to understand. For I also believe that 'Unless I believe, I shall not understand.'"[6]

Hard Work

2 TIMOTHY 2:15
> Be diligent to present yourself approved to God as a workman who does not need to be ashamed, accurately handling the word of truth.

The meaning of the word *diligence* (Greek *spoudazō*) includes the nuances of "haste," "eagerness," and "persistence." Paul is urging Timothy to "zealous persistence" in his study of the "word of truth." Study of the Bible and theology is not a task that one undertakes half-heartedly or with indifference. This is a task one takes up with the understanding that God Himself will judge one's effort and accuracy, and that one may be "approved" (Greek *dokimos*) or "ashamed." The task requires one to accurately handle the word of truth—the Scriptures or the gospel. "Handling accurately" (Greek *orthotomeō*) is literally "to cut straight." As a bricklayer must do his work following a "straight line" as he lays his bricks and as a farmer must follow a "straight line" in plowing the furrows in a field, so the one who handles the Word of God must be careful and conscientious as he aligns his teaching with the truth of the Word of God.

Humility

> **PROVERBS 3:5–6**
> Trust in the LORD with all your heart
> And do not lean on your own understanding.
> [6] In all your ways acknowledge Him,
> And He will make your paths straight.

> **PROVERBS 15:33**
> The fear of the LORD is the instruction for wisdom,
> And before honor *comes* humility.

These well-known verses are applicable not just to one's practical life of faith but to the practice of theology as well. It is imperative for theologians young and old to guard against the pride that allows one's own thoughts (and desires) to dominate and regulate one's theology.

SOLOMON ON HOW TO STUDY THEOLOGY

> **PROVERBS 2:1–5**
> My son, if you will receive my words
> And treasure my commandments within you,
> [2] Make your ear attentive to wisdom,
> Incline your heart to understanding;

> ³ For if you cry for discernment,
> Lift your voice for understanding;
> ⁴ If you seek her as silver
> And search for her as for hidden treasures;
> ⁵ Then you will discern the fear of the LORD
> And discover the knowledge of God.

Solomon indicates that the objectives to be achieved by the study of Proverbs will not be gained easily. The knowledge gained must not be merely received (an external hearing) but treasured (taken internally and personally valued). This knowledge will be gained only when one's ear is attentive (Hebrew *haqšîḇ*), given to thoughtful listening, and when there is an inclination (Hebrew *taṭṭeh*; lit. "bending toward") of one's heart's desire and one's mind. One must ask, even "cry" loudly ("lift your voice"), for wisdom. The term "cry" (Hebrew *qārā'*) has the notion of calling out after someone or to summon someone.

The idea here is that wisdom will not come to a passive learner. This knowledge will take effort like the effort to mine precious metals, which do not lie on the surface of the earth. Only focused, determined, and sustained effort will bring about the necessary skill of discernment and the true knowledge of God.

THEOLOGY AND THE BIBLICAL WORLDVIEW

Right Theology Is Crucial to Forming a Biblical Worldview

1 CORINTHIANS 1:18
For the word of the cross is foolishness to those who are perishing, but to us who are being saved it is the power of God.

1 CORINTHIANS 1:25
Because the foolishness of God is wiser than men, and the weakness of God is stronger than men.

> **1 CORINTHIANS 2:12–14**
>
> Now we have received, not the spirit of the world, but the Spirit who is from God, so that we may know the things freely given to us by God, [13] which things we also speak, not in words taught by human wisdom, but in those taught by the Spirit, combining spiritual *thoughts* with spiritual *words*.
>
> [14] But a natural man does not accept the things of the Spirit of God, for they are foolishness to him; and he cannot understand them, because they are spiritually appraised.

A "worldview" is a comprehensive set of ideas, values, beliefs, and convictions which a person holds (consciously or unconsciously) about reality, truth, ethics, beauty, etc. and how one is to live in the world. "A worldview is *the framework of our most basic beliefs that shapes our view **of** and **for** the world and is the basis of our decisions and actions.*"[7] The worldview of the Bible cannot be found in human wisdom. In fact, there is a fundamental antithesis between the biblical worldview and all man-centered, humanly conceived, and temporally focused worldviews. No humanly conceived philosophy or man-centered religion or ideology will enable one to understand who God is, or to make sense of the world God created, or live in a way pleasing to God, or provide a way of salvation to the knowledge of God, or enable a person to have fellowship with God (see Deut. 29:29).

In 1 Corinthians Paul is dealing with a church that was enamored with Greek philosophy. Many of the problems of this church stemmed from their attempt to combine Greek philosophical notions (man's wisdom) with elements of the teaching Paul had given to them when he preached the gospel to them (God's wisdom). Their division into factions that followed certain teachers (see 1 Cor. 1:12) was following the pattern of the students of Greek philosophy who divided up into rival schools of philosophy such as the Stoics and Epicureans (see Acts 17:18). Their problems with the resurrection (see 1 Cor. 15) stemmed from Greek philosophical views that held the physical world in contempt (as in Platonism) and saw the realm of the ideals or platonic (spiritual) forms as the only good. A bodily resurrection, which would be a return to this physical world, was unacceptable to them, as can be seen by the reactions of the philosophers to Paul's preaching of Christ's resurrection in Acts 17:32a.

Paul wants to make it clear to the Corinthians that when the gospel is preached ("the word of the cross," 1 Cor. 1:18a), it is foolishness to the world. And conversely, he wants them to know that "human wisdom" is foolishness to God (1 Cor. 1:20b; 1:25). Paul reminds them that they were not called because they were among the philosophically wise or worldly nobles (as judged by Greek philosophy or Greek social and class structures; 1 Cor. 1:26). Rather, God calls and saves (1 Cor. 1:27, 30) those the world considers foolish, weak, and base (1 Cor. 1:26–28) and He does this to emphatically "nullify" (1 Cor. 1:28b) worldly wisdom. He does this so that He is the One in whom we boast (i.e., we honor, revere, and trust Him alone) and so that our "faith would not rest on the wisdom of men [i.e., any other worldview, religion, philosophy, or ideology], but on the power of God" (1 Cor. 2:5), which is the "word of the cross" (1 Cor. 1:18).

However, it is to be understood that this "word of the cross" is true wisdom (1 Cor. 2:6ff). The so-called wise men of this world do not see it as such because it is not revealed to them (1 Cor. 2:9, 14); but this wisdom is revealed to those who have received "the Spirit who is from God" (1 Cor. 2:12), that is, to those who have been born again by the Spirit (see John 3:3–8; Titus 3:5–6; 1 Peter 1:3), to those who are taught by the Spirit (see 1 John 2:27).

Evangelicals understand that the concept of worldview has immense implications for Christianity. If everyone possesses a worldview—a comprehensive, unifying perspective in terms of which we interpret the cosmos and live our lives—then it is in terms of our worldview that Christians should live in the world to God's glory, defend the faith to unbelievers, and live out the implications of God's revealed will. The Christian worldview is rooted in the Bible: the transcendent, triune God, who sovereignly created and redeemed heaven and earth, provides the ultimate context for understanding all reality.[8]

> **COLOSSIANS 3:2**
>
> Set your mind on the things above, not on the things that are on earth.

A key aspect of the biblical worldview is not simply the belief in the transcendent reality of heaven, but a mind consistently attuned to the concerns of heaven (the glory of God; the eternal destiny of man) as opposed to the temporal concerns of this earthly life. The phrase "set your minds" is one term in the original (Greek *phroneite*) and is an imperative and is literally "think!" This is not a momentary thought but (in the present tense) it is a "habit of thinking," a "consistent mental perspective," a "constant mental orientation." This is not a mere emotional longing for future heavenly bliss but a frame of mind and thought, thoroughly and consistently informed by the Scriptures (see Col. 3:16), that sets one's priorities, informs one's values, and controls one's behavior. One cannot develop a biblical worldview if one's priorities, values, and actions are aligned with, or guided by, this temporal existence (see Matt. 6:34).

> **COLOSSIANS 3:16**
>
> Let the word of Christ richly dwell within you, with all wisdom teaching and admonishing one another with psalms *and* hymns *and* spiritual songs, singing with thankfulness in your hearts to God.

For Scripture to inform one's thinking (see Col. 3:2) there must be more than a superficial acquaintance with its content. The term "richly" (Greek *plousiōs*) has the notion of "abundantly," and the term "dwell" (Greek *enoikeitō*) has the notion of "to live in." The idea here is that the word of Christ (the gospel, the Scripture) must permeate one's heart and mind and be allowed to guide one's will.

Right Theology Is Crucial to Refuting False Worldviews

> **2 CORINTHIANS 10:3–5**
>
> For though we walk in the flesh, we do not war according to the flesh, [4] for the weapons of our warfare are not of the flesh, but divinely powerful for

> the destruction of fortresses. [5] *We are* destroying speculations and every lofty thing raised up against the knowledge of God, and *we are* taking every thought captive to the obedience of Christ.

In the spiritual battle that confronts the believer (in which the apostle Paul was himself engaged; see 2 Cor. 10:1–3), it is essential for believers not only to have a biblical worldview but to be engaged in confronting the many false worldviews with which they come into contact. The term "war" (Greek *strateuometha*; 2 Cor. 10:3) means to "engage in a battle," "to serve as a soldier." With this term, along with the reference to "the weapons of warfare" (Greek *tá hópla tés strateias*), Paul is using the metaphor of warfare (see Eph. 6:10–20), but he is not urging the Corinthians to armed confrontation. This is because the battle he has in mind here is not with actual men with actual physical weapons. The opponents Paul has in view here are human systems of thought. He speaks of "fortresses" (Greek *ochyrōmatōn*), yet these are not fortresses of stone but rather fortresses of thought ("speculations"; Greek *logismous*). These are all the man-centered religions, philosophies, and ideologies (see 1 Cor. 1–2, "man's wisdom") that are "raised up" or invented and disseminated to oppose "the knowledge of God" or simply God's wisdom (i.e., the gospel and the Scriptures; see 1 Cor. 1–2, above). All such false worldviews must be opposed and defeated (see Titus 1:9). Furthermore, in this battle (as Paul adjusts the metaphor from fighting an enemy to taking captives) the believer must bring "every thought captive" to be used only in "obedience to Christ." (The term "captive" here in Greek is *aichmalōtizontes*, "as a prisoner of war.") The idea here may be that we are to seek to defeat the false worldviews of others in order to bring them to submission to Christ. On the other hand, it may mean a believer must bring his own thoughts captive; that is, he must destroy every vestige of man-centered (self-centered) thinking in his own mind and heart and bring his every thought under the lordship of Christ.

COLOSSIANS 2:8

See to it that no one takes you captive through philosophy and empty deception, according to the tradition of men, according to the elementary principles of the world, rather than according to Christ.

Paul's warning here is the complement to his instructions to the Corinthians in 2 Corinthians 10:3–5. There he concluded that the final objective of the believers' battle with human systems of thought ("speculations . . . raised up against the knowledge of God") is to take "every thought captive to the obedience of Christ." However, believers must be aware that if they fail to conscientiously form a biblically grounded worldview, they are vulnerable to being "captive" (Greek *sylagōgōn*) themselves to false man-centered philosophies or ideologies. The term "captive" (Greek *sylagōgōn*, is used only here in the New Testament) means "to carry off" in robbery or as plunder.

The term "philosophy" (Greek *philosophias*; another term used only here in the New Testament) means "love of wisdom" but here means more than that and does not refer to the discipline of philosophical studies (although many times philosophy as such would fall under Paul's negative estimation). Paul has in mind the over-estimation, or errant-estimation, of the value of philosophy. Indeed, it is "empty deception." That is, it is empty, hollow, without real substance. The reason can be seen in Paul's next three statements. First, such philosophy is man-centered. It begins with man's speculation and builds on that speculation with further speculation until it becomes a tradition (Greek *paradosin*). This has the appearance of learning and wisdom but never really rises above the level of mere human speculation. Second, such philosophy is based in "elementary principles of the world." This has reference to the ideas and doctrines of the gnostic-like false teachers who were troubling the Colossians. It probably refers to their theories and conjectures about the origins of the physical universe. Finally, the false teachers are engaging in empty philosophy because the source of that philosophy is not "according to Christ"—it is not from, nor commensurate with, the Scriptures. All such philosophy is "deception" (Greek *apatēs*) and should be avoided (where such philosophy is incommensurate with the Scriptures) or brought into obedience to Christ (see 2 Cor. 10:5).

"In this short phrase ['according to Christ'] the dominant theological teaching of the letter is brought to bear on the central purpose of the letter. Christ is the one in whom God exclusively is to be found, the one through whom the world was created and through whom it is redeemed, and the one who has decisively defeated all the hostile powers. Any teaching that in any way detracts from Christ's exclusive role is by definition both wrong and ineffective."[9]

1. John Calvin, *Institutes of the Christian Religion*, ed. John T. McNeill, trans. Ford Lewis Battles (1559; repr., Louisville, KY: Westminster John Knox Press, 1960), 1:35. This is in Book One, Chapter 1, Section 1.
2. William D. Mounce, "Heart," in *Mounce's Complete Expository Dictionary of Old and New Testament Words* (Grand Rapids, MI: Zondervan, 2006), 327.
3. G. I. Williamson, *The Westminster Shorter Catechism* (Phillipsburg, NJ: P&R Publishing, 1970), 1.
4. John MacArthur, *The MacArthur New Testament Commentary: Titus* (Chicago: Moody Publishers, 1996), 48–49.
5. Ryrie, *Basic Theology*, 15.
6. Anselm, *Proslogion*, trans. Thomas Williams (Indianapolis: Hackett Publishing, 1995), 6.
7. W. Gary Philips, William E. Brown, and John Stonestreet, *Making Sense of Your World: A Biblical Worldview* (Salem, WI: Sheffield Publishing Company, 2008), 8.
8. W. Andrew Hoffecker, ed., "Preface," in *Revolutions in Worldview: Understanding the Flow of Western Thought* (Phillipsburg, NJ: P&R Publishing, 2007), xii.
9. Douglas J. Moo, *The Letters to the Colossians and to Philemon* (Grand Rapids, MI: William B. Eerdmans Publishing Company, 2008), 193.

CHAPTER 2

GOD'S WORD

Bibliology

Bibliology is the study of the nature and key characteristics of the Bible. It also includes the study of the different forms of God's self-revelation.

The knowledge of God's existence, character, and moral law, which comes through creation to all humanity, is often called '*general revelation*' (because it comes to all people generally). General revelation comes through observing nature, through seeing God's directing influence in history, and through an inner sense of God's existence and his laws that he has placed inside every person.[1]

THE DIFFERENT FORMS OF REVELATION

General Revelation

PSALM 19:1–4

The heavens are telling of the glory of God;
And their expanse is declaring the work of His hands.
[2] Day to day pours forth speech,
And night to night reveals knowledge.
[3] There is no speech, nor are there words;
Their voice is not heard.

> [4] Their line has gone out through all the earth,
> And their utterances to the end of the world.
> In them He has placed a tent for the sun.

By means of poetic parallelism and personification, the psalmist affirms that the physical heavens—the stars and planets, the sky, and the sun—reveal the creative wisdom, power, and grandeur of God. The order and constancy of the movements of the heavenly bodies—epitomized by the daily, unvarying movements of the sun—demonstrates clearly that, despite the fact that there are no actual words spoken, the creation itself declares that God is the glorious creator and He is the intelligent source of the design that is unmistakably displayed in the world every day.

> **ROMANS 1:19–20**
>
> Because that which is known about God is evident within them; for God made it evident to them. [20] For since the creation of the world His invisible attributes, His eternal power and divine nature, have been clearly seen, being understood through what has been made, so that they are without excuse.

Paul affirms that the very "creation of the world" reveals that God exists, that He is powerful and divine. Although God is "invisible" (Greek *aoratou*; see Col. 1:15; 1 Tim. 1:17), the attributes of God's power and wisdom can be "seen" in His creation. "God in his essence is hidden from human sight, yet much of him and much about him can be seen through the things he has made"[2] (see **Existence of God**).

Special Revelation

SPECIAL INSTRUMENTS OF SPECIAL REVELATION

The Lot

> **PROVERBS 16:33 (SEE ACTS 1:21–26)**
>
> The lot is cast into the lap,
> But its every decision is from the LORD.

Even events that seem the most random and fortuitous, such as the roll of a pair of dice, are determined by the sovereign direction of God. At times when men seek to use such means to make choices or seek fortunes, they should realize that God is the one who directs these seemingly arbitrary outcomes. That such means of revelation were apparently at one time affirmed by God does not mean such means of revelation are to be employed today. Those who have access to God's will through His inspired Word have all the sufficient revelation they need (see 2 Peter 1:3).

The Urim and Thummim

> **EXODUS 28:30 (SEE NUM. 27:21; DEUT. 33:8)**
> You shall put in the breastpiece of judgment the Urim and the Thummim, and they shall be over Aaron's heart when he goes in before the LORD; and Aaron shall carry the judgment of the sons of Israel over his heart before the LORD continually.

Exactly what these objects (Urim "lights" and Thummim "perfections") were, and how they were employed, is not known. Most likely they were stones, perhaps gemstones, attached in some fashion to the breastpiece of the High Priest (see Ex. 28:29). They were probably used on occasions when simple, concise directions or straightforward rulings (yes or no) were needed to adjudicate some matter before the nation of Israel in the wilderness period. Since they are not explicitly mentioned again after Deuteronomy, the type of guidance they afforded was not necessary or pertinent after that time.

SPECIAL MEANS OF SPECIAL REVELATION

Dreams and Visions

> **GENESIS 20:3, 6**
> But God came to Abimelech in a dream of the night, and said to him, "Behold, you are a dead man because of the woman whom you have taken, for she is married." . . .
> [6] Then God said to him in the dream, "Yes, I know that in the integrity

of your heart you have done this, and I also kept you from sinning against Me; therefore I did not let you touch her.

GENESIS 31:11, 24

[11] "Then the angel of God said to me in the dream, 'Jacob,' and I said, 'Here I am.'" . . .
[24] God came to Laban the Aramean in a dream of the night and said to him, "Be careful that you do not speak to Jacob either good or bad."

DANIEL 2:1, 3

[1] Now in the second year of the reign of Nebuchadnezzar, Nebuchadnezzar had dreams; and his spirit was troubled and his sleep left him. . . .
[3] The king said to them, "I had a dream and my spirit is anxious to understand the dream."

MATTHEW 1:20 (SEE 2:19)

[20] But when he had considered this, behold, an angel of the Lord appeared to him in a dream, saying, "Joseph, son of David, do not be afraid to take Mary as your wife; for the Child who has been conceived in her is of the Holy Spirit.

These instances undeniably indicate that God spoke to people through dreams. However, it is not entirely clear that what is being described as a "dream" in these biblical instances is exactly the same phenomenon as the common nightly brain activity of most human beings. In the two texts in Genesis it is explicitly stated that God was speaking ("God said") so it should be understood that the one having the "dream" was made to understand that this was no normal experience and was explicitly informed that God was using this means of revealing Himself. In the case of Mary's espoused husband Joseph, it was made clear to him that this was, indeed, a communication from God.

In the case of Nebuchadnezzar's dream, it was also indicated in some fashion that this experience carried meaning that needed divine explication. In other words, in none of these instances was there a question as to whether God was indeed revealing something. Therefore, if one must ask the question, "Is God speaking to me in my dream(s)?" the answer would be "No." If God is speaking in a dream He will make that quite obvious at the time.

But does God speak through dreams today? Again, the question is not, "Can He speak through dreams today?" That question has been answered: He has, and we must admit that He, being sovereign, could if He chose to. Setting aside the anecdotal data that He still does speak through dreams, the further question would have to be why would He communicate through dreams? Such information that He might communicate through a dream would have to be judged by the revelation of the written Word of God. Of course, if the information communicated by the dream contradicted the Word of God, it would have to be dismissed. On the other hand, if the information communicated by the dream was already revealed in the Word of God, it would be unnecessary. And if it claimed to reveal information not contradictory to the Word of God but merely repeating truth revealed in the Word, it would still not be necessary because Scripture is sufficient (see **Sufficiency of Scripture**).

> **ISAIAH 6:1**
>
> In the year of King Uzziah's death I saw the Lord sitting on a throne, lofty and exalted, with the train of His robe filling the temple.

While the term for vision is not found in this text, it is understood that Isaiah's experience was a vision (a supernatural experience that communicates a revelation from God). As with the matter of dreams, it is incontestable that God used visions to reveal Himself to men; but as with dreams, such visions were not nebulous visitations but were quite definite, immediate, and indisputable communications directly from God. The vision experienced by Isaiah was for the purpose of preparing him for the ministry to which the Lord was calling him, and to communicate to him the manner and purpose of that ministry.

SPECIAL AGENTS OF REVELATION

The Angel of the LORD

GENESIS 16:7–11

Now the angel of the LORD found her by a spring of water in the wilderness, by the spring on the way to Shur. [8] He said, "Hagar, Sarai's maid, where have you come from and where are you going?" And she said, "I am fleeing from the presence of my mistress Sarai." [9] Then the angel of the LORD said to her, "Return to your mistress, and submit yourself to her authority."

GENESIS 22:11 (SEE 22:15)

But the angel of the LORD called to him from heaven and said, "Abraham, Abraham!" And he said, "Here I am."

EXODUS 3:2

The angel of the LORD appeared to him in a blazing fire from the midst of a bush; and he looked, and behold, the bush was burning with fire, yet the bush was not consumed.

JUDGES 2:1

Now the angel of the LORD came up from Gilgal to Bochim. And he said, "I brought you up out of Egypt and led you into the land which I have sworn to your fathers; and I said, 'I will never break My covenant with you.'"

JUDGES 13:15, 16B-18

Then Manoah said to the angel of the LORD, "Please let us detain you so that we may prepare a young goat for you." . . . [16b] For Manoah did not know that he was the angel of the LORD. [17] Manoah said to the angel of the LORD, "What is your name, so that when your words come *to pass*, we may honor you?" [18] But the angel of the LORD said to him, "Why do you ask my name, seeing it is wonderful?"

The texts that refer to the Angel of the LORD (Hebrew *mal'āk yhwh*) clearly reveal that He is no ordinary angel. These appearances are often called "theophanies" (a manifestation of God that is discernible by the senses). However, it is possible that these should be called "Christophanies" or preincarnate manifestations of Christ, the Son of God. Several qualities of the Angel of the LORD argue that this entity is divine and the Son of God—Christ.

He is God: In the Genesis passage the Angel makes promises to Hagar (e.g., Gen. 16:10) that are promises like the promises the Lord made to Abraham (see Gen. 15:5) and Ishmael (see Gen. 17:20). In Genesis 22 the Angel speaks in such a way as to identify Himself with God; and reiterates the promises made to Abraham from God (see Gen. 22:15–18). In the Exodus passage the one identified as "the angel of the LORD" in verse 2 clearly identifies Him as "the LORD" (Ex. 3:4, 7, 14; see **The Attributes of God, Aseity**).

He is the preincarnate Christ: The fact that no man can see God (see Ex. 33:20; 1 John 4:12) and yet this divine one is "seen," would indicate that this Angel is the preincarnate Christ, for this—revealing and manifesting God—is the ministry of the Son (see John 1:18). While the phrase "an angel of the Lord" appears in the New Testament, no entity like "the Angel of the LORD" appears after the incarnation suggesting that the incarnate Christ and this Angel are one and the same. In the Judges passage the Angel identifies Himself with the designation "wonderful," which is a designation applied to the Messiah in Isaiah 9:6.

EXODUS 3:2, 5–6

The angel of the LORD appeared to him in a blazing fire from the midst of a bush; and he looked, and behold, the bush was burning with fire, yet the bush was not consumed. . . .
[5] Then He said, "Do not come near here; remove your sandals from your feet, for the place on which you are standing is holy ground." [6] He said also, "I am the God of your father, the God of Abraham, the God of Isaac, and the God of Jacob." Then Moses hid his face, for he was afraid to look at God.

Gabriel

> **DANIEL 9:21 (SEE 8:16)**
>
> While I was still speaking in prayer, then the man Gabriel, whom I had seen in the vision previously, came to me in *my* extreme weariness about the time of the evening offering.

> **LUKE 1:19**
>
> The angel answered and said to him, "I am Gabriel, who stands in the presence of God, and I have been sent to speak to you and to bring you this good news."

> **LUKE 1:26–27**
>
> Now in the sixth month the angel Gabriel was sent from God to a city in Galilee called Nazareth, [27] to a virgin engaged to a man whose name was Joseph, of the descendants of David; and the virgin's name was Mary.

The angel Gabriel is one of the two good angels named in the Bible (the other being Michael; see **Named Angels**). He is depicted in Scripture as the angel uniquely charged with communicating important messages from God to key individuals (e.g., Daniel and Mary) about very important events to come. He identified himself as the one "who stands in the presence of God." Precisely what this means is not specified. It may be an indication of his high rank and status but mainly this seems to be meant to indicate that his message is important and can be accepted as authentic and true. Since Gabriel is not mentioned as communicating to anyone after Mary (e.g., the apostles), it should be concluded that his unique ministry of revelation came to an end after his announcement to Mary.

The Incarnation of the Son

> **JOHN 1:1–2, 14**
>
> In the beginning was the Word, and the Word was with God, and the Word was God. [2] He was in the beginning with God. . . .
> [14] And the Word became flesh, and dwelt among us, and we saw His

> glory, glory as of the only begotten from the Father, full of grace and truth.

The very incarnation (God coming in human flesh) of the second person of the Trinity—the Son—is itself a type of special revelation. As a form of special revelation it is utterly unique and comparable only to the revelation of Jesus Christ at His second coming.

The Significance of the Term Scripture(s)

1 TIMOTHY 5:18

For the Scripture says, "YOU SHALL NOT MUZZLE THE OX WHILE HE IS THRESHING," and "The laborer is worthy of his wages."

2 PETER 3:16

As also in all *his* letters, speaking in them of these things, in which are some things hard to understand, which the untaught and unstable distort, as *they do* also the rest of the Scriptures, to their own destruction.

The term "Scripture" comes from the Greek term *graphē* which meant "writing" but came to be shorthand for "sacred writing." The word came to be used of the authoritative sacred writings of the Old Testament (see Matt. 21:42; Mark 12:10; Luke 24:27; John 5:39; Acts 17:2). The Scriptures carried inherent authority since they were considered the very word(s) of God (see **Inspiration of the Word of God** below.)

Here Paul cites two texts: one from Deuteronomy 25:4 and the other from Luke 10:7 and he calls both "Scripture," thereby indicating that the properties and qualities that made the Old Testament authoritative were applied to Luke's writings as well. Here Peter observes that Paul's letters were subject to misunderstanding and distortion just as were "the rest of the Scriptures." Thus, Peter applies the term "Scriptures" to Paul's letters.

THE CHARACTERISTICS OF SCRIPTURE

Inspiration of the Word of God

Inspiration is the doctrine that the words of Scripture are both the very words of God and, at the same time, the words of the human authors of Scripture.

THE VERY WORDS OF GOD

> **DEUTERONOMY 18:18**
>
> I will raise up a prophet from among their countrymen like you, and I will put My words in his mouth, and he shall speak to them all that I command him.

> **2 SAMUEL 23:2**
>
> "The Spirit of the LORD spoke by me,
> And His word was on my tongue."

> **JEREMIAH 1:9**
>
> Then the LORD stretched out His hand and touched my mouth, and the LORD said to me,
> "Behold, I have put My words in your mouth."

> **JEREMIAH 5:14**
>
> Therefore, thus says the LORD, the God of hosts,
> "Because you have spoken this word,
> Behold, I am making My words in your mouth fire
> And this people wood, and it will consume them."

> **JEREMIAH 30:1–2**
>
> The word which came to Jeremiah from the LORD, saying, [2] "Thus says the LORD, the God of Israel, 'Write all the words which I have spoken to you in a book.'"

When God communicated to and through the prophets and writers of the Old Testament, He communicated through words. Those words, Yahweh says, were "My words." While this might be taken by some to mean the prophets took direct dictation from Yahweh, it is more likely that this was

meant in a metaphorical or poetic sense, so that the words of the prophets
were to be regarded as the words Yahweh wanted spoken or written. It is
clear that each author of Scripture used his own vocabulary, style of writing,
and reflected his own personality in the written texts. And yet, it can be said
that the words of each one of these very individual authors were at the same
time "My words"—Yahweh's words. In the 2 Samuel text David affirms that
he spoke and he used his own tongue, but this was the word of the Spirit.

2 PETER 3:2

That you should remember the words spoken beforehand by the holy
prophets and the commandment of the Lord and Savior *spoken* by your
apostles.

In this brief comment Peter links the writings ("words") of the Old Testament ("holy") prophets and the commandments (Greek *entolēs*) of the Lord,
as those commandments (and generally His teaching) were conveyed by the
apostles. Thus, Peter has equated the value and authority of the teaching of
the Old Testament prophets and the teaching of New Testament apostles.
Just as the words and teaching of the prophets are God's, so the words and
teaching of the apostles are the Lord's.

> *Inspiration is that supernatural work of the Holy Spirit by which He*
> *superintended the writing process of Scripture so that all the words*
> *and every part of the original writings were at the same time the words*
> *of the human writers and the very words of God.*[3]

PLENARY INSPIRATION BY GOD, THE HOLY SPIRIT

2 TIMOTHY 3:16

All Scripture is inspired by God and profitable for teaching, for reproof, for
correction, for training in righteousness.

"All Scripture" refers to the New as well as the Old Testament (see Matt.
22:29; Mark 14:49; Luke 4:21; John 10:35). There are clear indications that

the gospels and epistles very early in the first century came to be recognized as "sacred writings" [see **The Significance of the Term Scripture(s)**].

The expression "is inspired by God" is *Theopneustos*, literally, "breathed out," and is intended to convey the fact that the Bible is "God's breath"—spoken by Him. Of course, this is a metaphorical way to say that "what Scripture speaks, God speaks" (see Rom. 9:17; Gal. 3:8); Scripture is called "the oracles of God" (Rom. 3:2). In the process of inspiration God used the minds, vocabularies, and experiences of the human authors to say precisely what He intended to say. The product of inspiration is the canonical books of the Bible (sixty-six in the Old Testament and twenty-seven in the New Testament).

The result of inspiration is a word from God that is useful, purposeful, and sufficient for "teaching"—doctrinal instruction, "reproof"—behavioral instruction, "correction"—restoration to proper direction in living, and "training"—discipline for right behavior and living.

> **2 PETER 1:20–21**
>
> But know this first of all, that no prophecy of Scripture is *a matter* of one's own interpretation, [21] for no prophecy was ever made by an act of human will, but men moved by the Holy Spirit spoke from God.

Peter's point is not about the interpretation of Scripture but rather its origin. No prophet or human author decided to write Scripture. The Bible is not the product of human ideas or desires, and it is not the product of mere human effort or will.

This phrase means the human authors of Scripture were "carried along," as a ship with sails might be "driven along" by the wind (see Acts 27:15). In an analogous way, as the human authors wrote their texts, the Holy Spirit superintended their very words to produce the "Word of God" (see Jer. 1:4; Rom. 3:2). Ultimately, the Holy Spirit is the divine author and originator of the Scriptures. The result is that what the human authors composed, out of their own capacities, ideas, experiences, and using their own words, was (in the original manuscripts) the inspired and inerrant "Word of God" (see **Inerrancy of the Word of God**).

JESUS' VIEW OF INSPIRATION

> **MATTHEW 5:18**
>
> For truly I say to you, until heaven and earth pass away, not the smallest letter or stroke shall pass from the Law until all is accomplished.

Jesus affirmed that the inspiration and authority of the Scriptures extended to its seemingly minor elements. Here Jesus likely had in mind the text of the Hebrew Old Testament. The smallest letter in the Hebrew alphabet was the *yōdh* which was only slightly larger than an apostrophe. The "stroke" (lit. "little horn") was the small pen-stroke that distinguished the different Hebrew letters of *he* and *het*. Here in Matthew "the smallest letter" translates *iota*, which is the smallest letter of the Greek alphabet.

Jesus' point here is that the purposes of God are revealed in written texts and every single element of those texts, down to what might be considered the insignificant elements, is a part of that revelation.

> **MATTHEW 22:31–32**
>
> "But regarding the resurrection of the dead, have you not read what was spoken to you by God: 32 'I AM THE GOD OF ABRAHAM, AND THE GOD OF ISAAC, AND THE GOD OF JACOB'? He is not the God of the dead but of the living."

The Sadducees denied the resurrection of the dead. Jesus explains that this makes no sense in light of the affirmation by God in Exodus 3:6 where God identifies Himself as the God of the patriarchs Abraham, Isaac, and Jacob. Jesus' argument turns on the present tense of the verb "I AM."

Of course, the patriarchs had died long ago, but Jesus affirms that God is—present tense—their God and that He is the God of the living, thus the Sadducees' denial of the resurrection is untenable. The point here is that Jesus apparently thought that even the verb tenses of the Old Testament were determinative of doctrine, and hence, were inspired.

> **MARK 12:36 (SEE MATT. 22:43)**
> "David himself said in the Holy Spirit,
>
> 'THE LORD SAID TO MY LORD,
> "SIT AT MY RIGHT HAND,
> UNTIL I PUT YOUR ENEMIES BENEATH YOUR FEET."'"

In a discussion with His opposition in the temple, Jesus quoted Psalm 110, a psalm written by David, but He adds that this was "said in" or by the Spirit. This indicates that Jesus Himself understood that the words of David were, at the same time, the words of the Holy Spirit.

Inerrancy of the Word of God

The doctrine of inerrancy affirms that the Bible is without error, fault, or defect in all that it affirms as fact, reports as history, or testifies as truthful, in any area of learning or science. It is acknowledged that this quality of Scripture applies absolutely only in the case of the original autographs and does not apply to copies and versions [translations] of the Bible.

> "Inerrancy is the view that when all the facts become known, they will demonstrate that the Bible, in its original autographs and correctly interpreted is entirely true and never false in all it affirms, whether that relates to the social, physical or life sciences."[4]

DESCRIPTIONS OF THE SOUNDNESS AND TRUTH OF SCRIPTURE

It Is Pure ("Tested")

> **PSALM 12:6**
> The words of the LORD are pure words;
> As silver tried in a furnace on the earth, refined seven times.

In contrast to those who "speak falsehood," and empty flattery (see Ps. 12:2–3), the speech of the Lord is "pure" (Hebrew *ṭāhôr*) or "clean." There may be a ceremonial connotation to this term ("clean" as opposed to "defiling" in a ceremonial setting) or an ethical connotation—morally upright. The words of the Lord are compared to ultrarefined silver and as such would contain no hint of error or deceit.

> **PSALM 18:30**
> As for God, His way is blameless;
> The word of the LORD is tried;
> He is a shield to all who take refuge in Him.

> **PROVERBS 30:5**
> Every word of God is tested;
> He is a shield to those who take refuge in Him.

The way of God is "blameless" (Hebrew *tāmîm*). The term means "to be complete, sound." Just so, the word of the Lord is "tried," "tested" (Hebrew *ṣārap*); this is to say it is "proven by testing." This affirms that the Word of God will perform as intended.

It Is Complete

> **PSALM 19:7**
> The law of the LORD is perfect, restoring the soul;
> The testimony of the LORD is sure, making wise the simple.

The word ("Law") is "perfect" (Hebrew *tāmîm*); the term means "to be complete, sound." In God's Word there is nothing to add and nothing to correct. It is perfectly suited to accomplish God's purposes (see **Sufficiency of Scripture** below).

It Is Lasting

> **ISAIAH 40:8 (SEE 1 PET. 1:25)**
> The grass withers, the flower fades,
> But the word of our God stands forever.

> **PSALM 119:89**
> Forever, O LORD,
> Your word is settled in heaven.

The term "stands" (Hebrew *yāqūm*) is used to convey the notion of something that is established and lasting (as the Noahic covenant, see Gen. 6:18; 9:9, 11). Thus the full expression "stands forever" (Hebrew *yāqūm le'ōwlām*) conveys the notion that the Word of God is fixed and durable. The term "settled" (Hebrew *niṣṣāḇ*) in this form often refers to an individual or object that is "standing" (see Gen. 24:13, 43; 35:20) in order to be seen. Because the Word is "standing" in heaven, it endures and will not wilt or be diminished. The Word of God is not a transient, passing revelation but one that transcends this temporal world. It is unchanging and eternal, as is its author.

It Is Truth

> PSALM 119:151
> You are near, O LORD,
> And all Your commandments are truth.

> PSALM 119:160
> The sum of Your word is truth,
> And every one of Your righteous ordinances is everlasting.

> JOHN 17:17
> Sanctify them in the truth; Your word is truth.

To say that the Word of God is *truth* is more than to say it is *true*. Indeed, it is true in the sense that everything it affirms corresponds with the reality of God and His creation. But the Word of God is not to be judged by some external standard or independent criteria that is somehow accessible to man, such as science or philosophy. Rather, God's Word *is truth*; it is *the standard* and *the criteria* by which all other truth claims are to be evaluated and judged.

Sufficiency of Scripture

> PSALM 19:7–11
> The law of the LORD is perfect, restoring the soul;

The testimony of the LORD is sure, making wise the simple.
⁸ The precepts of the LORD are right, rejoicing the heart;
The commandment of the LORD is pure, enlightening the eyes.
⁹ The fear of the LORD is clean, enduring forever;
The judgments of the LORD are true; they are righteous altogether.
¹⁰ They are more desirable than gold, yes, than much fine gold;
Sweeter also than honey and the drippings of the honeycomb.
¹¹ Moreover, by them Your servant is warned;
In keeping them there is great reward.

The psalmist describes the Word of God using various terms: law, testimony, precepts, commandment, fear, and judgments. The "law" is a term that identifies the word by the outward code of conduct for humans, which is based on the inner reality of God's own perfect moral righteousness. The "law" is a self-revelation of God's holiness (see Lev. 18–20). The term "testimony" identifies the Word as the self-referencing, self-verifying (self-attesting), self-revelation of God. The "precepts" are the principles to be discerned from the Word. The "commandments" identify the Word as the authoritative self-revelation of God. The "fear" identifies the Word of God by its effect on the unbelieving and unrepentant. The "judgments" identify God's Word as that word that displays God's actions in dealing both with the obedient and the recalcitrant.

The psalmist describes God's Word with six features or qualities: perfect, sure, right, pure, clean and true. The Word is "perfect" (Hebrew *tāmîm*)—complete, flawless; it is "sure" (Hebrew *ămēn*)—verified, confirmed; "right" (Hebrew *yāšar*)—morally exact; "pure" (Hebrew *bar*)—clean, innocent; "clean" (Hebrew *ṭāhôr*)—pure, undefiled; "true"(Hebrew *'emeth*)—reliable, faithful.

The psalmist describes the Word as to its outcomes and here is where the sufficiency of Scripture can be seen. The first effect or outcome is "restoring the soul." The first need of any human need is to have one's soul restored. This might mean simply "revived" in a physical sense," but it probably means more. If taken in a holistic sense it may mean "restored spiritually," a "spiritual renewal" (see Ps. 23:3a). It is the Word of God that brings needed spiritual renewal (even regeneration; see 1 Peter 1:23). The second effect is "making wise the simple." The "renewed soul" needs discernment to make spiritual progress. The simple person is not unintelligent but naïve and may be swayed by the "wisdom of the world" (see **Theology and the Biblical Worldview** above, Cor. 1–2). The Word of God is the renewed souls' (the believers') source for wisdom. "Wisdom" in the Old Testament has the notion of "having a skill" and the wisdom the simple person needs is "skill in living." The Word of God is the only reliable source for acquiring that skill. The third effect is "rejoicing the heart." Most people are seeking happiness, but only by the Word of God can true joy be found. The fourth effect is "enlightening the eyes." The "renewed soul" must live in a world that is characterized by darkness and filled with danger. Only the Word of God gives the necessary light; see Ps. 119:105, "Your word is a lamp to my feet and a light to my path." The fifth effect is righteous fear. The "renewed soul" will need the constant reminder that "The fear of the LORD is the instruction for wisdom" (Prov. 15:33). The tendency toward self-reliance, and inevitable subsequent failure (see Rom. 7), is prevented by a healthy and life-long "fear of God." The fear of the Lord is characterized by deep reverence, love, honor, praise, and submission. The sixth effect is the pleasure of knowledge and the reward of obedience. The psalmist speaks of the pleasure of knowing Scripture ("sweeter also than honey") and the reward of obedience ("in keeping them there is great reward.") This is not saying there will be a reward *after* the commandments and precepts are met, but that the reward is *in keeping* them. The most fulfilled life—joyful, satisfying, and eternally worthwhile life—is a life lived in obedience to the Word of God. It is through the Word of God that "His divine power has granted to us everything pertaining to life and godliness, through the true knowledge of Him who called us by His own glory and excellence" (2 Peter 1:3).

Power of the Word of God

HEBREWS 4:12
For the word of God is living and active and sharper than any two-edged sword, and piercing as far as the division of soul and spirit, of both joints and marrow, and able to judge the thoughts and intentions of the heart.

The metaphor here must not be understood by attempting to identify the actual type of sword the author has in mind but by paying close attention to the description of the sword and its action. The fact that it is a "two-edged sword" highlights the fact that it is sharp, hence penetrating, and that in action it cuts with precision. The Word is not dependent on a skilled swordsman but is itself "living and active," that is, has the vital energy of God working immediately in its operation.

The metaphor is not intended to teach lessons on anatomy since "joints and marrow" are not actually contiguous in a living body. And it is probably not helpful when it comes to the question of the constitution of human beings, since the supposed dichotomy of soul (Greek *psyche*) and spirit (Greek *pneuma*) is debated. (Compare John 12:27 and 13:21 where the same word for "troubled" is used both for Jesus' *psyche* and his *pneuma* respectively.) Furthermore, the metaphor is probably not all that helpful for analyzing human psychology by attempting to distinguish "the thoughts (Greek *enthumesis*) and intentions (Greek *ennoia*) of the heart." These two terms are, in many respects, synonyms and there is simply not enough in this text to suggest nuances to distinguish them. Indeed, this may be the very point the author is making. It is not the division (Greek *merismou*) between these various elements that is the main idea here but that these internal aspects of a person are not too deep or hidden to be exposed by the penetrating precision of the Word. The Word cuts precisely, it cuts deep, it cuts surely. And it exposes and "judges" (*kritikos*) these internal aspects of human nature, as a wielded sword might expose "joints and marrow" of a real body. As a result, nothing is hidden from sight but is seen for what it is (see Heb. 4:13).

THE CANONICITY OF THE BIBLE

The canonicity of the Bible refers to the collection of the inspired, authoritative books of the Bible. The English word "canon" comes from the Greek *kanon* (see the Hebrew *qāneh*) meaning "rule, ruler" or "measuring rod."

> **EXODUS 32:16**
>
> The tablets were God's work, and the writing was God's writing engraved on the tablets.

> **EXODUS 34:1**
>
> Now the LORD said to Moses, "Cut out for yourself two stone tablets like the former ones, and I will write on the tablets the words that were on the former tablets which you shattered."

These tablets were the stone tablets of the Ten Commandments upon which were the words engraved or written by God Himself. (The first set was shattered by Moses in anger when he observed the people worshiping the golden calf [see Ex. 32:19] and were replaced by a second set.) Among other factors this indicates the very idea of a written record of God's own words was originally God's idea. Thus, the initiative and design of preserving the Word(s) of God in written form was first proposed and instantiated by God Himself.

> **EXODUS 34:27**
>
> Then the LORD said to Moses, "Write down these words, for in accordance with these words I have made a covenant with you and with Israel."

In this context Moses was receiving instruction from Yahweh concerning the Sabbath (Ex. 34:21), the Feast of Weeks (Ex. 34:22–24), and the Passover (Ex. 34:25). The instruction to Moses to "write down these words" expands the idea of preserving the Word(s) of God in written form from stone tablets (see Ex. 34:27) to (presumably) a scroll or book (see Deut. 31:24). Thus, the very idea of a written Word of God, to be preserved for the instruction of God's people, was God's. Furthermore, this indicates that the subsequent notion of "sacred writings" (Scripture) began with the instructions of Yahweh to Moses to "write down these words."

> **DEUTERONOMY 31:24–26**
>
> It came about, when Moses finished writing the words of this law in a book until they were complete, [25] that Moses commanded the Levites who carried the ark of the covenant of the LORD, saying, [26] "Take this book of the

> law and place it beside the ark of the covenant of the LORD your God, that
> it may remain there as a witness against you."

At Yahweh's direction, Moses not only wrote down specific instructions for the people of God (see Ex. 34:27) but he recorded the entire Law in a book—the Pentateuch (the first five books of the Bible). These books were preserved in the ark of the covenant for use by future generations of God's people. Here are the biblical beginnings of the notion of canonicity. That is, it was by God's design that His people would know His ways and purposes by a collection of written texts that revealed His mind and will.

JOSHUA 24:26
> And Joshua wrote these words in the book of the law of God; and he took
> a large stone and set it up there under the oak that was by the sanctuary of
> the LORD.

Knowing the importance of the divinely inspired revelation from God preserved in the Law of Moses, Joshua continued the procedure of preserving—in a book—a record of God's Word and ways in the ongoing history of His people. This was a natural and reasonable development that apparently led subsequent generations of God's people to record and then collect these records of God's ways with His people. In other words, at this very early stage in the history of God's people, there was established an expectation that the recording of God's Word for a particular time and people would be preserved in books to be added to the collection (or canon) for use by later generations of God's people.

ISAIAH 8:1
> Then the LORD said to me, "Take for yourself a large tablet and write on it
> in ordinary letters: Swift is the booty, speedy is the prey."

JEREMIAH 36:2
> "Take a scroll and write on it all the words which I have spoken to you concerning Israel and concerning Judah, and concerning all the nations, from
> the day I *first* spoke to you, from the days of Josiah, even to this day."

Following the pattern established by Moses and Joshua, the prophets continued the practice of writing and preserving the record of God's mighty acts and
His very words. These prophets were directed by Yahweh to write down the
very words He spoke to them in books to preserve them for the people of God.

> **JOHN 14:26**
>
> "But the Helper, the Holy Spirit, whom the Father will send in My name,
> He will teach you all things, and bring to your remembrance all that I said
> to you."

> **JOHN 15:26**
>
> "When the Helper comes, whom I will send to you from the Father, *that is*
> the Spirit of truth who proceeds from the Father, He will testify about Me."

Jesus' promise to send the Holy Spirit—the Spirit of truth—was intended to
enable the disciples to recall His life and teaching and to learn from the Spirit
the truth they would need to know to accomplish the commission Jesus was
leaving with them (see Matt. 28:19–20). It was quite reasonable for them, following the pattern established by the Old Testament prophets, to put the record of Jesus' life and teaching in a book—which is exactly what happened
with the four gospels.

> **COLOSSIANS 4:16 (SEE 1 THESS. 5:27)**
>
> When this letter is read among you, have it also read in the church of the
> Laodiceans; and you, for your part read my letter *that is coming* from
> Laodicea.

> **2 PETER 3:15–16**
>
> And regard the patience of our Lord *as* salvation; just as also our beloved
> brother Paul, according to the wisdom given him, wrote to you, [16] as also
> in all *his* letters, speaking in them of these things, in which are some things
> hard to understand, which the untaught and unstable distort, as *they do*
> also the rest of the Scriptures, to their own destruction.

The very existence and preservation of the letters of Paul indicates that the
process, begun in the Old Testament, of writing down and preserving the

divinely given words of God continued with the New Testament apostles. Furthermore, it is clear from these verses that these letters were collected and shared among the local churches spread over the Greco-Roman world. The process of "canonization" was not invented by men but was God's design from the writings of Moses to the writings of the apostles.

> **REVELATION 22:18–19**
>
> I testify to everyone who hears the words of the prophecy of this book: if anyone adds to them, God will add to him the plagues which are written in this book; [19] and if anyone takes away from the words of the book of this prophecy, God will take away his part from the tree of life and from the holy city, which are written in this book.

The warning in these verses—to neither add to nor take away from the words of the book—is in the first instance to be applied to the book of Revelation itself. But the principle established may be reasonably applied to the whole of the biblical canon. Indeed, John may have had texts from the books of Moses in mind (see Deut. 4:2; 12:32). If so, that may imply that the warning covers more than this one book. The books that were inspired by God, and for that reason carry His own authority are to be accepted as such. No other books as such are needed and none should be added; and no books that are recognized as such should be dismissed (see Prov. 30:6).

---

1. Wayne Grudem, *Systematic Theology: An Introduction to Biblical Doctrine* (Grand Rapids, MI: Zondervan, 1994), 122–23.

2. Douglas J. Moo, *The Epistle to the Romans* (Grand Rapids, MI: William B. Eerdmans Publishing Company, 1996), 105.

3. David Finkbeiner, "Built Upon the Truth: Biblical Authority Yesterday and Today," in *Foundational Faith: Unchangeable Truth for an Ever-Changing World*, ed. John Koessler (Chicago: Moody Publishers, 2003), 51.

4. Paul D. Feinberg, "Bible, Inerrancy and Infallibility of," in *Evangelical Dictionary of Theology*, ed. Walter A. Elwell, 2nd ed. (Grand Rapids, MI: Baker Academic, 2001), 142.

CHAPTER 3

GOD THE FATHER

Theology Proper

Theology Proper is the study of God Himself: His existence, His attributes, the Trinity, and God's decrees.

> What comes into our minds when we think about God is the most important thing about us.[1]

EXISTENCE OF GOD

GENESIS 1:1

In the beginning God created the heavens and the earth.

The Bible does not begin with arguments for the existence of God but with the presupposition of the existence of God. Many people seem to think that mere creatures have or can find a place to stand—ontologically (being), epistemologically (knowing), or existentially (life experience)—from which they can pass judgment on the very existence (or not) of God, and from which they can discover and assess the mind of God, and from which they can appraise and rule (positive or negative) on the ways of God. But this is a denial of the creature/Creator distinction. This notion of a place for mere creatures to stand independently of God (human autonomy) fundamentally misses the basic reality that creatures are just that, creatures, and that God is their creator. Human beings are dependent on God for their very being, they are dependent on God to even be able to know anything, and their very lives are dependent on God (see Job 33:4). The idea that mere creatures have a place to stand from which they may judge God was completely debunked in the book of Job 38:1–42:6.

> **ACTS 14:17**
>
> "And yet He did not leave Himself without witness, in that He did good and gave you rains from heaven and fruitful seasons, satisfying your hearts with food and gladness."

God's goodness and care for His creatures is a witness to all peoples, not merely of His existence, but of His provision and benevolence.

> **ACTS 17:24–28**
>
> "The God who made the world and all things in it, since He is Lord of heaven and earth, does not dwell in temples made with hands; 25 nor is He served by human hands, as though He needed anything, since He Himself gives to all *people* life and breath and all things; 26 and He made from one *man* every nation of mankind to live on all the face of the earth, having determined *their* appointed times and the boundaries of their habitation, 27 that they would seek God, if perhaps they might grope for Him and find Him, though He is not far from each one of us; 28 for in Him we live and move and exist, as even some of your own poets have said, 'For we also are His children.'"

In his discourse in Athens, the apostle Paul was not attempting to show the Stoic and Epicurean philosophers what they "got right" by their own groping after God but that they were uninformed, in fact ignorant (see Acts 17:23 and Acts 17:30). Paul did not use different tactics to make his case in Athens (see Acts 17) than those he used in the synagogue in Pisidian Antioch (see Acts 13:13–31). In both cases his argument was grounded in Scripture. To the Jews in the synagogue he used Scripture to preach the truth of Christ (see Acts 13:22–23; 26–29) and his culminating argument was Christ's resurrection (Acts:13–30; 34–35). To the Gentiles in the Areopagus he used Scripture to preach the true God (Acts 17:24), the Creator, who is revealed in Christ as judge (Acts 17:31a), and his culminating argument was Christ's resurrection (Acts 17:31b).

Specifically, in Acts 17 Paul cites the truth of Genesis chapters 1 and 2 ("The God who made the world and all things in it"). He refers to Solomon's prayer at the dedication of the completed temple in 1 Kings 8:27 and to Isaiah's prophecy (indeed, the very words of Yahweh) in Isaiah 66:1–2 ("since He is Lord of heaven and earth, does not dwell in temples made with hands; nor is He served by human hands"). He refers to the self-sufficiency of God ("as though He needed anything"), which is what David reveals in Psalm 50:10–12. Paul asserts "He Himself gives to all people life and breath and all things" in line with what Job asserted in Job 27:3 and 33:4 and in Genesis 2:7. Paul makes a clear reference to Adam without using his name ("He made from one man every nation of mankind to live on all the face of the earth"), and the reference to "every nation" also recalls the truth that the nations as such are revealed in Genesis (see Gen. 10). Of those nations, Paul asserts God "determined their appointed times and the boundaries of their habitation," which is a truth found in Daniel 2:21 (see Ps. 75:6–7; Dan. 4:17, 32).

Paul explains that the provisions of "life and breath and all things" for all those who are the descendants of the "one man" (Adam) were intended to compel them to "seek God," and "find Him." However, Paul's very encounter with the "altar with this inscription, 'TO AN UNKNOWN GOD'" (Acts 17:23) attests to the fact that this intention has been frustrated. In spite of the fact that "He is not far from each one of us," and that men are utterly dependent upon Him for their existence ("for in Him we live and move and exist"), men remain ignorant of Him precisely because they are ignorant of the scriptural truths Paul has just laid before them. When Paul cites the Greek poets who affirm "we also are His children," he is not suggesting that those poets should be credited with discovering a truth. He is merely acknowledging that they have repeated a truth, regardless of how they came to fabricate it, or what they meant when they wrote it. Nevertheless, even this insight proves the inconsistency of the blatant idolatry that represents "Divine Nature" in images of precious metal and stone. In other words, the non-stony nature of "the children of God" should have been enough to expose the impropriety of depicting the divine nature in metals or stone.

Paul does not build a case for God upon the pagan notions and idolatry of these Greeks. At every point he challenges their philosophy with the revealed truth of Scripture. He does not take what they "got right" on their own and construct rationalistic arguments and present evidences for their consideration on their terms (in their own pagan worldview). Paul knows that "times of ignorance" (i.e., reliance upon man's wisdom; see 1 Cor. 1–2) do not call for dialogue with these worldly wise men; but what is needed in such times is the proclamation of the command that "all people everywhere should repent" (Acts 17:30). Furthermore, this is the most considerate and most compassionate message to proclaim, "because He has fixed a day in which He will judge the world in righteousness through a Man whom He has appointed" (Acts 17:31). The coming judgment required that Paul warn these men of the certainty of that coming judgment.

Paul's discourse was not a dialogue of scholars exchanging metaphysical ideas, but a truth-based, Christ-honoring (see 1 Peter 3:15), compassionately motivated "destroying [of] speculations and every lofty thing raised up against the knowledge of God," and the "taking [of] every thought captive to the obedience of Christ" (2 Cor. 10:5).

ROMANS 1:18–22

For the wrath of God is revealed from heaven against all ungodliness and unrighteousness of men who suppress the truth in unrighteousness, [19] because that which is known about God is evident within them; for God made it evident to them. [20] For since the creation of the world His invisible attributes, His eternal power and divine nature, have been clearly seen, being understood through what has been made, so that they are without excuse. [21] For even though they knew God, they did not honor Him as God or give thanks, but they became futile in their speculations, and their foolish heart was darkened. [22] Professing to be wise, they became fools.

Paul has expressed his eagerness to preach the gospel in Rome (see Rom. 1:15) and he explains in the book of Romans what that gospel is (see **Justification**). However, he begins where the gospel ("good news") must begin and that is with the "bad news" of God's wrath. (On the "wrath of God" see **The Attributes of God**.) In brief, the gospel is necessary because of the "ungodliness and unrighteousness of men" and thus God's judgment stands over the whole world (see Rom. 3:19) because "all have sinned" (see Rom. 3:23). What is more they "suppress the truth in unrighteousness." In the following verses Paul explains this "suppression." First, the nature and content of the truth suppressed leaves men under the wrath of God and without excuse (Rom. 1:19–20), and second, the manner and method of truth suppression leaves men under the wrath of God and without excuse (Rom. 1:21–23). The term "suppress" (Greek *kateksō*) means "to hinder," "to repress," "to restrain." The "suppressors" are actually everyone in the world (before they regenerated).

Paul first explains what it is that they suppress. Surprisingly, Paul affirms that everyone knows God exists! The expression "that which is known about God" (Greek *to gnōston tou Theou*) conveys the idea that He Himself (His existence) is known and information about Him is knowable. All men know God exists because He has made it "evident within" (NASB margin "among") them and "evident to them." The term "evident" (Greek *phaneron*) means "manifest," "apparent and clear." This knowledge is "within" (Greek *en*) them; this could be taken to mean "an inner personal awareness" or it could be indicating that what is known is known by (among) all people. This knowledge of God has been made evident, made plain, through God's creation which exhibits "His eternal power and divine nature." The creation of all things displays God's "invisible attributes": God's eternity—for He had to exist before He created all things in space and time; God's power—which must be the supernatural power to create all that is "natural" from nothing; God's "divine nature"—the term here is *theotais* and has the idea of "divinity" or "deity"— that which transcends everything in (created) nature. Paul is not saying that the knowledge of God can be gained by a program of investigation, research, deduction, and rational argument. Even though men know there is a God and they know something about Him, yet they suppress it! "To say that the unbeliever suppresses the truth is to say that he both possesses it and that he suppresses it."[2] "But Paul's main point is that seeing, people do not see; perceiving, they do not perceive. They see creation (see Job 40:15–41; Pss. 8; 19; 104; Isa. 40:21–26, etc.) But because they reject the knowledge of God they have thrown away the key to it all."[3]

So do unbelievers "know God"? The answer to this question is both yes and no. "Deep down in his mind every man knows that he is a creature of God and responsible to God. . . . But every man acts and talks as though this were not so."[4]

This is not a proof text for "natural theology" because what Paul is saying here makes a "natural theology" (if it were even possible) moot. Men do not have to be convinced of God's existence or His divine nature; they already know! However, it is this knowledge that is suppressed! (The attempt to argue the evidence and the reasons to believe in God's existence with those who already know that God exists but who have successfully suppressed that knowledge is a fool's errand [Prov. 26:4].) It is a case of "while seeing, they may see and not perceive, and while hearing, they may hear and not understand" (see Mark 4:12; Isa. 6:9).

Paul moves from the fact of their suppression of truth to the way they have suppressed the truth. First, they do not honor God as God. The Greek term for "honor" is *edoxasan* from the Greek term *doxazō*, "to glorify." They did not give Him the glory He deserved as God. They refused to acknowledge God *as* the self-existent, the one and only God. Second, they did not give Him the thanks He deserved. They refused to acknowledge God *as* the creator and provider of every good and perfect gift. Third, they engaged in futile speculations (see Eph. 4:17–18). The word "became futile" (Greek *emataiōthēsan*) comes from the Greek term *mataioō* (only here in the New Testament) and means vain or foolish (see Ps. 94:11). They refused to acknowledge God *as* the source and first principle of all "reason." Fourth, they became foolish and dark-hearted. The heart (Greek *kardia*) is the seat of a person's inner life. It is the place of one's thoughts, emotions, and decisions. To have a foolish and darkened heart means one's thoughts are unreliable, one's emotions are misplaced and unstable, one's decisions are defective and corrupt. As a result, they refused to acknowledge God *as* He has revealed Himself in the "light" of His Word! Fifth, they profess wisdom but become foolish. The term "profess" (Greek *phaskontes*) has the notion of "to assert," "to affirm," "to allege," "to make the claim." In this form (present active participle) it has the notion of a continuing action—they keep making this assertion as if they are trying to convince themselves. The idea is not merely that they claimed to be wise while in reality they became fools, but that they made themselves into fools by this constant unwarranted profession of wisdom. They refused to acknowledge God *as* the One who *is* wisdom and "whose thoughts are higher than our thoughts" (Isa. 55:8–9). Sixth, they become idolaters (Rom. 1:23). They refused to "acknowledge God" *as* the only living and true God.

The suppression of the truth of God and about God is a serious matter which, if persisted in, brings temporal judgment (see Rom. 1:24, 26, 28 "God gave them over") and eternal loss.

ROMANS 2:14–16

For when Gentiles who do not have the Law do instinctively the things of the Law, these, not having the Law, are a law to themselves, [15] in that they show the work of the Law written in their hearts, their conscience bearing witness and their thoughts alternately accusing or else defending them, [16] on the day when, according to my gospel, God will judge the secrets of men through Christ Jesus.

Paul is not suggesting that the Gentiles he has in mind actually kept the Law and thereby either gained favor with God or excused themselves. He is making the rather pedestrian observation that there are times and places where Gentiles—in the natural course of events, perhaps somewhat inadvertently—do "the things of the Law." That is, for whatever reason—perhaps simply because it seemed good to them at the time—they decide to live in such a way that they do things that are in accord with the Law. (The term "when" [Greek *hotan*] is more exactly expressed by "whenever." The idea is "Gentiles do not always do what is right, but sometimes they do."[5]) Paul is saying that this is only possible because they have "the Law written in their hearts." This is, of course, not actually the Law of the Torah but it is the inner sense of God's moral law which all human beings possess. This inner moral sense is itself based on the moral sense of God's own nature, which is also the basis of the moral sense of the Law of the Torah. Human beings have this inner "moral sense" because they are made in the image of God, and at certain times they find that being guided by that moral sense serves them better than going against that moral sense. The reason why being guided by that moral sense seems to work in their lives is because God made them, and God gave them that moral sense, *and* God made the world in which they live. In Paul's argument here he is not saying the Gentiles who do follow the guidance of their inner moral sense will be justified by doing so, but that when they do so they are a rebuke to the Jews who have the written Law, and claim to be doers of the Law but then also turn out to be transgressors of the Law (see Rom. 2:17–29).

> **HEBREWS 11:6**
>
> And without faith it is impossible to please *Him*, for he who comes to God must believe that He is and *that* He is a rewarder of those who seek Him.

The starting point for the knowledge of God is not rational arguments or empirical evidences but faith in God. The knowledge of God is never true knowledge if it is abstract and impersonal. This requires faith in Him—personal faith in a personal God. That is, one does not first come to know there is a god and then comes to have faith in God. This knowledge that comes by faith is not attained by a gradual process but is holistic. True faith is the personal knowledge of God which comes through God's own self-revelation. It is not achieved by the mental efforts or empirical investigations of man. True faith includes personal assent—the personal acceptance and appreciation (love)—for what God has given in His self-revelation. True faith embraces a personal commitment from the heart to conform one's life and actions to the self-revelation of God. All three of those elements—knowledge, assent, commitment—must come together at the same time if the faith is genuine; and only genuine faith leads to the true knowledge of God. In short, this faith is genuine only if it accepts the position of the dependent creature before a sovereign Creator and from the outset intends to be submissive and obedient to the self-revelation of God. True faith is personal trust in the promises of God which demonstrates itself in love for (see Ps. 119:97), and obedience to, the Word of God. This faith also knows and trusts that God is actively involved in the lives of His creatures, actively rewarding those who come to faith in Him.

THE ONLY GOD

DEUTERONOMY 4:35

"To you it was shown that you might know that the LORD, He is God; there is no other besides Him."

2 SAMUEL 7:22 (SEE 1 CHRON. 17:20; SEE NEH. 9:6; SEE PS. 86:10)

For this reason You are great, O Lord GOD; for there is none like You, and there is no God besides You, according to all that we have heard with our ears.

JOEL 2:27

"Thus you will know that I am in the midst of Israel,
And that I am the LORD your God,
And there is no other;
And My people will never be put to shame."

JOHN 17:3

"This is eternal life, that they may know You, the only true God, and Jesus Christ whom You have sent."

EPHESIANS 4:6

One God and Father of all who is over all and through all and in all.

1 TIMOTHY 2:5

For there is one God, *and* one mediator also between God and men, *the* man Christ Jesus.

JAMES 2:19

You believe that God is one. You do well; the demons also believe, and shudder.

Beginning with Moses, through the prophets, the psalms, the histories of the Old Testament, into the New Testament and the apostles, and the Lord Jesus Christ Himself, the testimony of Scripture is consistent in the affirmation that there is only one God. He is the Lord, Yahweh. This excludes all forms of polytheism, pantheism, and atheism.

TRANSCENDENCE AND IMMANENCE OF GOD

ISAIAH 40:22 (SEE PS. 99:1)

It is He who sits above the circle of the earth,
And its inhabitants are like grasshoppers,
Who stretches out the heavens like a curtain
And spreads them out like a tent to dwell in.

ISAIAH 66:1

Thus says the LORD,
"Heaven is My throne and the earth is My footstool.
Where then is a house you could build for Me?
And where is a place that I may rest?"

PSALM 113:4–7

The LORD is high above all nations;
His glory is above the heavens.
⁵Who is like the LORD our God,
Who is enthroned on high,
⁶Who humbles Himself to behold
The things that are in heaven and in the earth?

PSALM 145:18

The LORD is near to all who call upon Him,
To all who call upon Him in truth.

> **JEREMIAH 23:23**
>
> "Am I a God who is near," declares the LORD,
> "And not a God far off?"

> **ISAIAH 57:15**
>
> For thus says the high and exalted One
> Who lives forever, whose name is Holy,
> "I dwell *on* a high and holy place,
> And *also* with the contrite and lowly of spirit
> In order to revive the spirit of the lowly
> And to revive the heart of the contrite."

The transcendence of God is His utter "otherness"; He is *sui generis*. This is usually expressed in Scripture in metaphorical terms: in terms of size, He is immense—the heavens are His "tent" and "throne," the earth is His "footstool"; in terms of distance, He is high above—"above the circle of the earth," "above the heavens," "high and exalted"; in terms of moral purity, He is holy and glorious. God's immanence is His presence with, and involvement in, the affairs of this world. This is often expressed in Scripture as His nearness (especially in prayer), and His tender care of the poor and needy. Scripture does not attempt to explain how both can be true at the same time. Indeed, in several texts (e.g., above Ps. 113:4–7 and Isa. 57:15) both are affirmed in the same verses. The failure to affirm both God's transcendence and His immanence has been the source of many aberrant views of God. An overemphasis on transcendence can lead to Deism; an overemphasis on immanence can lead to theologies that say God is experiencing all the ups-and-downs of life and history just as we are, as Process Theology[6] suggests. Rightly understood, transcendence and immanence are not contrary concepts but complementary concepts. Even if they cannot be fully understood by believers, if held in faith, they lead to a greater appreciation of God's greatness and goodness.

ATTRIBUTES OF GOD

The attributes of God are His perfections and the distinguishing characteristics He has revealed about Himself, and by which He manifests His nature to

His creation. The Scriptures do not reveal these attributes in a way that indicates that they fall into various classifications or categories.

Question 4: What is God?

Answer: God is a Spirit, infinite, eternal, and unchangeable, in his being, wisdom, power, holiness, justice, goodness, and truth.[7]

EXCURSUS: An Illustration in Place of Classification

Instead of a system of classification of the attributes, what Scripture actually reveals is the interrelatedness of God's attributes or perfections. Perhaps an illustration will help us to understand this interrelatedness of the attributes. If we look at a diamond, what do we see? If it is a cut diamond, we see one thing, made up of one substance (carbon), with a number of facets. Each facet is identifiable on its own, but each facet is still the diamond and is still made of the same stuff as the diamond. Actually, we can never really see one facet because to "see" one facet is to see it in relation to the facets next to it, and we see those facets in relation to the facets next to those facets; indeed, to see any facet we really see it only in relation to all the facets, even if we can only concentrate on one facet at a time. Furthermore, the several facets are visible as such only because of the light that comes into the diamond through all the other facets.

If we think of the attributes of God like the facets on a diamond (granting the limitations inherent to all illustrations that use God's creation to describe God!), we perhaps have a better picture of how the attributes of God relate to each other and to God Himself. As with the facets on the diamond, so each attribute of God is what it is only in relation to other attributes related to it, and in relation to all the attributes, and in relation to God as He is in Himself. So, for instance, in considering God's eternality, we are in fact talking about His attribute of His infinity in relation to time. But here we are also talking about His aseity—His self-existence, because His existence just "is" and always (eternally) has been. When we refer to His infinity with respect to space, we are talking about His immensity or omnipresence. It is even possible to describe Him as "infinite in holiness," or "infinite in goodness" to describe the absolute nature of those qualities in Him. Likewise, in speaking of His attribute of truthfulness we are affirming that He is "true in His person"—which is His attribute of faithfulness or constancy, and He is "true when He speaks in His revelation"—which is His attribute of veracity or reliability. Thus, no attribute is ever really distinct from any of the other attributes, for again, each attribute is what it is only in relation to all the attributes considered together. "God is not the particular instantiation of a wonderful set of properties. Rather, there is nothing in God that is not identical with His divinity, nothing that is not just God Himself."[8] Thus, in considering each attribute (facet), the following comments will inevitably at times refer to His other attributes to display this interrelatedness of attributes.

Aseity (Self-Existence)/Being

EXODUS 3:14

God said to Moses, "I AM WHO I AM"; and He said, "Thus you shall say to the sons of Israel, 'I AM has sent me to you.'"

ISAIAH 44:24

Thus says the LORD, your Redeemer, and the one who formed you from the womb,

"I, the LORD, am the maker of all things,
Stretching out the heavens by Myself
And spreading out the earth all alone."

ISAIAH 45:22

"Turn to Me and be saved, all the ends of the earth;
For I am God, and there is no other."

From the "burning bush" God called Moses to lead His people out of bondage in Egypt (see Ex. 3:1–10). However, Moses demurred and began to offer excuses for why he should not be the one to undertake this commission. He claimed to be insignificant (Ex. 3:11), he claimed that no one would believe God had spoken to him (Ex. 4:1), he claimed to lack eloquence (Ex. 4:10).

At one point he argued that if he went to the people they would ask for the name of the God who had sent him (Ex. 3:13). Here God gave to Moses the stunning revelation of His name, "I AM WHO I AM" (Hebrew *'ehyeh 'asher 'ehyeh*). The name "I AM" (Hebrew *'ehyeh*) is the first person singular of the Hebrew verb *hayah* (Hebrew *hwh*—"to be, become"). When this is put into the third person singular ("he is"), it becomes *yahweh or Yahweh*—which is His name!

He is the God whose most basic attribute is "is-ness," or "being-itself." There is no "being-in-general" outside of God. He is the source and ground of ALL being (including human beings; "in Him we live and move and exist" [Acts 17:28]). He is ALL necessity and everything else is mere contingency. He has ALL priority, and from that ALL preeminence, and from that ALL power, and from that ALL authority. Yahweh is the maker of all things; He was not "made" and He did not "become." He has eternally been the one and only "God who is." The term used to describe this "aseity" means "self-existent" (Latin: "a," from and "se," self). He is not derived, dependent, or beholden to anyone or anything else; in fact, everything in creation is derived from, dependent on, and beholden to Him.

Spirituality

EXODUS 20:4
"You shall not make for yourself an idol, or any likeness of what is in heaven above or on the earth beneath or in the water under the earth."

EXODUS 33:20
But He said, "You cannot see My face, for no man can see Me and live!"

JOHN 1:18
No one has seen God at any time; the only begotten God who is in the bosom of the Father, He has explained *Him*.

JOHN 4:24
"God is spirit, and those who worship Him must worship in spirit and truth."

> **1 TIMOTHY 1:17**
> Now to the King eternal, immortal, invisible, the only God, *be* honor and
> glory forever and ever. Amen.

The gospel of John records a conversation Jesus had with a Samaritan
woman at a well (see John 4:5–6ff). At one point the conversation turned
to the subject of worship. Specifically, the woman had a question about the
most appropriate place for worship (see John 4:20). Jesus told the woman
that the question was actually moot, since God is not concerned about the
place where He is worshiped as much as He is concerned about the worshipers themselves (they must be "true worshipers" [John 4:23]) and the qualities
of worship ("in spirit and truth" [John 4:24]). The reason a particular location is not necessary, and these other aspects are vital, is because, Jesus says,
"God is spirit" (Greek *pneuma ho Theos*). The expression here is meant to
convey not that God is one spirit among many, but that His nature is "spirit."
A spirit does not have a corporeal body. When Jesus wanted to reassure the
disciples that He was indeed raised bodily from the dead, He invited them
to "see My hands and My feet, that it is I Myself; touch Me and see," and He
explained "for a spirit does not have flesh and bones as you see that I have"
(Luke 24:39). As spirit God has no characteristics of physical matter—no extension in space, no parts, no weight. As a spirit He is invisible, and therefore
cannot be seen with the physical eyes. It is this attribute that makes all physical representations of Him invalid, indeed idolatrous.

Eternity/Infinity

> **DEUTERONOMY 33:27A**
> "The eternal God is a dwelling place,
> And underneath are the everlasting arms."

> **PSALM 90:2**
> Before the mountains were born
> Or You gave birth to the earth and the world,
> Even from everlasting to everlasting, You are God.

PSALM 102:12

But You, O LORD, abide forever,
And Your name to all generations.

1 TIMOTHY 1:17

Now to the King eternal, immortal, invisible, the only God, *be* honor and
glory forever and ever. Amen.

"Eternity" and "infinity" are words that we can recognize but they refer to
concepts that are quite beyond the capacity of finite human minds to fully
grasp. To affirm that God is "eternal" is to say He is timeless in His being.
This is actually a corollary concept to His aseity—"He is" and always has
been "is." He is above and beyond time, and He experiences all time as one
moment.

The scriptural language is meant to convey these notions of timelessness by contrasting the existence and experiences of His creatures and
creation *in time* to God's existence *beyond time*. The psalmist makes reference to the mountains as the most ancient and lasting monuments in creation. Few things in this world seem as solid, lasting, and unchangeable as
the mountains. And yet He existed before the mountains, indeed, He "gave
birth" to them. His existence transcends the existence of those exemplars of
lasting-ness; He is "everlasting." The Hebrew term *'ôlām* indicates a period
of very long duration; used twice in the expression "from everlasting to everlasting," it indicates a stretch of incalculable, unfathomable time—which
is what eternity is. Furthermore, God's existence spans and exceeds the existence of "all generations" of mankind. His existence transcends not just
one life, not just one generation, but all generations of human lives. The very
transitory-ness of human life is the archetypical opposite of God's everlasting existence. God's immutable timelessness is a great comfort to His human
creatures. The expression "everlasting arms" is an anthropomorphism describing His tender care and protection, as a mother would tenderly take up
and care for a sleeping infant. His "everlasting arms" are a place of security
and hope for those who live in this ever-changing, unstable, transient world.

Simplicity/Unity

DEUTERONOMY 6:4

"Hear, O Israel! The LORD is our God, the LORD is one!"

God is one numerically and God is one in substance. He is one thing—God. He is not made up of parts. In the expression "the Lord is one," the term "one" (Hebrew *eḥad*) can be understood as indicating a compound unity (see Gen. 2:24). Thus, here is an affirmation of monotheism that allows for the later revelation of the Trinity.

> The principle claim of divine simplicity is that God is not composed of parts. Whatever is composed of parts depends upon its parts to be as it is. A part is anything in a subject that is less than the whole and without which the subject would be really different than it is. In short, composite beings need their parts to exist as they do. Moreover, the parts in an integrated whole require a composer distinct from themselves to unify them, an extrinsic source of unity. If God should be composed of parts—of components that were prior to Him in being—He would be doubly dependent: first, on the parts, and second, on the composer of the parts. But God is absolute in being, alone the sufficient reason for Himself and all other beings, and so cannot in any respect derive His being from another. Because God cannot depend on what is not God in order to be God, theologians traditionally insist that all that is in God is God.[9]

Immutability

PSALM 102:27

"But You are the same,
And Your years will not come to an end."

MALACHI 3:6

"For I, the LORD, do not change; therefore you, O sons of Jacob, are not consumed."

JAMES 1:17

Every good thing given and every perfect gift is from above, coming down from the Father of lights, with whom there is no variation or shifting shadow.

Immutability means unchangeability; that is, God does not change. He does not change in His being. He cannot improve because He is perfect, and has been, and will be, eternally. He does not change His mind or change His plans. He does not need to because those plans never fail—He is all powerful and nothing can thwart His purpose. Nothing can happen that would compel Him to change His plans—He already knows everything that will happen; indeed He is the one who has decreed what will happen (see Eph. 1:11; 3:11; Isa. 46:11).

Immutability is most often referred to in Scripture in relation to God's promises to His people. Malachi has in mind both the promises of God and the faithlessness of the people (Israel). They deserve God's judgment but because God is immutable in His promises, the people, the "sons of Jacob, are not consumed"—are not judged. James is reminding his readers that all the good things of life are gifts from God and believers can expect that He can be counted on to continue to provide good gifts.

Omnipresence

1 KINGS 8:27

"But will God indeed dwell on the earth? Behold, heaven and the highest heaven cannot contain You, how much less this house which I have built!"

PSALM 139:7–10

Where can I go from Your Spirit?
Or where can I flee from Your presence?
[8] If I ascend to heaven, You are there;
If I make my bed in Sheol, behold, You are there.
[9] If I take the wings of the dawn,
If I dwell in the remotest part of the sea,
[10] Even there Your hand will lead me,
And Your right hand will lay hold of me.

This and the next two attributes use the prefix "omni." This is from Latin and simply means "all."

Omnipresence simply means God is "everywhere present." Solomon recognizes that even the magnificent temple he has built is utterly inadequate to be called "God's house" because even the vast expanse of space is too small to encompass God.

Omnipotence

PSALM 147:5
Great is our Lord and abundant in strength;
His understanding is infinite.

ISAIAH 14:27
"For the LORD of hosts has planned, and who can frustrate *it*? And as for His stretched-out hand, who can turn it back?"

JEREMIAH 32:17 (SEE GEN. 18:14)
"'Ah Lord GOD! Behold, You have made the heavens and the earth by Your great power and by Your outstretched arm! Nothing is too difficult for You.'"

MARK 10:27
Looking at them, Jesus said, "With people it is impossible, but not with God; for all things are possible with God."

LUKE 1:37
"For nothing will be impossible with God."

Omnipotence means God is "all powerful." The epitome of God's all-mightyness is the creation of the universe. This power is often described using anthropomorphic terms (i.e., descriptions of God using human terms such as "stretched-out hand," "outstretched arm").

When Scripture says nothing is impossible for God, the idea is that actions or exploits that would be beyond human capacity (such as a virgin birth or saving sinners) are not beyond the power of God. God's power is only limited by His own nature; He cannot do anything contrary to His nature (see Heb. 6:18).

Omniscience

HIS KNOWLEDGE IS EXTENSIVE

PSALM 139:1–4

O Lord, You have searched me and known *me*.
2 You know when I sit down and when I rise up;
You understand my thought from afar.
3 You scrutinize my path and my lying down,
And are intimately acquainted with all my ways.
4 Even before there is a word on my tongue,
Behold, O Lord, You know it all.

PSALM 147:4–5

He counts the number of the stars;
He gives names to all of them.
5 Great is our Lord and abundant in strength;
His understanding is infinite.

ISAIAH 40:13–14

13 Who has directed the Spirit of the Lord,
Or as His counselor has informed Him?
14 With whom did He consult and *who* gave Him understanding?
And *who* taught Him in the path of justice and taught Him knowledge
And informed Him of the way of understanding?

HEBREWS 4:13

And there is no creature hidden from His sight, but all things are open and
laid bare to the eyes of Him with whom we have to do.

Omniscience means that God is "all knowing"; He has "all knowledge." God's knowledge is never supplemented by man's knowledge or man's understanding. God learns nothing from human science or human philosophical speculation. Indeed, God knows all the actions, even the intentions of a man. He knows the thoughts and intentions of man's heart (see Jer. 17:10) and a man's words before he even speaks them.

HIS KNOWLEDGE IS BEYOND HUMAN UNDERSTANDING

PSALM 145:3

Great is the LORD, and highly to be praised,
And His greatness is unsearchable.

ISAIAH 40:28

Do you not know? Have you not heard?
The Everlasting God, the LORD, the Creator of the ends of the earth
Does not become weary or tired.
His understanding is inscrutable.

ROMANS 11:33–36

Oh, the depth of the riches both of the wisdom and knowledge of God!
How unsearchable are His judgments and unfathomable His ways! [34] For
WHO HAS KNOWN THE MIND OF THE LORD, OR WHO BECAME HIS COUNSELOR?
[35] Or WHO HAS FIRST GIVEN TO HIM THAT IT MIGHT BE PAID BACK TO HIM
AGAIN? [36] For from Him and through Him and to Him are all things. To Him
be the glory forever. Amen.

God's knowledge is not just more extensive than human knowledge but is in fact incomprehensible to human minds. This is not to say that there is nothing that can be known about God and His ways. Human beings can know what God has revealed (see Deut. 29:29). But even granted this relative human understanding, humans can never grasp the height and depth and breadth of God's mind. We can know truly, but we will never have the knowledge God has exhaustively.

The "wisdom and knowledge of God" which Paul extols in this doxology is found in his revelation of the way of salvation in the gospel of Jesus Christ (see Rom. 1–8), and in what God has revealed about His plans and purposes for the nation of Israel (see Rom. 9–11). Paul describes this "wisdom and knowledge" as "unsearchable" and "unfathomable." Again, these terms do not mean nothing can be known about God's ways (Paul has just spent eleven chapters of doctrine and teaching for the Romans to know and understand!). The term "unsearchable" (Greek *anexeraunēta*) is rare and refers to something "beyond searching out," perhaps in the sense that it cannot be discovered by a pursuit or quest. The term "unfathomable" (Greek *anex-ichniastoi*) is also rare and has the idea of something that cannot be traced or tracked (as one might follow someone's footprints on a pathway). The point being made in this great doxology is that the capacity humans have on their own could never ascertain or discover the ways of God.

Goodness

PSALM 100:5

For the LORD is good;
His lovingkindness is everlasting
And His faithfulness to all generations.

PSALM 145:6–9

Men shall speak of the power of Your awesome acts,
And I will tell of Your greatness.
[7] They shall eagerly utter the memory of Your abundant goodness
And will shout joyfully of Your righteousness.
[8] The LORD is gracious and merciful;
Slow to anger and great in lovingkindness.
[9] The LORD is good to all,
And His mercies are over all His works.

LAMENTATIONS 3:25

The LORD is good to those who wait for Him,
To the person who seeks Him.

MATTHEW 5:45

"So that you may be sons of your Father who is in heaven; for He causes His sun to rise on *the* evil and *the* good, and sends rain on *the* righteous and *the* unrighteous."

MATTHEW 7:11

"If you then, being evil, know how to give good gifts to your children, how much more will your Father who is in heaven give what is good to those who ask Him!"

ACTS 14:17

"And yet He did not leave Himself without witness, in that He did good and gave you rains from heaven and fruitful seasons, satisfying your hearts with food and gladness."

God's goodness is His benevolence. The psalmist links His greatness to His goodness, and His goodness to His righteousness and His mercy and His patience and His lovingkindness (*ḥesed*). His goodness is mostly seen in His provision for His creation. He gives sun and rain in order that His creation will produce the food they need for life, and the food He gives is good and brings His creatures much joy (see Ps. 104:15; Eccl. 10:19). His goodness exceeds the relative goodness of an earthly father.

Wisdom

PSALM 104:24

O Lᴏʀᴅ, how many are Your works!
In wisdom You have made them all;
The earth is full of Your possessions.

DANIEL 2:20–21

Daniel said,
   "Let the name of God be blessed forever and ever,
   For wisdom and power belong to Him.
   [21] "It is He who changes the times and the epochs;
   He removes kings and establishes kings;
   He gives wisdom to wise men
   And knowledge to men of understanding."

ROMANS 16:27

To the only wise God, through Jesus Christ, be the glory forever. Amen.

1 CORINTHIANS 2:7 (SEE ROM. 11:33)

But we speak God's wisdom in a mystery, the hidden *wisdom* which God predestined before the ages to our glory.

The wisdom of God is not just His knowledge (omniscience) but it is the application of His knowledge, particularly in the outworking of His eternal purpose (see Eph. 1:11). God employs everything in His creation wisely and for the purpose of accomplishing His ends. One way God's wisdom is displayed is in the outworking of His purpose for the nations in history. All of history—the rise and fall of nations and empires—is in God's control and according to His wise plan. God's wisdom is preeminently seen in the outworking of His plan of redemption in Christ. The unwise rulers of this world see that plan as foolish (see 1 Cor. 1:18–20; 2:8) but in fact it is the plan that began before the foundation of the world (see Eph. 1:4) and will continue into eternity.

Holiness (Transcendence and Purity)

EXODUS 15:11

"Who is like You among the gods, O LORD?
Who is like You, majestic in holiness,
Awesome in praises, working wonders?

LEVITICUS 11:44

"'For I am the LORD your God. Consecrate yourselves therefore, and be holy, for I am holy. And you shall not make yourselves unclean with any of the swarming things that swarm on the earth.'"

ISAIAH 6:1–3 (SEE JOHN 12:41)

In the year of King Uzziah's death I saw the Lord sitting on a throne, lofty and exalted, with the train of His robe filling the temple. [2] Seraphim stood above Him, each having six wings: with two he covered his face, and with two he covered his feet, and with two he flew. [3] And one called out to another and said,

"Holy, Holy, Holy, is the LORD of hosts,
The whole earth is full of His glory."

1 PETER 1:15–16

But like the Holy One who called you, be holy yourselves also in all *your* behavior; [16] because it is written, "YOU SHALL BE HOLY, FOR I AM HOLY."

REVELATION 4:8

And the four living creatures, each one of them having six wings, are full of eyes around and within; and day and night they do not cease to say,

"HOLY, HOLY, HOLY *is* THE LORD GOD, THE ALMIGHTY, WHO WAS AND WHO IS AND WHO IS TO COME."

In his great vision Isaiah was given an awesome display of the holiness of God. In a sense, Moses's words in Exodus 15:11 are a commentary on Isaiah's vision. Here the Lord God is seen (in vision) in majestic holiness, in awesome exaltation. He is on a throne, which speaks of His power and sovereign authority. He is "lofty and exalted" which indicates He is above and separated from everything and everyone else. His robe is also a symbol of His authority and power. And this robe fills the temple, which indicates He makes the environment majestic (not the other way around). He is attended by seraphim (a classification of angels mentioned only here) whose only function is to cry out and extol the holiness of God. The seraphim are themselves magnificent heavenly beings, and yet they must cover themselves and conceal themselves from the direct gaze of God. Their threefold cry (likely antiphonally) is "Holy, Holy, Holy" (Hebrew *qādôsh*). The repetition raises the declaration to the superlative level—He is "the holiest." The term "holy" (Hebrew *qādôsh* along with the equivalent Greek term *hagiazō*) has the notion of something distinct, separated from the profane (anything "unclean"), utterly pure, and without any moral deficiencies. This describes God's holiness perfectly and Isaiah uses this term of God twenty-six times in his prophecy (see Isa. 1:4; 5:19; 10:20; 12:6; 29:19; 37:23; and more). When the angels affirm "the whole earth is full of His glory," they bridge the gap between heaven and earth and affirm that His holy transcendence does not prevent His genuine immanence (see **Transcendence and Immanence of God** above). Indeed, the whole of creation reflects the glory (*qābôd*) of God.

The prophet's reaction (see Isa. 6:5) is itself a statement on the holiness of God. He recognizes his own utter lack of holiness and pronounces a curse on himself ("Woe is me"), and he confesses his sinfulness and impurity. Isaiah was a man of God, a prophet who spoke for God, but in the presence of the

Holy Lord of Hosts even his lips are unclean. Anything less than God is less than holy. God's holiness is the utter opposite of man's sinfulness. Nevertheless, God's holiness is the archetype for God's people (see 1 Peter 1:15) and they are to strive to be conformed to His holiness (see Heb. 12:14).

Justice/Righteousness

PSALM 36:6
Your righteousness is like the mountains of God;
Your judgments are *like* a great deep.
O LORD, You preserve man and beast.

PSALM 72:2
May he judge Your people with righteousness
And Your afflicted with justice.

PSALM 89:14
Righteousness and justice are the foundation of Your throne;
Lovingkindness and truth go before You.

PSALM 98:9
Before the LORD, for He is coming to judge the earth;
He will judge the world with righteousness
And the peoples with equity.

ACTS 17:31
"Because He has fixed a day in which He will judge the world in righteousness through a Man whom He has appointed, having furnished proof to all men by raising Him from the dead."

2 PETER 1:1
Simon Peter, a bond-servant and apostle of Jesus Christ,
To those who have received a faith of the same kind as ours, by the righteousness of our God and Savior, Jesus Christ.

The righteousness or justice (Hebrew *ṣedāqâ* and Greek *dikaiosynē*) of God can be understood as the application of His holiness. When God judges, He does so with perfect uprightness in Himself and He applies perfect rectitude toward those over whom He passes judgment.

Lovingkindness

PSALM 42:8

The LORD will command His lovingkindness in the daytime;
And His song will be with me in the night,
A prayer to the God of my life.

PSALM 63:3

Because Your lovingkindness is better than life,
My lips will praise You.

PSALM 145:8

The LORD is gracious and merciful;
Slow to anger and great in lovingkindness.

ISAIAH 54:10

"For the mountains may be removed and the hills may shake,
But My lovingkindness will not be removed from you,
And My covenant of peace will not be shaken,"
Says the LORD who has compassion on you.

ISAIAH 63:7

I shall make mention of the lovingkindnesses of the LORD, the praises of
the LORD,
According to all that the LORD has granted us,
And the great goodness toward the house of Israel,
Which He has granted them according to His compassion
And according to the abundance of His lovingkindnesses.

The term "lovingkindness" in the Old Testament is the Hebrew term *ḥesed*. It is a rich and deeply meaningful word but the concept it is meant to convey is not easily translated by any single term in Greek (LXX), Latin, or English. "For centuries the word *ḥesed* was translated with words like mercy, kindness, love. The LXX [Greek version of the Old Testament] usually uses *eleos* 'mercy,' and the Latin *misericordia*."[10] Expressed between humans, *ḥesed* conveyed the notions of kindness, sympathy, care, loyalty, mercy, and fidelity one might expect among members of an extended family. With respect to God's special, covenantal relationship with Israel, He displays *ḥesed*—"steadfast-love," "loyal-love," and "faithful-love." God's *ḥesed* is why He keeps His covenant promises in spite of Israel's many failures.[11]

Love

JOHN 3:16

"For God so loved the world, that He gave His only begotten Son, that whoever believes in Him shall not perish, but have eternal life."

ROMANS 5:8

But God demonstrates His own love toward us, in that while we were yet sinners, Christ died for us.

EPHESIANS 2:4–5

But God, being rich in mercy, because of His great love with which He loved us, [5] even when we were dead in our transgressions, made us alive together with Christ (by grace you have been saved).

1 JOHN 4:8

The one who does not love does not know God, for God is love.

The highest type of love mentioned in the New Testament is that love captured in the Greek term *agape*. This love is self-giving, even sacrificial love. And this is the love that describes this attribute of God. The self-sacrificial quality of God's love can be seen in the gift of the Son by the Father, in the self-sacrificial death of the Son for those who were at enmity with Him, and in the new life He freely and sovereignly gave to those dead in their transgressions and sins.

Love is so central to His being that the apostle John can say "God is love." John is not limiting God's essence to love—he is not saying "Love is God." He is affirming that love is central to all that God is and does.

Mercy

> **ROMANS 9:14–15, 18**
> What shall we say then? There is no injustice with God, is there? May it never be! ¹⁵ For He says to Moses, "I WILL HAVE MERCY ON WHOM I HAVE MERCY, AND I WILL HAVE COMPASSION ON WHOM I HAVE COMPASSION." . . . ¹⁸ So then He has mercy on whom He desires, and He hardens whom He desires.

> **TITUS 3:5**
> He saved us, not on the basis of deeds which we have done in righteousness, but according to His mercy, by the washing of regeneration and renewing by the Holy Spirit.

Mercy (Greek *eleos*) is a quality that is displayed in the face of misery and is related to His compassion. The object of mercy is most often in a state of abject wretchedness and unable to find restoration by any means of self-effort. God's mercy is freely given, is not earned by our actions or efforts, and for that reason it is related to God's grace.

Grace/Favor

> **GENESIS 6:8**
> But Noah found favor in the eyes of the LORD.

> **EXODUS 33:19**
> And He said, "I Myself will make all My goodness pass before you, and will proclaim the name of the LORD before you; and I will be gracious to whom I will be gracious, and will show compassion on whom I will show compassion."

> **ROMANS 3:23–24**
> For all have sinned and fall short of the glory of God, ²⁴ being justified as a gift by His grace through the redemption which is in Christ Jesus.

> **EPHESIANS 1:4B–8**
> In love ⁵ He predestined us to adoption as sons through Jesus Christ to

Himself, according to the kind intention of His will, [6] to the praise of the glory of His grace, which He freely bestowed on us in the Beloved. [7] In Him we have redemption through His blood, the forgiveness of our trespasses, according to the riches of His grace [8] which He lavished on us. In all wisdom and insight.

EPHESIANS 2:5, 8–9

Even when we were dead in our transgressions, made us alive together with Christ (by grace you have been saved). . . . [8] For by grace you have been saved through faith; and that not of yourselves, *it is* the gift of God; [9] not as a result of works, so that no one may boast.

TITUS 2:11

For the grace of God has appeared, bringing salvation to all men.

A well-known definition of grace is "the unmerited favor of God," and the texts certainly bear out the accuracy of that definition. Grace is not given to those who deserve it; indeed, it would cease to be grace if the benefit could be earned (see Rom. 4:4–5) because grace is a gift, a free and undeserved provision.

Patience/Longsuffering

NUMBERS 14:18

"'The LORD is slow to anger and abundant in lovingkindness, forgiving iniquity and transgression; but He will by no means clear *the guilty*, visiting the iniquity of the fathers on the children to the third and the fourth *generations*.'"

PSALM 86:15

But You, O Lord, are a God merciful and gracious,
Slow to anger and abundant in lovingkindness and truth.

ROMANS 2:4

Or do you think lightly of the riches of His kindness and tolerance and patience, not knowing that the kindness of God leads you to repentance?

ROMANS 9:22

What if God, although willing to demonstrate His wrath and to make His power known, endured with much patience vessels of wrath prepared for destruction?

2 PETER 3:9, 15A

The Lord is not slow about His promise, as some count slowness, but is patient toward you, not wishing for any to perish but for all to come to repentance . . . [15] and regard the patience of our Lord *as* salvation.

The patience or longsuffering of God is not a minor theme in the Bible. It is most often related to His attributes of mercy and compassion but with an eye to His justice and even His wrath. Sinners must not presume upon His patience but see it as an evidence of His mercy and repent.

Truthfulness/Veracity

NUMBERS 23:19

God is not a man, that He should lie,
Nor a son of man, that He should repent;
Has He said, and will He not do it?
Or has He spoken, and will He not make it good?

PSALM 33:4

For the word of the LORD is upright,
And all His work is *done* in faithfulness.

PSALM 119:151

You are near, O LORD,
And all Your commandments are truth.

PSALM 119:160

The sum of Your word is truth,
And every one of Your righteous ordinances is everlasting.

ROMANS 3:3–4

What then? If some did not believe, their unbelief will not nullify the faithfulness of God, will it? [4] May it never be! Rather, let God be found true,

though every man *be found* a liar, as it is written,
"THAT YOU MAY BE JUSTIFIED IN YOUR WORDS,
AND PREVAIL WHEN YOU ARE JUDGED."

God is a God of truth and always speaks the truth. The fact that Moses says simply "God is not a man, that He should lie" says a great deal about the pervasive tendency toward mendacity and prevarication of humanity. In fact, God cannot lie (see Titus 1:2). God's truthfulness is most pertinent when considering His self-revelation particularly in the Scriptures. We need to know that when God speaks to us, we can rely on His words to be true and accurate and what they say to reflect (correspond to) reality.

Faithfulness

DEUTERONOMY 7:9
Know therefore that the LORD your God, He is God, the faithful God, who keeps His covenant and His lovingkindness to a thousandth generation with those who love Him and keep His commandments.

DEUTERONOMY 32:4
The Rock! His work is perfect,
For all His ways are just;
A God of faithfulness and without injustice,
Righteous and upright is He.

PSALM 89:1–2
I will sing of the lovingkindness of the LORD forever;
To all generations I will make known Your faithfulness with my mouth.
² For I have said, "Lovingkindness will be built up forever;
In the heavens You will establish Your faithfulness."

LAMENTATIONS 3:21–23
This I recall to my mind,
Therefore I have hope.
²² The LORD'S lovingkindnesses indeed never cease,
For His compassions never fail.

> [23] *They* are new every morning;
> Great is Your faithfulness.

1 THESSALONIANS 5:24

Faithful is He who calls you, and He also will bring it to pass.

The faithfulness of God is most important in terms of His relationship with His people. His commitment to His people means they can rely on His lovingkindness in the course of life and can trust in His promises yet to be realized. His faithfulness is something experienced by His people through life—"they are new every morning." And His faithfulness sustains their hope in promises yet unrealized. Indeed, His faithfulness extends to future generations. Paul reminded the Thessalonians of the calling they had received and in which they lived, and that reminder was meant to reassure them that all His promises would be kept.

Glory

EXODUS 24:16

The glory of the LORD rested on Mount Sinai, and the cloud covered it for six days; and on the seventh day He called to Moses from the midst of the cloud.

DEUTERONOMY 5:24

"You said, 'Behold, the LORD our God has shown us His glory and His greatness, and we have heard His voice from the midst of the fire; we have seen today that God speaks with man, yet he lives.'"

1 KINGS 8:10–11

It happened that when the priests came from the holy place, the cloud filled the house of the LORD, [11] so that the priests could not stand to minister because of the cloud, for the glory of the LORD filled the house of the LORD.

PSALM 24:8

Who is the King of glory?
The LORD strong and mighty,
The LORD mighty in battle.

PSALM 29:3

The voice of the LORD is upon the waters;
The God of glory thunders,
The LORD is over many waters.

PSALM 57:5

Be exalted above the heavens, O God;
Let Your glory be above all the earth.

JOHN 1:14

And the Word became flesh, and dwelt among us, and we saw His glory, glory as of the only begotten from the Father, full of grace and truth.

HEBREWS 1:3A

And He is the radiance of His glory and the exact representation of His nature.

The glory of God is a major theme in the Bible. The Hebrew term for glory, *kābōd*, originally meant "heavy" or "weighty" (perhaps as precious metal like gold is heavy). It came to be used of persons and things that were "weighty" in importance, such persons or things that demanded honor, respect, or should be highly valued. The depictions of the glory of God coming into a space, typically the temple or appearing in the heavens, also often included manifestations of light (a fire or lightning) so the idea of glory also conveyed the idea of brilliance or splendor. This latter idea is prominent in the Greek term for glory, *doxa*, which has the nuances of "brightness, splendor, and radiance." The glory of God elicits praise or doxology from His people. In a sense, the glory of God (brightness) is what men see when the transcendence of God is allowed to shine through to the earthly realm (see Isa. 6:3; Matt. 17:2, the transfiguration).

Wrath

NAHUM 1:2

A jealous and avenging God is the LORD;
The LORD is avenging and wrathful.

The LORD takes vengeance on His adversaries,
And He reserves wrath for His enemies.

ROMANS 1:18

For the wrath of God is revealed from heaven against all ungodliness and unrighteousness of men who suppress the truth in unrighteousness.

ROMANS 9:22

What if God, although willing to demonstrate His wrath and to make His power known, endured with much patience vessels of wrath prepared for destruction?

EPHESIANS 5:6

Let no one deceive you with empty words, for because of these things the wrath of God comes upon the sons of disobedience.

REVELATION 6:16–17

And they said to the mountains and to the rocks, "Fall on us and hide us from the presence of Him who sits on the throne, and from the wrath of the Lamb; [17] for the great day of their wrath has come, and who is able to stand?"

REVELATION 19:15

From His mouth comes a sharp sword, so that with it He may strike down the nations, and He will rule them with a rod of iron; and He treads the wine press of the fierce wrath of God, the Almighty.

The wrath (Hebrew *ḥēmāh*; Greek *orgē*) of God is not a minor theme in the Bible. The wrath of God is His righteous, angry reaction to sin. God has a righteous aversion to sin (see Hab. 1:13) and is rightly indignant toward sin (see Ps. 145:20). Sin calls forth God's upright and resolute vengeance. God's wrath is directed toward and against His enemies and the disobedient— in other words, toward those who deserve it. His wrath is inevitable (it will come) and inexorable (it will be unrelenting). However, the many references to the wrath of God are intended to warn men and to call them to repentance.

NAMES OF GOD

Yahweh

GENESIS 2:4 (SEE GEN. 2:5, 7, 8)

This is the account of the heavens and the earth when they were created, in the day that the LORD God made earth and heaven.

EXODUS 3:4–5, 14–15

When the LORD saw that he turned aside to look, God called to him from the midst of the bush and said, "Moses, Moses!" And he said, "Here I am." ⁵ Then He said, "Do not come near here; remove your sandals from your feet, for the place on which you are standing is holy ground." . . . ¹⁴ God said to Moses, "I AM WHO I AM"; and He said, "Thus you shall say to the sons of Israel, 'I AM has sent me to you.'" ¹⁵ God, furthermore, said to Moses, "Thus you shall say to the sons of Israel, 'The LORD, the God of your fathers, the God of Abraham, the God of Isaac, and the God of Jacob, has sent me to you.' This is My name forever, and this is My memorial-name to all generations."

The name of the God of Abraham, Isaac, and Jacob is "Yahweh." This name appears over 6,800 times in the Old Testament. In English translations the name is commonly rendered "the LORD," using all capital letters (L O R D) to distinguish it from another name, Adonai ("Lord"). The four letters of the Hebrew name YHWH are called the "tetragrammaton" ("four-lettered"). This name was considered too sacred to be pronounced and so the vowels for Adonai were placed around the letters YHWH which effectively made the name unpronounceable. It is from this non-name that the appellation "Jehovah" was devised.

This name expresses His self-existence (see **Aseity [Self-existence]/Being** above) and is His "covenant name" by which He is identified specifically with the people (nation) of Israel.

Yahweh Sabaoth

PSALM 24:10 (SEE ISA. 9:7)

Who is this King of glory?

The LORD of hosts,

He is the King of glory. . . .

HAGGAI 2:6–9 (SEE ZECH. 4:6)

"For thus says the LORD of hosts, 'Once more in a little while, I am going to shake the heavens and the earth, the sea also and the dry land. [7] I will shake all the nations; and they will come with the wealth of all nations, and I will fill this house with glory,' says the LORD of hosts. [8] 'The silver is Mine and the gold is Mine,' declares the LORD of hosts. [9] 'The latter glory of this house will be greater than the former,' says the LORD of hosts, 'and in this place I will give peace,' declares the LORD of hosts."

LUKE 2:13

And suddenly there appeared with the angel a multitude of the heavenly host praising God and saying,

The term "hosts" (Hebrew *ṣābā, ṣebāʾōth*) refers to armies or to the vast number (as in an army) of the angels in heaven. In Luke 2:13 the term "hosts" is *strateia*, which—like *ṣābāʾ, ṣebāʾōth*—refers to an army. In these references the terms are meant to indicate the transcendent power and authority of Yahweh as He is the Lord over the vast army of heavenly angels who do His bidding in either judgment or praise.

Yahweh Yireh

GENESIS 22:14

Abraham called the name of that place The LORD Will Provide, as it is said to this day, "In the mount of the LORD it will be provided."

The term "Yireh" (Hebrew *yirʾeh*) is from a root that means "to see" (Hebrew *rāʾâ*) and in certain forms, as in Genesis 22:14, has the notion of "to see" in a sustaining way. This name is appropriate for God since it was He who "provided" the ram to be sacrificed in place of Isaac.

Yahweh Shalom

JUDGES 6:24A

Then Gideon built an altar there to the LORD and named it The LORD is Peace.

The Hebrew term "Shalom" (*šālôm*) is the term for "peace." In order to reassure Gideon of God's presence and favor, the angel of the Lord accepted Gideon's offering of meat and bread in a blaze of fire (Judg. 6:21). However, this manifestation unnerved the timid Gideon who cried out in fear (Judg. 6:22). He had to be reassured by Yahweh who calmed him with the words, "Peace to you, do not fear; you shall not die." (Judg. 6:23). The altar built and named by Gideon was an expression of his faith in God, and his newfound understanding that the one who has the presence and favor (grace) of God need not fear for he is at peace with God.

Yahweh Tsidkenu

JEREMIAH 23:6

"In His days Judah will be saved,
And Israel will dwell securely;
And this is His name by which He will be called,
'The LORD our righteousness.'"

The term "Tsidkenu" (from the Hebrew *ṣedeq, ṣedāqâ*) means "our righteousness." The context of this naming is the messianic promise of the Davidic "Branch" (Jer. 23:5a; see Jer. 33:15; Isa. 4:2; Zech. 6:12–13). The reign of the coming Messiah will be a reign of wisdom, justice, and righteousness (Jer. 23:5b) in which the reunited nation (both Judah and Israel are mentioned) will "be saved" and will "dwell securely" (Jer. 23:6a). This name ("our righteousness") indicates the source of the salvation and security which He brings. (See **Justification**.)

El

> **GENESIS 31:13A**
>
> I am the God *of* Bethel, where you anointed a pillar, where you made a vow to Me.

> **PSALM 77:14**
>
> You are the God who works wonders;
> You have made known Your strength among the peoples.

The name *El* is the basic name for the, or a, "deity" and is normally translated as "God." Often, when the one true God is meant, the context or surrounding terms (e.g., "the God of heaven" Ps. 136:26; "the living God" Josh. 3:10; Ps. 84:2) or the use of the article ("*h*"; e.g., Gen. 31:13, Hebrew *hāʾēl*) will make this clear. The God who had met Jacob at Bethel was Yahweh, the God of the Patriarchs (see Gen. 28:13, 19)—the true God. He is the God who "works wonders," that is, has power and strength.

Elohim

> **GENESIS 1:1–4**
>
> In the beginning God created the heavens and the earth. ² The earth was formless and void, and darkness was over the surface of the deep, and the Spirit of God was moving over the surface of the waters. ³ Then God said, "Let there be light"; and there was light. ⁴ God saw that the light was good; and God separated the light from the darkness.

> **GENESIS 1:26–27**
>
> Then God said, "Let Us make man in Our image, according to Our likeness; and let them rule over the fish of the sea and over the birds of the sky and over the cattle and over all the earth, and over every creeping thing that creeps on the earth." ²⁷ God created man in His own image, in the image of God He created him; male and female He created them.

The name "Elohim" appears over 2,000 times in the Old Testament and is often translated simply "God" as it is in Genesis 1. In Hebrew the ending "-im" usually indicates a plural noun. When used of God, this ending is a "plural of majesty" or a "plural of intensity." This name for God appears first in Scripture, at the head of the creation account where the transcendent power of God is displayed in the creation of the universe and everything in it. The plural form of this name is not a proof of His Triunity but it is harmonious with later revelation that does reveal that God is Triune. (See **The Trinity.**)

El Shaddai

> **GENESIS 17:1**
> Now when Abram was ninety-nine years old, the LORD appeared to Abram and said to him,
>> "I am God Almighty;
>> Walk before Me, and be blameless."

> **RUTH 1:20–21**
> She said to them, "Do not call me Naomi; call me Mara, for the Almighty has dealt very bitterly with me. ²¹ I went out full, but the LORD has brought me back empty. Why do you call me Naomi, since the LORD has witnessed against me and the Almighty has afflicted me?"

The term "Shaddai" is generally translated "almighty" (Hebrew *šadday*). The basic meaning of this term has to do with "power." The "power" in view, however, is not so much the absolute power of God's omnipotence but His power over life circumstances of His people. From the human perspective, it seemed hopeless that the aged Abraham would have a son, and likewise it seemed that Naomi had reached a hopeless condition in life. Both were powerless to change the circumstances of their lives. However, the Almighty God has the power to change the lives of those who trust Him.

El Elyon

> **GENESIS 14:18–20, 22**
> And Melchizedek king of Salem brought out bread and wine; now he was a priest of God Most High. ¹⁹ He blessed him and said,

"Blessed be Abram of God Most High,
Possessor of heaven and earth;
[20] And blessed be God Most High,
Who has delivered your enemies into your hand." . . .
Abram said to the king of Sodom, "I have sworn to the LORD God Most
High, possessor of heaven and earth."

PSALM 91:1–2, 9

He who dwells in the shelter of the Most High
Will abide in the shadow of the Almighty.
[2] I will say to the LORD, "My refuge and my fortress,
My God, in whom I trust!" . . .
[9] For you have made the LORD, my refuge,
Even the Most High, your dwelling place.

The term or name "Elyon" comes from a root term (Hebrew *ʿālâ*) that means "to ascend," or "to go up." When it is used of God—"God Most High"—it refers to His elevated status above all of creation. By extension it refers to His absolute sovereignty. This sovereignty is revered by all who know Him and at the same time it is an endless source of comfort because He is a place of refuge.

El Olam

GENESIS 21:33

Abraham planted a tamarisk tree at Beersheba, and there he called on the
name of the LORD, the Everlasting God.

ISAIAH 40:28

Do you not know? Have you not heard?
The Everlasting God, the LORD, the Creator of the ends of the earth
Does not become weary or tired.
His understanding is inscrutable.

The Hebrew term *ʿôlām* means "lasting" or "eternal" (see **Eternity/Infinity**). This name means He is the everlasting God, or simply the eternal God.

Adonai

> **GENESIS 15:2 (SEE 15:8)**
> Abram said, "O Lord GOD, what will You give me, since I am childless, and the heir of my house is Eliezer of Damascus?"

> **EXODUS 4:10A**
> Then Moses said to the LORD, "Please, Lord, I have never been eloquent."

The term "Adonai" (Hebrew *ʾadōnāy*) is the generic title "lord." In the Old Testament it is a title used as a general term of respect for anyone in authority (e.g., a husband, Gen. 18:12; a master, Ex. 21:4–8; a king, 1 Sam. 22:12; a governor, Neh. 3:5; and others). It is used as a name for God, but usually in a context with other divine names or with descriptions which indicate that the one being referred to is the true God.

When the names Adonai and Yahweh (YHWH) occur together in the Hebrew Bible, the convention of translating YHWH as "the LORD" would be confusing ("the Lord [Adonai] the LORD [YHWH]) and so in such cases LORD becomes GOD—using the capitals G O D.

THE TRINITY

> We believe in one God, the Father Almighty, Maker of heaven and earth and of all things visible and invisible; And in one Lord Jesus Christ, the only-begotten Son of God, begotten from the Father before all ages, Light from Light, true God from true God, begotten, not made, of one substance with the Father through Whom all things were made. . . . And [we believe] in the Holy Spirit, the Lord and Giver of life, Who proceeds from the Father, Who with the Father and the Son is jointly worshipped and jointly glorified. . . .[12]

There Is One God

> **DEUTERONOMY 6:4**
> "Hear, O Israel! The LORD is our God, the LORD is one!"

The Scriptures are clear that there is one and only one God. The term "one" (Hebrew *'ehād*) may be understood as a "oneness of unity" (only by way of illustrating the meaning of the word *'ehād* and not as an illustration of the Trinity; see Gen. 2:24, e.g., the oneness of man and wife).

There Are Three Persons

THE FATHER IS GOD

> **1 CORINTHIANS 8:6A**
> Yet for us there is *but* one God, the Father, from whom are all things and we *exist* for Him.

> **EPHESIANS 4:6**
> One God and Father of all who is over all and through all and in all.

THE SON IS GOD
(see **The Deity of Christ**)

THE SPIRIT IS GOD
(see **His Deity**)

The Scriptures are clear that there are three (persons) who may rightly be called God. Paul's assertion that "there is but one God" establishes his belief in the one God based on the monotheism of the Old Testament. His reference to "the Father" is not meant to say this one God is the Father only, but that "the Father" is God. Other passages indicate that "the Son" is God and yet other passages indicate that "the Spirit" is God. This is not to suggest that there are three gods (i.e., tritheism) but that each one of the persons may rightly be called God. At the same time, the three are not merely three different names of the one God, as if there are times when the one God is called "Father," and at other times He is called "the Son," and yet other times He is called "the Holy Spirit" (i.e., modalism). The Scriptures reveal that there is one God (substance, essence; Greek *ousia*) in three persons (subsistence; Greek *hypostasis*).

Summary: While the term "Trinity" is not used in the Bible, the Scriptures clearly reveal that there is one God, and just as clearly, they speak of three who may be rightly called God, and the three each have the characteristics of personhood. The Father, the Son, and the Spirit each possess knowledge, show emotion, demonstrate will. The creedal statement—one God in three persons—is an accurate summary of what the Bible says about the one God who is the Father, the Son, and the Spirit. In short, the doctrine of the Trinity is not imposed upon the texts of Scripture but emerges from what the Scriptures reveal about the one God and the three, who are distinct persons who deserve to be called God.

> We teach that there is but one living and true God (Deut. 6:4; Isa. 45:5–7; 1 Cor. 8:4), an infinite, all-knowing Spirit (John 4:24), perfect in all His attributes, *one in essence, eternally existing in three Persons—Father, Son, and Holy Spirit* (Matt. 28:19; 2 Cor. 13:14)—each equally deserving worship and obedience.[13]

Indications in the Old Testament

There are no texts in the Old Testament that explicitly teach the Trinity. There are texts that can be seen as indications of, and which are in harmony with, the doctrine of the Trinity.

INDICATIONS OF A PLURALITY IN GOD

> **GENESIS 1:26A**
> Then God said, "Let Us make man in Our image, according to Our likeness."

> **GENESIS 3:22A**
> Then the LORD God said, "Behold, the man has become like one of Us, knowing good and evil."

> **GENESIS 11:7**
> "Come, let Us go down and there confuse their language."

> **ISAIAH 6:8A**
>
> Then I heard the voice of the Lord, saying, "Whom shall I send, and who
> will go for Us?"

In Genesis 1:26 God is speaking and the Hebrew text uses a first-person plural verb to describe that speaking, in the expression "Let Us make." Also, God uses a plural pronoun "Our" when He refers to the "image" in which He is making man. Again, in Genesis 11:7 God uses a first-person plural verb: "let Us go down." In both Genesis 3:22 and Isaiah 6:8 God uses a plural pronoun ("Us") to refer to Himself. As noted in the name "Elohim," these plurals may be indications of majesty and intensity, but with the clearer revelation of the Trinity given in the New Testament these texts seem to reveal a divine acknowledgment of His actual plurality.

INDICATIONS IN MESSIANIC PROPHECY

> **ISAIAH 61:1A**
>
> The Spirit of the Lord GOD is upon me,
> Because the LORD has anointed me.

In this text the Messiah is speaking. (This text was read by Jesus in the synagogue at Nazareth. On that occasion He affirmed that the prophecy was fulfilled in His ministry [see Luke 4:16–21].) The Messiah is describing His empowerment by the Spirit and His commission by Yahweh. In this text He makes reference to the Lord (Yahweh) and to the Spirit of the Lord (Yahweh) in such a way that these titles may be understood to refer to two distinct entities, both of which are identified by the name Yahweh. If the Messiah is still speaking through verse 8 ("For I, the Lord (Yahweh), love justice"), then He identifies Himself by the name Yahweh. Again, this is an indication of a plurality in God and prepares for the full revelation of the Trinity in the New Testament.

Indications in the New Testament

THREE NAMES

MATTHEW 28:19

"Go therefore and make disciples of all the nations, baptizing them in the name of the Father and the Son and the Holy Spirit."

2 CORINTHIANS 13:14

The grace of the Lord Jesus Christ, and the love of God, and the fellowship of the Holy Spirit, be with you all.

The references in Scripture to the names (Father, Son, Holy Spirit) and the separate identities indicated (God, Jesus Christ, Holy Spirit) within one verse is significant. These are indications that each name stands for a distinct person and each identity belongs to a distinct person. Consequently, this is indicative of the reality of the Trinity. In these texts the Trinity is not something that is being argued, rather it is simply assumed. These are the kind of texts that were studied and debated by the scholars and bishops of the church in the second through the fourth centuries and those debates led to the orthodox creeds of the church. What the church later succinctly articulated in creeds (such as the Nicene-Constantinopolitan Creed AD 381) is squarely-based on what the church read in the New Testament. In other words, the Trinity was not invented by the framers of the creeds, but it was discerned by them to be the teaching of Scripture.

THE DECREE OF GOD

Question #7: What are the decrees of God?

Answer: The decrees of God are his eternal purpose according to the counsel of his will, whereby, for his own glory, he hath foreordained whatsoever comes to pass.[14]

Is One decree

EPHESIANS 1:11B

Having been predestined according to His purpose who works all things after the counsel of His will.

Is Eternal

EPHESIANS 3:11

This was in accordance with the eternal purpose which He carried out in Christ Jesus our Lord.

Is Enduring

PSALM 33:11

The counsel of the LORD stands forever,
The plans of His heart from generation to generation.

ISAIAH 46:10

"Declaring the end from the beginning,
And from ancient times things which have not been done,
Saying, 'My purpose will be established,
And I will accomplish all My good pleasure.'"

Is Immutable

JOB 23:13–14

But He is unique and who can turn Him?
And *what* His soul desires, that He does.
For He performs what is appointed for me,
And many such *decrees* are with Him.

Is for God's Own Glory

EPHESIANS 1:6

To the praise of the glory of His grace, which He freely bestowed on us in the Beloved.

The Decree Is Worked Out through Creation

GENESIS 1:1–2 (SEE GEN. 1–2)

In the beginning God created the heavens and the earth. ² The earth was formless and void, and darkness was over the surface of the deep, and the Spirit of God was moving over the surface of the waters.

NEHEMIAH 9:5B–6

"O may Your glorious name be blessed
And exalted above all blessing and praise!
⁶ "You alone are the LORD.
You have made the heavens,
The heaven of heavens with all their host,
The earth and all that is on it,
The seas and all that is in them.
You give life to all of them
And the heavenly host bows down before You."

PSALM 33:6

By the word of the LORD the heavens were made,
And by the breath of His mouth all their host.

COLOSSIANS 1:16

For by Him all things were created, *both* in the heavens and on earth, visible and invisible, whether thrones or dominions or rulers or authorities—all things have been created through Him and for Him.

HEBREWS 11:3

By faith we understand that the worlds were prepared by the word of God, so that what is seen was not made out of things which are visible.

The Pattern of Creation: The outworking of God's decree in creation follows a pattern that began in the first chapters of Genesis. The first two verses of the Bible reveal this pattern. God begins with creating the material universe—"heavens and the earth." This expression is a merism, which may simply be defined as a statement of opposites to indicate totality. Everything that is the material universe is "just there"—it is "formless and void," or unformed and unfilled. It is all watery, and dark, and devoid of life. (In anticipation of a key point to be made below, it is interesting to note that the apostle John informs his readers that on the new earth "there is no longer any sea" [Rev. 21:1].)

But then immediately God begins to refine His creation. He overcomes the darkness with the creation of light, which is separated from the darkness (Gen. 1:4); He separates the waters (Gen. 1:6) and then creates dry land (Gen. 1:9). This "create and refine" pattern continues through the chapter. That pattern can be seen in the progress through the days of creation. Many Bible scholars have observed that the six days of creation should be seen as two groups of three and that the days of group one (days one through three) correspond to the days of group two (days four through six). Thus, on day one light was created (Gen. 1:3) and on day four the heavenly bodies that are the holders—the mechanisms to furnish the light—are created (Gen. 1:14). On day two the waters were separated into sea and sky (Gen. 1:6–8) and on day five the living creatures that were to fill the sea and sky, fish and birds, are created (Gen. 1:20–22). Likewise, on day three, the earth, with all the plant life on it, is created (Gen. 1:9–12), and on day six, the animal life that will sustain itself on those plants is created (Gen. 1:24–25). Of course, the culmination of the sixth day is the creation of man and woman (Gen. 1:26–27). The pattern is "create and refine."

Some scholars have argued that the second chapter of Genesis is a second, and in some ways incommensurate, account of creation. They suggest this for several reasons: the style of writing and the opening of the account in Genesis 2 (see Gen. 2:4) is different; the names used for God in these chapters are different (God/Elohim in chapter 1 and LORD God/Yahweh Elohim in chapter 2); the creation of man and woman is different. However, these differences are not as stark as these scholars suggest. Actually, many of the differences between the chapters can be explained by the pattern of "create and refine." For instance, the mandates that God gave to man and woman in Genesis 1:26 and 28 to "rule" (Hebrew *rādā*) and "subdue" (Hebrew *kābaš*) the earth are refined by placing the man in the garden (Gen. 2:8) and commanding him to "cultivate it and keep it" (Gen. 2:15). The mandate to "be fruitful and multiply, and fill the earth" (Gen. 1:28) is refined by the creation of Eve (Gen. 2:22–23) and the institution of marriage (Gen. 2:24–25).

This pattern of "create and refine" continues throughout the outworking of God's decree. With respect to the nation of Israel, God calls and makes a covenant with Abraham and then He refines that covenant with the later biblical covenants—the Mosaic (Ex. 19–24), the Davidic (Sam. 7; Ps. 89), the New Covenant (Jer. 31). Even with respect to the salvation of sinners, the pattern "create and refine" can be seen in the regeneration of the elect, which is followed by the lifelong process of their sanctification, and ultimately in their glorification.

This pattern will culminate in a final phase of refinement when Christ returns to establish His millennial kingdom. When Adam sinned he plunged the creation over which he was to rule into a curse (see Gen. 3:17–19) and so that creation, the apostle Paul says, is "subjected to futility" (Rom. 8:20); that is, this cursed world cannot be refined by Adam's posterity in the way God originally intended. Thus, at the present time that creation "groans and suffers" (Rom. 8:22), but that creation awaits the time when it "will be set free from its slavery to corruption into the freedom of the glory of the children of God" (Rom. 8:21). That time will come when Christ establishes His earthly kingdom. In that kingdom Christ, the second Adam, will fulfill the creation mandate to rule over and subdue the earth. "The reversal of the curse will also enable the earth to once again be amazingly productive, being freed from thorns and thistles (e.g., Isa. 32:13–15)"[15]; (see Isa. 35:1–7). Death and sickness will be mitigated (see Isa. 33:24; 35:5–6; 61:1–2). "With the earth being freed from the curse and becoming universally fertile, and with disease and death being almost nonexistent, we can understand why peace, prosperity, and a sense of well-being will characterize Messiah's kingdom (e.g., Isa. 25:8–9; 35:1–2; 30:23–25; 60:15; 61:7; Amos 9:13–15; Ezek. 36:29–30; Zech. 8:11–12; 9:16–17)."[16] In short, this will be the time of ultimate refinement of God's creation by the second Adam (see Rom. 5:14; 1 Cor. 15:22, 45).

The pattern of "create and refine" will end with the re-creation of the new heavens and new earth (see Rev. 21–22). This present creation will be completely burned (see 2 Peter 3:7, 10) and "the first heaven and the first earth [will pass] away" (Rev. 21:1). The new heavens and the new earth will be a complete and final creation where God's purposes for His glory will be realized for eternity.

The Decree Is Worked Out in Providence

The providence of God is His continuing preservation and active governance of all that He has created in accord with His original purpose and His ultimate ends. This preservation and governance includes the processes of nature, the actions of His creatures, the happenings of history and even apparently serendipitous (chance) events.

IN NATURE

JOB 5:10
He gives rain on the earth
And sends water on the fields.

PSALM 65:9
You visit the earth and cause it to overflow;
You greatly enrich it;
The stream of God is full of water;
You prepare their grain, for thus You prepare the earth.

PSALM 104:5, 14–15
He established the earth upon its foundations,
So that it will not totter forever and ever. . . .
[14] He causes the grass to grow for the cattle,
And vegetation for the labor of man,
So that he may bring forth food from the earth,
[15] And wine which makes man's heart glad,
So that he may make *his* face glisten with oil,
And food which sustains man's heart.

MATTHEW 6:26
Look at the birds of the air, that they do not sow, nor reap nor gather into barns, and *yet* your heavenly Father feeds them. Are you not worth much more than they?

ACTS 14:17

and yet He did not leave Himself without witness, in that He did good and gave you rains from heaven and fruitful seasons, satisfying your hearts with food and gladness.

IN HISTORY

JOB 12:23

He makes the nations great, then destroys them;
He enlarges the nations, then leads them away.

PSALM 22:28

For the kingdom is the LORD's
And He rules over the nations.

JEREMIAH 27:5

I have made the earth, the men and the beasts which are on the face of the earth by My great power and by My outstretched arm, and I will give it to the one who is pleasing in My sight.

DANIEL 2:21

It is He who changes the times and the epochs;
He removes kings and establishes kings;
He gives wisdom to wise men
And knowledge to men of understanding.

DANIEL 4:17B

"In order that the living may know
That the Most High is ruler over the realm of mankind,
And bestows it on whom He wishes
And sets over it the lowliest of men."

ACTS 17:26

"And He made from one *man* every nation of mankind to live on all the face of the earth, having determined *their* appointed times and the boundaries of their habitation."

The Decree Is Worked Out in Personal Circumstances

GENESIS 45:8

"Now, therefore, it was not you who sent me here, but God; and He has made me a father to Pharaoh and lord of all his household and ruler over all the land of Egypt."

GENESIS 50:20

As for you, you meant evil against me, *but* God meant it for good in order to bring about this present result, to preserve many people alive.

JOB 14:5

Since his days are determined,
The number of his months is with You;
And his limits You have set so that he cannot pass.

PSALM 139:16

Your eyes have seen my unformed substance;
And in Your book were all written
The days that were ordained *for me*,
When as yet there was not one of them.

MATTHEW 10:29–31

Are not two sparrows sold for a cent? And *yet* not one of them will fall to the ground apart from your Father. [30] But the very hairs of your head are all numbered. [31] So do not fear; you are more valuable than many sparrows.

God's Decree and Evil / God Is Sovereign Over Evil

The Bible does not attempt to provide a philosophical answer to the problem of evil, nor does it attempt to provide a psychologically satisfying answer to the problem of evil from a purely man-centered point of view. The Bible does offer a philosophically credible and psychologically satisfying answer from its own (God's own) point of view.[17] The Bible clearly teaches that God stands opposed to evil, will judge evil, and He is sovereign over evil.

GOD HATES EVIL

PSALM 5:4

For You are not a God who takes pleasure in wickedness;
No evil dwells with You.

HABAKKUK 1:13A

Your eyes are too pure to approve evil,
And You can not look on wickedness *with favor*.

GOD USES EVIL ACTIONS FOR HIS PURPOSES

GENESIS 50:20A

As for you, you meant evil against me, *but* God meant it for good.

PROVERBS 16:4

The LORD has made everything for its own purpose,
Even the wicked for the day of evil.

ISAIAH 10:5–7

Woe to Assyria, the rod of My anger
And the staff in whose hands is My indignation,
[6] I send it against a godless nation
And commission it against the people of My fury
To capture booty and to seize plunder,
And to trample them down like mud in the streets.
[7] Yet it does not so intend,
Nor does it plan so in its heart,
But rather it is its purpose to destroy
And to cut off many nations.

GOD DOES NOT TEMPT TO EVIL

JAMES 1:14–15

But each one is tempted when he is carried away and enticed by his own
lust. [15] Then when lust has conceived, it gives birth to sin; and when sin is
accomplished, it brings forth death.

GOD WILL JUDGE SIN AND EVIL

PSALM 1:5

Therefore the wicked will not stand in the judgment,
Nor sinners in the assembly of the righteous.

PSALM 37:28

For the LORD loves justice
And does not forsake His godly ones;
They are preserved forever,
But the descendants of the wicked will be cut off.

MALACHI 4:3

You will tread down the wicked, for they will be ashes under the soles of
your feet on the day which I am preparing," says the LORD of hosts.

MATTHEW 13:41

The Son of Man will send forth His angels, and they will gather out of His
kingdom all stumbling blocks, and those who commit lawlessness.

GOD OVERRULES EVIL TO ACCOMPLISH HIS WILL

GENESIS 50:19–20

But Joseph said to them, "Do not be afraid, for am I in God's place? [20] As
for you, you meant evil against me, *but* God meant it for good in order to
bring about this present result, to preserve many people alive."

ROMANS 8:28

And we know that God causes all things to work together for good to
those who love God, to those who are called according to *His* purpose.

ROMANS 9:20

On the contrary, who are you, O man, who answers back to God? The
thing molded will not say to the molder, "Why did you make me like this,"
will it?

These texts are indicative of the principle that while humans often do not
have the sufficient knowledge, nor sufficient perspective (of times, of exigent

circumstances, of objectives, of purposes, etc.) to understand why God allows evil, believers can have confidence that God does have sufficient reasons (moral, eternal, purposeful) for the evil that happens.

1. A. W. Tozer, *The Knowledge of the Holy* (New York: Harper & Brothers, 1961), 9.

2. Greg L. Bahnsen, *Van Til's Apologetic: Readings and Analysis* (Phillipsburg, NJ: P&R Publishing, 1998), 442.

3. Leon Morris, *The Epistle to the Romans* (Grand Rapids, MI: William B. Eerdmans Publishing Company, 1988), 82.

4. Bahnsen, *Van Til's Apologetic*, 443; quoting Cornelius Van Til, *Defense of the Faith*, 3rd ed. (Philadelphia, PA: P&R Publishing, 1967), 111.

5. Morris, *Romans*, 124.

6. See T. Bradshaw, "Process Theology," in *New Dictionary of Theology: Historical and Systematic*, eds. Martin Davie et al. (Downers Grove, IL: InterVarsity Press, 2016), 707–09.

7. Williamson, *The Westminster Shorter Catechism*, 16.

8. James E. Dolezal, *All That Is in God: Evangelical Theology and the Challenge of Classical Christian Theism* (Grand Rapids, MI: Reformation Heritage Books, 2017), 43.

9. Dolezal, *All That Is in God*, 40–41.

10. R. Laird Harris, "ḥesed," in *Theological Wordbook of the Old Testament*, eds. R. Laird Harris, Gleason L. Archer, Jr., and Bruce K. Waltke (Chicago: Moody Publishers, 1980), 1:305.

11. See William D. Mounce, ed., "Love," *Mounce's Complete Expository Dictionary of Old and New Testament Words* (Grand Rapids, MI: Zondervan, 2006), 426.

12. Leo Donald Davis, *The First Seven Ecumenical Councils (325–787): Their History and Theology* (Collegeville, MN: The Liturgical Press, 1983), 122.

13. John MacArthur and Richard Mayhue, eds., *Biblical Doctrine: A Systematic Summary of Bible Truth* (Wheaton, IL; Crossway, 2017), 345. Emphasis added.

14. Williamson, *The Westminster Shorter Catechism*, 27.

15. Paul N. Benware, *Understanding End Times Prophecy: A Comprehensive Approach* (Chicago: Moody Publishers, 2006), 336.

16. Ibid., 337.

17. For a practical response to the problem of evil on logical and psychological grounds, see Greg L. Bahnsen, *Always Ready: Directions for Defending the Faith*, ed. Robert R. Booth (Nacogdoches, TX: Covenant Media Press, 1996), 163–75.

CHAPTER 4

GOD THE SON

Christology

Christology is the study of the person and work of Jesus Christ.

PREEXISTENCE AND ETERNITY OF THE SON

ISAIAH 9:6

For a child will be born to us, a son will be given to us;
And the government will rest on His shoulders;
And His name will be called Wonderful Counselor, Mighty God,
Eternal Father, Prince of Peace.

MICAH 5:2

"But as for you, Bethlehem Ephrathah,
Too little to be among the clans of Judah,
From you One will go forth for Me to be ruler in Israel.
His goings forth are from long ago,
From the days of eternity."

JOHN 1:1–3

In the beginning was the Word, and the Word was with God, and the Word was God. [2] He was in the beginning with God. [3] All things came into being through Him, and apart from Him nothing came into being that has come into being.

JOHN 8:56–58

"Your father Abraham rejoiced to see My day, and he saw *it* and was glad."
⁵⁷ So the Jews said to Him, "You are not yet fifty years old, and have You
seen Abraham?" ⁵⁸ Jesus said to them, "Truly, truly, I say to you, before
Abraham was born, I am."

GALATIANS 4:4

But when the fullness of the time came, God sent forth His Son, born of a
woman, born under the Law.

COLOSSIANS 1:17

He is before all things, and in Him all things hold together.

PHILIPPIANS 2:5–7

Have this attitude in yourselves which was also in Christ Jesus, ⁶ who,
although He existed in the form of God, did not regard equality with God a
thing to be grasped, ⁷ but emptied Himself, taking the form of a bond-servant, *and* being made in the likeness of men.

The preexistence of Christ is a teaching that is woven into the scriptural revelation about Christ. That is, it is not a truth about Christ that is asserted separate
from other truths about Him but is integral to the revelation of His person and
His work. The fact that He is the Messiah affirms His preexistence, for the Messiah is called "Eternal Father," and "His goings forth are from long ago, From the
days of eternity." Virtually every affirmation of His deity also obviously affirms
His preexistence; thus, every phrase in John 1:1 assumes His preexistence as
does His own self-declaration to be "I AM." The very fact of His incarnation as
such assumes his preexistence, for He was already the Son who was "sent forth"
and then "born of a woman" (see **The Incarnation of the Son**). The assertions
in Paul's two Christological hymns (see **Direct Affirmations of Christ's Deity /
The Epistles of Paul**) affirm He was "before all things," and that "He existed"
before He was "made in the likeness of men."

It has been said that without belief in the preexistence of Christ, Christianity would no longer be recognizable. "The doctrine of Christ's preexistence
did not result from theological curiosity or speculation. As early as the first
decade of the church, Christians saw preexistence as necessary for understanding Christ's person and significance in human salvation."[1]

PROPHECIES OF THE MESSIAH (CHRIST)

The narrative of the gospels is replete with references and allusions to Old Testament messianic prophecy. These quotations and allusions are meant to establish that Jesus of Nazareth is indeed the long-expected Messiah. Those Old Testament prophecies had become clouded with the temporal desires of the people who developed messianic expectations that were distortions or misunderstandings of what the Old Testament had actually prophesied about the Messiah. In the first coming Jesus did fulfill what the Old Testament actually predicted, and the New Testament writers wanted to make this very clear.

The Fact of His Birth

ISAIAH 9:6

For a child will be born to us, a son will be given to us;
And the government will rest on His shoulders;
And His name will be called Wonderful Counselor, Mighty God,
Eternal Father, Prince of Peace.

The Place of His Birth

MICAH 5:2

"But as for you, Bethlehem Ephrathah,
Too little to be among the clans of Judah,
From you One will go forth for Me to be ruler in Israel.
His goings forth are from long ago,
From the days of eternity."

MATTHEW 2:4–6

Gathering together all the chief priests and scribes of the people, he inquired of them where the Messiah was to be born. [5] They said to him, "In Bethlehem of Judea; for this is what has been written by the prophet:

[6] 'AND YOU, BETHLEHEM, LAND OF JUDAH,
ARE BY NO MEANS LEAST AMONG THE LEADERS OF JUDAH;

> FOR OUT OF YOU SHALL COME FORTH A RULER
> WHO WILL SHEPHERD MY PEOPLE ISRAEL.'"

This prophecy is remarkable for its accuracy and clarity. Micah predicted the Messiah would be born in Bethlehem, and indeed that is where Jesus was born. However, Micah also alluded to His preexistence, and therefore to His deity, which made this birth even more significant.

The Fulfillment of Covenant Promises

ABRAHAMIC COVENANT

GENESIS 17:9–10A

God said further to Abraham, "Now as for you, you shall keep My covenant, you and your descendants after you throughout their generations. [10] This is My covenant, which you shall keep, between Me and you and your descendants after you."

LUKE 1:55

As He spoke to our fathers,
To Abraham and his descendants forever.

LUKE 1:72–73

"To show mercy toward our fathers,
And to remember His holy covenant,
[73] The oath which He swore to Abraham our father."

DAVIDIC COVENANT

Son of David

2 SAMUEL 7:12–13

"'"When your days are complete and you lie down with your fathers, I will raise up your descendant after you, who will come forth from you, and I will establish his kingdom. [13] He shall build a house for My name, and I will establish the throne of his kingdom forever."'"

> **LUKE 1:31–33**
>
> "And behold, you will conceive in your womb and bear a son, and you shall name Him Jesus. [32] He will be great and will be called the Son of the Most High; and the Lord God will give Him the throne of His father David; [33] and He will reign over the house of Jacob forever, and His kingdom will have no end."

> **LUKE 1:69–70**
>
> "And has raised up a horn of salvation for us
> In the house of David His servant—
> [70] As He spoke by the mouth of His holy prophets from of old."

In both Mary's "Magnificat" (see Luke 1:46–55) and Zacharias's "Benedictus" (Luke 1:67–79) the birth of Jesus was viewed as the fulfillment, or rather the inauguration of the fulfillment, of the covenant promises to Abraham and David. Why did Mary and Zacharias see the fulfillment of those promises in the birth of the child Jesus? Both had received an angelic messenger who revealed to them the significance of this birth (see Luke 1:17 and 1:32–33); both had a deep understanding of the Old Testament (as evidenced by the content of their respective songs); and both lived in the context of a nation and people who were living in constant expectation that the Lord (Yahweh) would keep His ancient promises. For Luke's readers these assurances are meant for the reader to know, keep in mind, and see them vindicated in the narrative to follow.

The Promise of a Davidic King

> **2 SAMUEL 7:16**
>
> "'"Your house and your kingdom shall endure before Me forever; your throne shall be established forever."'"

> **PSALM 2:6–7**
>
> "But as for Me, I have installed My King
> Upon Zion, My holy mountain."
> [7] "I will surely tell of the decree of the LORD:
> He said to Me, 'You are My Son,
> Today I have begotten You.'"

> **JEREMIAH 33:17**
>
> "For thus says the LORD, 'David shall never lack a man to sit on the throne of the house of Israel.'"

> **LUKE 1:32–33**
>
> "He will be great and will be called the Son of the Most High; and the Lord God will give Him the throne of His father David; [33] and He will reign over the house of Jacob forever, and His kingdom will have no end."

> **MATTHEW 20:30–31 (SEE MATT. 9:27)**
>
> And two blind men sitting by the road, hearing that Jesus was passing by, cried out, "Lord, have mercy on us, Son of David!" [31] The crowd sternly told them to be quiet, but they cried out all the more, "Lord, Son of David, have mercy on us!"

The two blind men of Jericho obviously wanted to be healed and they cried out to Jesus for mercy. The name by which they called Jesus—"Son of David"—expressed their faith that He was the Messiah and the coming king in the line of David (see Matt. 1:1).[2]

The Promise of a High Priest

> **PSALM 110:4**
>
> The LORD has sworn and will not change His mind,
> "You are a priest forever
> According to the order of Melchizedek."

> **HEBREWS 4:14**
>
> Therefore, since we have a great high priest who has passed through the heavens, Jesus the Son of God, let us hold fast our confession.

> **HEBREWS 5:10**
>
> Being designated by God as a high priest according to the order of Melchizedek.

Virgin Birth of Christ / Incarnation

The Virgin Birth was the means God chose for the Son to be "incarnate." "Incarnation" is the doctrine that means the second person of the Trinity (the Son) took on human nature and body.

> **ISAIAH 7:14**
>
> Therefore the Lord Himself will give you a sign: Behold, a virgin will be with child and bear a son, and she will call His name Immanuel.

> **MATTHEW 1:18**
>
> Now the birth of Jesus Christ was as follows: when His mother Mary had been betrothed to Joseph, before they came together she was found to be with child by the Holy Spirit.

> **LUKE 1:34–37**
>
> Mary said to the angel, "How can this be, since I am a virgin?" [35] The angel answered and said to her, "The Holy Spirit will come upon you, and the power of the Most High will overshadow you; and for that reason the holy Child shall be called the Son of God. [36] And behold, even your relative Elizabeth has also conceived a son in her old age; and she who was called barren is now in her sixth month. [37] For nothing will be impossible with God."

The first of the Old Testament prophecies which Matthew cites is the prophecy of the Virgin Birth of Jesus Christ. The facts asserted are plain: "Behold, a virgin will be with child and bear a son." Matthew does not argue either the plausibility or possibility of such a miracle, nor did he expound on what Isaiah (in Isa. 7:14) intended.

Isaiah pronounced the prophecy of the virgin who would "be with child and bear a son." This pronouncement was given to the faithless king Ahaz. It was given to Ahaz as a sign that the Lord would protect and save the people of Judah from the threat posed by "Rezin the king of Aram and Pekah the son of Remaliah, king of Israel" (Isa. 7:1). The meaning of the sign and the child was given in the child's name: "and she will call His name Immanuel." Matthew provides the translation of the name "God with us." The birth of the virgin Mary's Son is the fulfillment of all the promises God made to protect and save His people.

EXCURSUS: Why Believe in the Virgin Birth?

There are at least three reasons to hold to the fact of a literal virgin birth of Jesus Christ. First, there is no reason to make it up if it did not happen. The question of Jesus' birth might have been left a mystery and the truth of His sinlessness, His preexistence, and His divine nature (taught clearly in other texts) would have been sufficient to sustain all the other biblical doctrines of the person and work of Christ. The only reason to include such a doctrine so contrary to nature and experience is that this was the truth about His birth. Second, more to the point, this is what the inspired and inerrant Word of God teaches in Matthew's gospel and in Luke's. The term used for virgin (Greek *parthenos*) along with other expressions used in the gospel accounts (e.g., the expression in Luke 1:34 "I am a virgin" is literally "I know not a man," a euphemism for virginity) affirm that the gospel writers recorded that Mary was a virgin *before* the conception, *during* her pregnancy, and until Christ's birth. To deny the virgin birth is to reject the Word of God. Thirdly, it must be observed that while both Matthew and Luke clearly affirm that Mary was a virgin, their accounts are very different and are written from completely different points of view. Virtually the only element that is the same in both accounts is the fact of Mary's virginity. This argues strongly that these were independent accounts that betray no collusion and they are each simply relating the facts of what actually occurred.[3]

His Life and Ministry

Virtually everything in Jesus' life and ministry was prophesied in the Old Testament. (The following texts are arranged with the Old Testament prophetic text followed by the text of New Testament fulfillment.)

TEACHING AND MIRACLES

PSALM 78:2

I will open my mouth in a parable;
I will utter dark sayings of old.

MATTHEW 13:34–35

All these things Jesus spoke to the crowds in parables, and He did not speak to them without a parable. [35] *This was* to fulfill what was spoken through the prophet:

"I WILL OPEN MY MOUTH IN PARABLES;
I WILL UTTER THINGS HIDDEN SINCE THE FOUNDATION OF THE WORLD."

ISAIAH 29:18

On that day the deaf will hear words of a book,
And out of *their* gloom and darkness the eyes of the blind will see.

ISAIAH 61:1

The Spirit of the Lord GOD is upon me,
Because the LORD has anointed me
To bring good news to the afflicted;
He has sent me to bind up the brokenhearted,
To proclaim liberty to captives
And freedom to prisoners.

MATTHEW 11:5

"*The* BLIND RECEIVE SIGHT and *the* lame walk, *the* lepers are cleansed and *the* deaf hear, *the* dead are raised up, and *the* POOR HAVE THE GOSPEL PREACHED TO THEM."

JOHN 9:39

And Jesus said, "For judgment I came into this world, so that those who do not see may see, and that those who see may become blind."

ISAIAH 35:5–6

Then the eyes of the blind will be opened
And the ears of the deaf will be unstopped.
[6] Then the lame will leap like a deer,
And the tongue of the mute will shout for joy.

For waters will break forth in the wilderness
And streams in the Arabah.

MATTHEW 9:29–30A

Then He touched their eyes, saying, "It shall be done to you according to your faith." [30] And their eyes were opened.

LUKE 4:16–21

And He came to Nazareth, where He had been brought up; and as was His custom, He entered the synagogue on the Sabbath, and stood up to read. [17] And the book of the prophet Isaiah was handed to Him. And He opened the book and found the place where it was written,

[18] "THE SPIRIT OF THE LORD IS UPON ME,
BECAUSE HE ANOINTED ME TO PREACH THE GOSPEL TO THE POOR.
HE HAS SENT ME TO PROCLAIM RELEASE TO THE CAPTIVES,
AND RECOVERY OF SIGHT TO THE BLIND,
TO SET FREE THOSE WHO ARE OPPRESSED,
[19] TO PROCLAIM THE FAVORABLE YEAR OF THE LORD."

[20] And He closed the book, gave it back to the attendant and sat down; and the eyes of all in the synagogue were fixed on Him. [21] And He began to say to them, "Today this Scripture has been fulfilled in your hearing."

The text in Isaiah (61:1ff) is very clearly a text that refers to the Messiah and was understood as such in Jesus' day. When Jesus read from that text in His hometown of Nazareth and declared, "Today this Scripture has been fulfilled in your hearing," He was making a stunning claim to be the Messiah. And, of course, the narrative of His ministry of compassion, healing, and teaching gave evident testimony to that claim for He indeed preached good news, healed the afflicted, and set free those who were captive to demons.

However, according to the narrative in Luke 4, Jesus stopped the reading after the phrase "to proclaim the favorable year of the Lord." This was intentional because the next line in Isaiah 61, "And the day of vengeance of our God," refers to the day of the Lord, the day of judgment and tribulation. In the first coming Jesus had not come to fulfill that part of the prophecy. That fulfillment is yet to come. This illustrates a feature of Old Testament prophecy. Many times in Old Testament messianic texts both the first and second coming of the Lord are woven together. That is, the Old Testament prophet does not indicate that some of his prophecy will be fulfilled at the Lord's first coming and some at the second coming. The Old Testament prophets knew of the coming Messiah, but it was not understood until the Messiah was born that there would be not one but two comings. The first coming was for salvation (see Luke 19:10) and the second would be for judgment (see Rev. 19:11–21) and to set up His kingdom (see Rev. 20:1–6).

TRIUMPHAL ENTRY (AND COMING REIGN)

ZECHARIAH 9:9–10

Rejoice greatly, O daughter of Zion!
Shout *in triumph*, O daughter of Jerusalem!
Behold, your king is coming to you;
He is just and endowed with salvation,
Humble, and mounted on a donkey,
Even on a colt, the foal of a donkey.
[10] I will cut off the chariot from Ephraim
And the horse from Jerusalem;
And the bow of war will be cut off.
And He will speak peace to the nations;
And His dominion will be from sea to sea,
And from the River to the ends of the earth.

MATTHEW 21:1–5 (SEE MARK 11:1–14; LUKE 19:28–40; JOHN 12:12–19)

When they had approached Jerusalem and had come to Bethphage, at the Mount of Olives, then Jesus sent two disciples, [2] saying to them, "Go into the village opposite you, and immediately you will find a donkey tied *there* and a colt with her; untie them and bring them to Me. [3] If anyone says anything to you, you shall say, 'The Lord has need of them,' and immediately he will send them." [4] This took place to fulfill what was spoken through the prophet:
[5] "SAY TO THE DAUGHTER OF ZION,
'BEHOLD YOUR KING IS COMING TO YOU,
GENTLE, AND MOUNTED ON A DONKEY,
EVEN ON A COLT, THE FOAL OF A BEAST OF BURDEN.'"

The prophecy of Zechariah 9:9–10 is one of the most recognizable messianic prophecies in the Old Testament due to the fact that one portion of this prophecy is quoted in the Gospels in the account of Jesus' triumphal entry into Jerusalem (Matt. 21:5; John 12:15).[4] This prophecy appears in the third section of Zechariah's prophecy, which is made up of two extended messages or burdens of the prophet concerning the coming of the Messiah (chapters 9–14). The term *burden* (Hebrew *massâ*; lit. a heavy load, a substantial weight to be borne) is used to introduce "an oracle" of a prophet (see Isa. 13:1; 14:28; Jer. 23:33, 34, 36, 38). The first burden is in two parts: 9:1–8 and 9:9–10:12. Part one (9:1–8) concerns the Lord's judgment that will come (through the instrument of Alexander the Great) upon the northern and coastal nations of the Levant. This prophetic word of conquest and destruction stands in contrast to part two (9:9–10:12) the coming of the Lord's Messiah.

This entire section (9:9–10:12) concerns the simple but glorious fact that the Lord's Messiah (the long-awaited King; see Gen. 49:10; Ps. 14:7) is coming ("your king is coming to you"; see Zech. 2:10). He is described as "just," "righteous" (*şaddîq*). His coming brings several benefits.

The manner of His coming is surprising for He will come in humility (Hebrew *'ănî*). This term was used with the notion of 'poor' (see Zech. 7:10; 11:7, 11 RV) or 'afflicted' (Isa. 14:32; 51:21; 54:11; see Isa. 53:7). He will be riding "on a donkey, even on a colt, the foal of a donkey." This was not altogether unheard of for a king who was coming in peace (see Judg. 5:10; 10:4; 12:14; 2 Sam. 16:1–2). However, given the description in verse 10, this is something incongruous and unexpected.

The first benefit the coming of the King will bring is great joy: "Rejoice greatly, O daughter of Zion! Shout in triumph, O daughter of Jerusalem!" The phrase "daughter(s) of Zion" and the equivalent phrase "daughter(s) of Judah/Jerusalem" occurs over thirty times in the Old Testament; it is a personification of Jerusalem. The idea is all of Jerusalem will rejoice at His coming.

The second benefit is "salvation." The "salvation" in view here is not limited to the notion most often associated with the term—a soteriological sense. However, there is another sense of salvation which may be understood more in terms of deliverance (mainly from enemy nations). This is the sort of salvation the psalmist has in mind in psalms like Psalm 14:7 and Psalm 44:7, which is a deliverance from or victory over one's enemies. This whole phrase has the notion that in His coming He is empowered and authorized to deliver a victory. However, the notion of salvation from sin is not missing (see Ps. 85:4, 9).

The third benefit is peace and an end to warfare. The armaments of war—the "chariots," "the warhorses," and the "battle bow" will be "cut off" (from the Hebrew verb *kārat*). The sense of the term here indicates a breaking, destroying, or disabling. Then the Messiah will "speak peace to the nations" and bring in the fourth benefit, the establishment of "dominion." The extent of this "dominion" is "from sea to sea" and "from the River to the ends of the earth." These descriptions cannot be restricted to the Holy Land and indicate a worldwide dominion or kingdom (see Ps. 72:8).

It is quite clear that the prophecy of verse 9 was literally fulfilled when Jesus of Nazareth entered Jerusalem on a foal of a donkey (Matt. 21:1–11, v. 5; Mark 11:1–10; Luke 19:29–39; John 12:12–19, v. 15) in the so-called "Triumphal Entry." But it is just as obvious that the rest of the prophecy (verse 10) was *not fulfilled* at the same time. Here is an instance of what some have called "prophetic foreshortening." This is when a prophet depicts two future events as virtually one event but later revelation and fulfillment reveals that there are actually two events. Here, the first coming of the Messiah and His second coming are depicted as one event.

There are several implications to be made from this "prophetic foreshortening." First, it is clear that the events prophesied that were fulfilled in the first coming (verse 9; the Triumphal Entry) were fulfilled literally. Second, it stands to reason that what is revealed about the second coming (verse 10) will be fulfilled just as literally. This also helps to answer the question of the meaning of "salvation" in this context. The one sense of salvation, that of salvation from sin, was accomplished at the first coming (Matt. 1:21; Luke 19:10) and the other sense of salvation, that of deliverance and victory over enemy nations, will be accomplished at the second coming (see Ps. 2:8–9; Rev. 2:27; 19:15).

HIS CRUCIFIXION

PSALM 22:1, 6–18 (SEE MATT. 27:33–50; MARK 15:22–39;
LUKE 23:33–49; JOHN 19:16–30)

My God, my God, why have You forsaken me?
Far from my deliverance are the words of my groaning. . . .
⁶ But I am a worm and not a man,
A reproach of men and despised by the people.
⁷ All who see me sneer at me;
They separate with the lip, they wag the head, *saying*,
⁸ "Commit *yourself* to the LORD; let Him deliver him;
Let Him rescue him, because He delights in him."
⁹ Yet You are He who brought me forth from the womb;
You made me trust *when* upon my mother's breasts.
¹⁰ Upon You I was cast from birth;
You have been my God from my mother's womb.
¹¹ Be not far from me, for trouble is near;
For there is none to help.
¹² Many bulls have surrounded me;
Strong *bulls* of Bashan have encircled me.
¹³ They open wide their mouth at me,
As a ravening and a roaring lion.
¹⁴ I am poured out like water,
And all my bones are out of joint;
My heart is like wax;
It is melted within me.
¹⁵ My strength is dried up like a potsherd,
And my tongue cleaves to my jaws;
And You lay me in the dust of death.
¹⁶ For dogs have surrounded me;
A band of evildoers has encompassed me;
They pierced my hands and my feet.
¹⁷ I can count all my bones.
They look, they stare at me;
¹⁸ They divide my garments among them,
And for my clothing they cast lots.

Psalm 22 begins with one of the most familiar lines in the Bible—but not because it is here in Psalm 22. These words "My God, my God, why have You forsaken me?" are familiar because it is a line quoted by Christ (in Aramaic, as Matthew records) while He was being crucified. However, this is only part of what ties this prophetic psalm to the experience of Christ on the cross. Actually, what appears here as David's experience in hyperbole is a stunning description of Christ's experience in fact. Psalm 22 is essentially a description of the crucifixion from Jesus' own point of view.

The psalm describes "Christ's cry of desolation" (Ps. 22:1–2); then "Christ's experience of humiliation" (Ps. 22:6–8); then "Christ's experience of rejection" (Ps. 22:11–16). The description given here in the psalm so clearly details the actual experience of Jesus that some have dubbed this psalm "the fifth gospel." Beside the mockery Jesus endured ("despised by the people. All who see me sneer at me," "They open wide their mouth at me," Ps. 22:6b-7a, 13; compare, "And those passing by were hurling abuse at Him, wagging their heads," with this from Matthew's gospel: "In the same way the chief priests also, along with the scribes and elders, were mocking Him" [see Matt. 27:39, 41]) the description of the physical suffering recorded (in verses 14–15a, 16b, 17) is virtually a clinical description of a body in the throes of crucifixion (e.g., dislocation of joints, loss of strength, excessive thirst, the piercing of hands and feet) and each is mentioned or alluded to in the gospel accounts of the crucifixion. Perhaps the most surprising note is in verse 18, "They divide my garments among them, And for my clothing they cast lots." This describes with stunning accuracy the callous actions of the Roman guards who crucified Jesus ("And when they had crucified Him, they divided up His garments among themselves by casting lots," Matt. 27:35). When Jesus cried, "*Eli, Eli, lama sabachthani?*" (Matt. 27:46), He was in effect applying this psalm to Himself and directing any who would pay attention to the fact that on the cross He was fulfilling messianic prophecy.

It must be noted that the psalmist, David, despite the desolation, humiliation, and rejection, weaves through his experience affirmations of trust in God (Ps. 22:3–5), care from God (Ps. 22:9–10), and prayer to God (Ps. 22:19–21), that culminates in praise to God and confidence in God (Ps.

22:22–31). It may be assumed that this too was part of what Jesus from the cross was telling the chief priests, the scribes, and the mocking onlookers; He had not lost His faith in God and even then He put His trust in God.

HIS RESURRECTION

> **PSALM 16:10**
> For You will not abandon my soul to Sheol;
> Nor will You allow Your Holy One to undergo decay.

> **ACTS 2:27**
> "'BECAUSE YOU WILL NOT ABANDON MY SOUL TO HADES,
> NOR ALLOW YOUR HOLY ONE TO UNDERGO DECAY.'"

THE PERSON OF CHRIST

The doctrine of the person of Christ concerns His identity as the Son of God, His deity, His humanity, and His work.

His Name/Title—the Son of God

The expression "Son of . . ." is quite common in Hebrew and Aramaic and is an expression picked up and used frequently in the New Testament. While obviously this was often used to refer to the relationship of an actual son to an actual father, in many instances it is used as an idiomatic expression to express a person's character or nature. In Deuteronomy 13:13, the terms "some worthless men" is literally "sons (Hebrew benê) of Belial (Hebrew beliyya'al)" meaning "the men who have the character of Belial." Jesus gave the nickname *Boanerges* to James and John, the sons of Zebedee, which means "sons of thunder" (see Mark 3:17). Perhaps this was because they were hot-tempered men or perhaps this is a mild antiphrasis by Jesus, where He gave them a name opposite to their naturally timid demeanor; the metaphorical sense is evident either way.

It is likely that the name or title "Son of God" when used of Jesus had both connotations. It was meant to convey the truth of His (Trinitarian) sonship relation to the Father (minus any notion of physical begetting). And it was intended to express the idea that He had the character and nature of God. Everyone who used this name or title was making a profound claim about the person of Christ—He is God.

THE NAME/TITLE USED BY AN ANGEL

> **LUKE 1:35**
>
> The angel answered and said to her, "The Holy Spirit will come upon you, and the power of the Most High will overshadow you; and for that reason the holy Child shall be called the Son of God."

At the announcement of the birth of the Messiah, to the mother of the Messiah, it is an angel from the Lord who affirms that the child is the "holy Child" and "shall be called the Son of God."

THE NAME/TITLE USED BY A DISCIPLE

> **MATTHEW 16:13–17**
>
> Now when Jesus came into the district of Caesarea Philippi, He was asking His disciples, "Who do people say that the Son of Man is?" [14] And they said, "Some *say* John the Baptist; and others, Elijah; but still others, Jeremiah, or one of the prophets." [15] He said to them, "But who do you say that I am?" [16] Simon Peter answered, "You are the Christ, the Son of the living God." [17] And Jesus said to him, "Blessed are you, Simon Barjona, because flesh and blood did not reveal *this* to you, but My Father who is in heaven."

In Matthew's gospel the narrative portions (very broadly) revolve around Jesus' interaction with three groups—the crowds (see 4:23–25; 14:13–21; 15:29–31), the opposition (see 12:1–8, 9–21; 15:1–9; 16:1–4), and the disciples (see 4:18–22; 10:1–15). At this point (16:13–20) in Matthew's narrative Jesus turns His attention expressly toward His disciples. The next several chapters are about Jesus preparing His disciples for His death, resurrection, and departure (see 16:21, 17:9, 22–23, 20:17–19), and this account is part of that preparation.

The location of "Caesarea Philippi" was strategic. This place was about twenty-five miles north of the Sea of Galilee and was always a center of pagan worship. It was technically outside the land of Israel and therefore removed from the crowds and the opposition. Here the disciples were removed from the religious pressure of the opposition, the social stresses of the crowds, and the demands of ministry. This was the "perfect setting for rest and reflection and to gauge their faith and understanding of Jesus.

Jesus began with a question, "Who do people say that the Son of Man is?" The title "Son of Man" was Jesus' favorite self-designation (used about eighty times in the NT). It was a title that had clear messianic associations (used in Dan. 7:13 as a title of the Messiah). Jesus probably used it to emphasize His humanity and so also His humility and submission, but beyond that, it meant He was self-aware of His unique person.

The "people" Jesus had in mind are the crowds who had been following Jesus throughout His ministry. The responses of the crowds showed their lack of understanding of Jesus. John the Baptist was a revered figure who had gained a significant following before his arrest and execution. Perhaps some could not accept that he was really dead or perhaps they thought he'd been resurrected (as Herod had, see 14:1–2). Elijah was not as improbable a suggestion as it might seem since the OT account does not record his death and the OT prophet Malachi had foretold his (Elijah's) return (Mal. 4:5). Jeremiah was a revered prophet and has been called the "weeping prophet" (which may say something about the demeanor of Jesus during His ministry). Some Jewish writings even predicted the return of Jeremiah (see 2 Esdras 2:18; see 2 Maccabees 15:14). The catch-all answer, "Or one of the prophets," indicates that the crowds could see something of the power and authority of those "men of God" in Jesus' own ministry. It is notable that none of these views reflect the hostility of the opposition and yet none were so bold as to suggest He was the Messiah. He did not seem to match up to their messianic expectations.

Jesus asked a second question, "But who do you say that I am?" And the response, from Peter (speaking for all the disciples) is ringing affirmation of not just the Messiahship of Jesus, but of His deity: "You are the Christ, the

Son of the living God." In affirming that Jesus is "the Christ," literally "the anointed" (i.e., the Messiah), Peter had to repudiate the accusations and lies of the opposition (see Matt. 12:22–29), he had to ignore the undiscerning opinions of the crowds, and he had to overcome the disciples' own short-sighted perception of Jesus (which was not completely surmounted until after the resurrection).

When Peter added, "the Son of the living God," he was making a statement that was stunning in its implications. The expression "son of" was a well-known Hebraic expression: to be "son of something, or someone" meant "to have the nature of that something, or someone." Thus, to call Jesus "the Son of the living God," is to call Him God. For Peter, a pious Jew, committed to the faith of Israel (see Deut. 6:4ff), to utter this stunning declaration is quite amazing. It meant that all that religious tradition taught had to be reconceived, and all that popular opinion conjectured had to be ignored. Jesus, the Son of God, has the nature of God and is God.

That Peter's great declaration was true and accurate is affirmed by Jesus' response, "Blessed are you, Simon Barjona."

THE NAME/TITLE ACKNOWLEDGED BY JESUS HIMSELF

MATTHEW 26:63–64

But Jesus kept silent. And the high priest said to Him, "I adjure You by the living God, that You tell us whether You are the Christ, the Son of God." [64] Jesus said to him, "You have said it *yourself*; nevertheless I tell you, hereafter you will see THE SON OF MAN SITTING AT THE RIGHT HAND OF POWER, and COMING ON THE CLOUDS OF HEAVEN."

THE NAME/TITLE APPLIED TO THE MESSIAH BY YAHWEH

PSALM 2:7

"I will surely tell of the decree of the LORD:
He said to Me, 'You are My Son,
Today I have begotten You.'"

ACTS 13:33

"That God has fulfilled this *promise* to our children in that He raised up Jesus, as it is also written in the second Psalm, 'YOU ARE MY SON; TODAY I HAVE BEGOTTEN YOU.'"

HEBREWS 1:5 (SEE HEB. 5:5)

For to which of the angels did He ever say,

   "YOU ARE MY SON,

   TODAY I HAVE BEGOTTEN YOU"?

And again,

   "I WILL BE A FATHER TO HIM

   AND HE SHALL BE A SON TO ME"?

Each of these texts cites Psalm 2:7. In this Psalm it is the Messiah Himself who gives testimony that Yahweh declared and affirmed Him as "My Son." Each New Testament citation of this declaration, when applied to Jesus Christ, is affirming that He is indeed the Son of God, and hence, that He is God.

THE DEITY OF CHRIST

His Self-Conscious Affirmations of His Deity

The following claims of Jesus affirm that He knew Himself to be equal to the Father and hence one with the Father in divine nature and essence.

HE CLAIMED EQUALITY WITH THE FATHER/HE CLAIMED TO BE THE SON OF THE FATHER

JOHN 5:18–21 (SEE JOHN 14:23)

For this reason therefore the Jews were seeking all the more to kill Him, because He not only was breaking the Sabbath, but also was calling God His own Father, making Himself equal with God. [19] Therefore Jesus answered and was saying to them, "Truly, truly, I say to you, the Son can do nothing of Himself, unless *it is* something He sees the Father doing; for whatever the Father does, these things the Son also does in like manner. [20] For the Father loves the Son, and shows Him all things that He Himself is doing; and *the Father* will show Him greater works than these, so that you will marvel. [21] For just as the Father raises the dead and gives them life, even so the Son also gives life to whom He wishes."

JOHN 8:19

So they were saying to Him, "Where is Your Father?" Jesus answered, "You know neither Me nor My Father; if you knew Me, you would know My Father also."

JOHN 10:29–30

"My Father, who has given *them* to Me, is greater than all; and no one is able to snatch *them* out of the Father's hand. [30] I and the Father are one."

JOHN 14:11 (SEE VV. 7–11; V. 20)

"Believe Me that I am in the Father and the Father is in Me; otherwise believe because of the works themselves."

JOHN 17:10

"And all things that are Mine are Yours, and Yours are Mine; and I have been glorified in them."

JOHN 17:11 (SEE V. 21)

"I am no longer in the world; and *yet* they themselves are in the world, and I come to You. Holy Father, keep them in Your name, *the name* which You have given Me, that they may be one even as We *are*."

HE CLAIMED TO BE REVEALER OF THE FATHER

MATTHEW 11:27

"All things have been handed over to Me by My Father; and no one knows the Son except the Father; nor does anyone know the Father except the Son, and anyone to whom the Son wills to reveal *Him*."

JOHN 1:18

No one has seen God at any time; the only begotten God who is in the bosom of the Father, He has explained *Him*.

HE CLAIMED TO BE THE UNIQUE AGENT OF THE FATHER

JOHN 5:43A

"I have come in My Father's name, and you do not receive Me."

JOHN 5:24A

"Truly, truly, I say to you, he who hears My word, and believes Him who sent Me, has eternal life."

JOHN 5:30

"I can do nothing on My own initiative. As I hear, I judge; and My judgment is just, because I do not seek My own will, but the will of Him who sent Me."

JOHN 5:37–38

"And the Father who sent Me, He has testified of Me. You have neither heard His voice at any time nor seen His form. [38] You do not have His word abiding in you, for you do not believe Him whom He sent."

JOHN 6:44

"No one can come to Me unless the Father who sent Me draws him; and I will raise him up on the last day."

In these verses (and more!) Jesus claims to be "sent" by the Father. This expression indicates both a mission and the authority to carry out that mission. In effect, Jesus claimed to be *the agent* or ambassador of the Father while He was here on earth.

HE CLAIMED TO BE "I AM"

JOHN 8:58

Jesus said to them, "Truly, truly, I say to you, before Abraham was born, I am."

This is the most direct claim to deity made by Jesus. In this declaration Jesus is affirming His preexistence, which is in itself a claim to deity. Even more startling than that, He is claiming to be "I AM." The Greek expression *ego eimi* is the emphatic first person singular for the verb "to be" and reflects the Hebrew *'ehyeh*, which is the equivalent to *ego eimi*, that is, the first person singular for the verb "to be." When Jesus spoke those words, everyone who heard Him would immediately have thought of the text in Exodus 3:14 where God declared His name to Moses as "I AM THAT I AM." In short, Jesus was making a claim not just to deity, but to be Yahweh. The name Yahweh is actually the third person singular for the verb "to be"—He Is.

He Claimed to Be the Source of Eternal Life

JOHN 10:27–29

"My sheep hear My voice, and I know them, and they follow Me; 28 and I give eternal life to them, and they will never perish; and no one will snatch them out of My hand. 29 My Father, who has given *them* to Me, is greater than all; and no one is able to snatch *them* out of the Father's hand."

JOHN 11:25–26

Jesus said to her, "I am the resurrection and the life; he who believes in Me will live even if he dies, 26 and everyone who lives and believes in Me will never die. Do you believe this?"

Direct Affirmations of Christ's Deity

THE GOSPEL OF JOHN

JOHN 1:1–3

In the beginning was the Word, and the Word was with God, and the Word was God. 2 He was in the beginning with God. 3 All things came into being through Him, and apart from Him nothing came into being that has come into being.

John begins his gospel with a striking prologue that declares unequivocally the deity of the incarnate Word, Jesus Christ. When John refers to the "Word," he is referring to the one who became incarnate, namely Jesus Christ, as verse 14 makes clear. John's brief assertions make several claims about the "existence" of the "Word."

With obvious allusion to Genesis 1, John affirms both the *absolute preexistence*, and the *eternal* existence of the Word—"In the beginning was the Word." Next, he affirms the *distinct* existence of the Word from God—"the Word was with God." He continues with an affirmation of the *divine* existence of the Word—"the Word was God." And he summarizes all three of these with a reiteration—"He was in the beginning with God." That last phrase alone (but informed by the three previous affirmations) affirms He existed before there was a "beginning"; in other words, this affirms His eternal preexistence. (It should be noted that while the words "eternal preexistence" are intelligible to us, that to which they are meant to refer is quite beyond our cognitive grasp.) Furthermore, since eternality is a quality or attribute of God alone, this is also an affirmation of the deity of the Word. And, this affirms that the Word was distinct from God, as indicated by the preposition "with." He existed in relation with, or to, God. Finally, here in this last affirmation, and in all the instances where John refers to "the Word" by the personal pronoun—"He" (lit. "this one")—the personal existence of the Word is affirmed.

To emphasize the thrust of these affirmations of the pre-, distinct, divine, and personal existence of the Word, John makes a further affirmation of the existence of the Word relative to all other existent things. He affirms that the Word is the creator of all things that exist. This obviously excludes Himself and God. Just as obviously, this makes His existence "other than" the existence of all He created. In other words, His is not a "created existence" (He is not a creature—He is the Creator). Furthermore, this affirms a priority that includes but transcends mere temporal priority.

John's prologue is not meant to reveal everything about the eternal relations of the Godhead, the ontological status of the Father *viz* the Son, or the complexities of the Trinity—much less explain them. But these verses are the starting point of understanding the person of the Son (Christology). They are meant to establish the basic existential (if nebulous) boundaries which are necessary to understand what the rest of the gospel of John (and the New Testament) reveals about the Word—the person of the Son. When one considers the different ways the opponents of orthodoxy (in Jesus' own lifetime and throughout the first four centuries of the church, and ever after) invented distorted views of the Son, one can appreciate the importance and value of articulating and maintaining the truth of these affirmations. Had these boundaries been respected, the list of heresies (Trinitarian and Christological) would have been a great deal shorter.

> **JOHN 20:28**
> Thomas answered and said to Him, "My Lord and my God!"

This declaration by Thomas is all the more dramatic since it comes after Thomas had displayed a settled skepticism about the bodily resurrection of Jesus (see John 20:24–25). When the Lord Jesus appeared to Thomas and personally challenged that skepticism, Thomas responded not with "I now believe in the resurrection" but with a declaration significantly stronger. The proof of the bodily resurrection of Jesus led Thomas to an even more profound insight, namely that Jesus was God! The author of the gospel employed Thomas's declaration as a narrative capstone for his main thesis, namely that Jesus is God (see John 1:1–3; 20:31).

THE EPISTLES OF PAUL

> **ROMANS 9:4–5**
> Who are Israelites, to whom belongs the adoption as sons, and the glory and the covenants and the giving of the Law and the *temple* service and the promises, ⁵ whose are the fathers, and from whom is the Christ according to the flesh, who is over all, God blessed forever. Amen.

In Romans chapters 9 through 11, Paul is making his argument for the ongoing viability of God's purposes and program for national Israel. In Romans 9:4–5 he begins by noting a few of the ongoing privileges of the Jews, Paul's "kinsmen according to the flesh" (Rom. 9:3). These privileges include their unique relationship with God ("adoption as sons"), the giving of the Law and the services in the temple and, most significant, the promises given to the fathers in the covenant (or covenants, i.e., Abrahamic, Davidic, New Covenant). One of these privileges is the Messiah, Christ. Here Paul identifies Christ with several descriptions. A more literal rendering of verse 5b is "and from them, according to the flesh, is the Christ, who is overall God, blessed forever." In effect, Paul is saying the Jews are privileged to be the nation from which comes the Messiah, Christ. This Christ is God, and He is ever blessed. While this view is not the consensus of all commentators, "arguments in favor of taking 'God' as an appellation (or title designation) of 'Messiah' greatly outweigh those that support the alternative."[5] Thus, "Paul here calls the Messiah, Jesus, 'God,' attributing to him full divine status."[6]

PHILIPPIANS 2:6–11

Who, although He existed in the form of God, did not regard equality with God a thing to be grasped, [7] but emptied Himself, taking the form of a bond-servant, *and* being made in the likeness of men. [8] Being found in appearance as a man, He humbled Himself by becoming obedient to the point of death, even death on a cross. [9] For this reason also, God highly exalted Him, and bestowed on Him the name which is above every name, [10] so that at the name of Jesus EVERY KNEE WILL BOW, of those who are in heaven and on earth and under the earth, [11] and that every tongue will confess that Jesus Christ is Lord, to the glory of God the Father.

Because there are a number of poetic elements in these verses, they are regarded by many as an early hymn. This has led to much speculation as to the origin and authorship of the hymn. However, those discussions are rendered (mostly) moot in light of the fact that Paul wrote this letter and this hymn appears in it. He surely agreed with its theology.

The hymn consists of two stanzas: the first is verses 6 through 8 in which Paul describes the condescension of Christ—from preexistent deity, to incarnate humanity, to ignominious crucifixion. The second stanza is verses 9 through 11 in which Paul describes the exaltation of Christ—in which God the Father gives Him a "name above every name," and He is given homage from every realm of creation, and He is acknowledged as Lord by "every tongue." The deity of Christ is affirmed in both stanzas.

In stanza one, Paul affirms Christ's deity in verse 6 in two expressions. In the first expression ("He existed in the form of God") there is an affirmation of Christ's preexistence but a preexistence of a unique nature—"in the form of God." The term *form* (Greek *morphē*) is the key term in this entire hymn.[7] This term essentially means "what is seen on the outside is what is really there on the inside." Christ "had himself known a prior existence in the 'form' of God—not meaning that he was 'like God but really not' but that he was characterized by what was essential to being God."[8] Before He was incarnate, Christ was already "existing" (Greek *hyparchōn*) in all that was essential to God.

In the second expression in verse 6 Paul elaborates on the meaning of "form" (Greek *morphē*). He "did not regard equality with God a thing to be grasped." The term *equality* (Greek *isa*) means "to have the same value," or "to be equivalent." It is found in English terms such as "*iso*sceles," which in geometry means to have two sides of equal length. This equality with God was not something Christ sought to "grasp." The idea here is that He did not seek to retain His advantages as God.

"The net result, therefore, is that these two phrases together make explicit what Paul has implied in a variety of ways throughout the [Pauline] corpus: Christ had preexistence as the Son of God, and his sonship was that of one who was fully and equally divine with the Father."[9]

In stanza two, Paul affirms Christ's deity by the exaltation Christ shall receive. He is not only given a name above all names, but He will be given universal homage when at the name of Jesus "every knee will bow . . . and . . . every tongue will confess that Jesus Christ is Lord." This is actually an allusion to Isaiah 45:23. In that context it is Yahweh who is speaking (see Isa. 45:21–22, 24–25) and it is Yahweh who says, "That to Me every knee will bow, every tongue will swear allegiance." Paul has boldly applied this text to Christ in such a way that it is clear he thinks Jesus Christ is Yahweh. Christ is not just deity—God, He is the one true God. Paul's additional phrase, "to the glory of God the Father" should be taken as an indication that the Father is also God. Although he does not elaborate the point here, this is a clear indication that Paul's theology was trinitarian.

It is remarkable that this magnificent hymn, which affirms deeply significant truths about the person of Christ, is here in Paul's letter to the

Philippians in order to encourage them to follow Christ's example ("Have this attitude in yourselves" of humility, self-sacrifice, and obedience).

> **COLOSSIANS 1:15–20**
>
> He is the image of the invisible God, the firstborn of all creation. [16] For by Him all things were created, *both* in the heavens and on earth, visible and invisible, whether thrones or dominions or rulers or authorities—all things have been created through Him and for Him. [17] He is before all things, and in Him all things hold together. [18] He is also head of the body, the church; and He is the beginning, the firstborn from the dead, so that He Himself will come to have first place in everything. [19] For it was the *Father's* good pleasure for all the fullness to dwell in Him, [20] and through Him to reconcile all things to Himself, having made peace through the blood of His cross; through Him, *I say*, whether things on earth or things in heaven.

> **COLOSSIANS 2:9**
>
> For in Him all the fullness of Deity dwells in bodily form.

Paul's letter to the Colossians was written in response to some false teachers that infiltrated the church in Colossae. The nature of that false teaching was apparently a mixture of gnostic-like ideas, based in Greek (generally Platonic and Stoic) philosophy with some Judaistic legalism and ceremonialism. In this letter, and particularly in this hymn, Paul counters that heresy with the truth about the person of Jesus Christ. Broadly speaking, Paul's point is that whatever the false teachers offered in terms of insight into spiritual matters, access to God and His power (see Col. 2:16–20), and wisdom for this life (see Col. 1:9, 28) and the next, are to be found in truth in Christ.

These verses are clearly a hymn, as can be seen in the variations from Paul's usual style and language. For instance, the surrounding context has a number of personal pronouns (referring to Paul and his readers) and a number of first-person and second-person verbs—but these features are not found in Col. 1:15–20. He probably used a preexisting hymn but adapted it to make his own statement.

In this hymn the deity of Christ is revealed six ways: His Person (v. 15); His Power (v. 16); His Priority and dominion (vv. 17–18); His *Plērōma*

(Greek for "Fullness") (v. 19) (see 2:9); His Program of (Comprehensive) reconciliation (v. 20.)

In describing His person, Paul says, "He is the image (Greek *eikōn*) of the invisible God." The term "image" (Greek *eikōn*) may have the notion of a likeness or representation, a reflection in a mirror or an image on a coin. However, it does not indicate "mere likeness" or "incidental likeness," but a likeness or representation that conveys something of nature and authenticity of the original. In contrast to Adam who was *made* in the image of God, Christ *is* the image of God—He manifests God. But God is invisible (Greek *aoratou*) (see 1 Tim. 6:15). This is not simply a "paradox," much less a logical contradiction. The perception of this image is not by the external sense of physical sight but by an inner insight (faith) that "sees" where mere physical sight cannot see.

Furthermore, He is "the firstborn (Greek *prōtotokos*) of all creation." This is a very important term. The *prōtotokos* can mean "first in birth-order," "first in place, order or time" but here has the idea of "foremost in rank or dignity." It refers primarily to position, rank, or priority of position and emphasizes a preeminence of quality or preeminence of kind. Christ has *priority* to all creation and *sovereignty* over all creation.

Paul refers to three aspects of His creative power. First, there is the reality of it ("For by Him all things were created"). Since the power of creation belongs to God alone, Paul is affirming the deity of Christ. Second, there are the realms over which this power is exerted ("both in the heavens and on earth, visible and invisible, whether thrones or dominions or rulers or authorities"). These expressions are meant to indicate the completeness of Christ's power. He is above all these created realms; He is not a part of those realms but over them. Finally, Paul states the reason for exercising this power ("all things have been created through Him and for Him"). He is the source, the agent and the goal of creation. This could only be true of one who is God.

The somewhat enigmatic expression, "He is before all things," may be taken as a statement of His preexistence as well as a statement of His superiority. The key is His relationship to "all things." The preceding verse affirms He created "all things," so quite obviously that implies He existed before them. And the following phrase affirms He holds "all things" together, implying a certain sovereignty over them. The idea of the verb "hold together" (Greek *synestēken* from *synistēmi*) has the notion of "to cohere," "hold together." This "coherence" is not merely physical. Paul is probably alluding to Greek philosophical ideas about the basic metaphysical realities that keep the world and the universe together. Those speculative metaphysical ideas are rendered invalid and proven to be puerile by the truth about Christ. He is the one that keeps planets in their orbits, grounds moral laws, and "upholds all things by the word of His power" (Heb. 1:3).

Paul further acknowledges His priority and dominion by affirming that He is the "head of the body, the church." This might seem an odd addition because the church is certainly one of the "all things" just mentioned. Why does Paul mention His headship over the church specifically? Paul is actually elevating the significance of the church in relation to "all things." In this headship He is the "beginning" of a new creation because He is the firstborn (Greek *prōtotokos*—again, first in rank and position) "from the dead." In contrast to the gnostic and Greek philosophical ideas, He transcends the temporal reality not by rising up the chain of being but by rising from the dead. It is not by escaping this physical, material world (by esoteric knowledge as in Gnosticism) but by redeeming it through resurrection and new creation that Christ "will come to have first place in everything."

When Paul affirms that "it was the Father's good pleasure for all the fullness (see Col. 2:9) to dwell in Him," he makes the most direct contradiction to the Greek (gnostic) notions. The "fullness" (Greek *plērōma*) was a vague term used in Greek philosophy in a number of ways, but Paul co-opts all of that and uses it to express the incarnation (see Col. 2:9). The incarnation ("in bodily form") of "deity" (Greek *theotes*; "divine nature") virtually demolishes (see 2 Cor. 10:5) all the esoteric notions and metaphysical speculations of Greek philosophy (and thereby defeats the false teachers harassing the Colossian church.)

The final affirmation of the hymn gives the reason for the incarnation, namely the reconciliation of "all things." The mere mention of reconciliation implies enmity and the mention of the cost of that reconciliation—"the blood of His cross"—recalls Paul's words in Colossians 1:15–16. The rescue the Colossians needed, the redemption and forgiveness they now possessed, was not accomplished by Greek philosophical speculation or esoteric gnostic doctrines but by the "Beloved Son," the magnificent One Paul has described in this amazing hymn.

---

1 TIMOTHY 3:16

By common confession, great is the mystery of godliness:

He who was revealed in the flesh,

Was vindicated in the Spirit,

Seen by angels,

Proclaimed among the nations,

Believed on in the world,

Taken up in glory.

In this brief transition in Paul's letter to Timothy (from his instructions on church order [1 Tim. 2:1–3:15] to the discussion of the false teachers [1 Tim. 4:1–5]), Paul records what most scholars would agree is a six-line hymn that summarizes several important features of his convictions about Christ. (Whether Paul composed or simply quotes an early church hymn written by someone else is a fairly moot issue; since he records it here we can assume Paul agreed with all that it affirms.)

He begins with two introductory statements. "By common confession" means that what Paul states here is an affirmation that all true believers would openly affirm. (Paul likely has the false teachers in mind who would abjure this forthright affirmation.) In the New Testament the term *mystery* refers to a truth that was not fully revealed and understood in the Old Testament but is now revealed. Here the "mystery of godliness" refers to the incarnation of Jesus Christ.

The six lines of the hymn describe some aspect of the incarnation of the Son of God.

First, Christ was revealed ("manifested"; Greek *ephanerothe*) "in the flesh." The Greek term *ephanerothe* does not mean "to bring into existence," or "to create," but "to make visible." In the incarnation, the Son of God took on human flesh and was seen as a man (see John 1:14; 1 John 1:1–3). The term *flesh* is used to describe Christ's humanity; it does not, as in Romans 7, refer to fallen human nature. This made it possible for Christ to sympathize with humanity and to serve as a faithful high priest (see Heb. 2:11, 14). This is an affirmation of His true humanity.

Second, Christ "was vindicated in the Spirit." The term *vindicated* is the Greek term *dikaioō* and is related to the idea of "justification." The notion here is not that Jesus needed to be justified from sin as humans must be, but rather that He was declared or acknowledged to be who He is by the Spirit. It may be that this refers to Jesus' baptism where He was declared by the Father's voice to be the "beloved Son" with the further acknowledgment of the Spirit (see Matt. 3:16–17). This is an acknowledgment of His deity.

Third, Christ was beheld by angels. Jesus' incarnation was announced by an angel (see Luke 1:26–38), angels celebrated His birth (see Luke 2:8–14), angels ministered to Him (see Mark 1:13), and angels were present at His empty tomb (see Matt. 28:2). The presence of the holy angels was a further acknowledgment of His heavenly origins.

Fourth, Christ was "proclaimed among the nations." This was true during His earthly ministry; He and His disciples ministered in Judea, Galilee, Samaria (see John 4:4ff), Gerasene, the Decapolis (Gentile cities east of the Sea of Galilee, see Mark 5:1, 20), and the regions of Tyre and Sidon (see Mark 7:24–26, 32). Of course, after his resurrection the gospel spread beyond the regions of the eastern Mediterranean (see Matt. 28:19–20).

Fifth, Christ was "believed on in the world." The four gospels, the book of Acts, and indeed the rest of the New Testament confirm this as fact.

Sixth, Christ was "taken up in glory" (see Acts 1:9–10). This refers to the ascension and Christ's return to heavenly glory (see John 17:4–5). The ascension was the final confirmation that Jesus Christ was indeed God incarnate and that His mission on earth had been accomplished.

These six lines roughly tell the story of the incarnation and as such they form the core of what must be believed about Jesus Christ.

THE GENERAL EPISTLES

> **HEBREWS 1:1–3**
>
> God, after He spoke long ago to the fathers in the prophets in many portions and in many ways, ² in these last days has spoken to us in His Son, whom He appointed heir of all things, through whom also He made the world. ³ And He is the radiance of His glory and the exact representation of His nature, and upholds all things by the word of His power. When He had made purification of sins, He sat down at the right hand of the Majesty on high.

The basic theme of the letter to the Hebrews is the superiority of Jesus Christ, the Son, to everything and everyone. The readers of the letter needed to know that superiority in order to keep them from returning from devotion to Jesus back to Judaism (see the so-called "warning passages," 2:1–4, 3:7–4:13, 5:11–6:12, 10:19–39, 12:14–29). The reference to "His Son" is meant to remind the readers of the declaration in Psalm 2:7, "He said to Me, 'You are My Son; Today I have begotten You.'" This reference is made explicit in Hebrews 1:5. The author expects his readers to known that this Son is Jesus Christ (see Matt. 3:17; 17:5).

In the opening verse the author asserts the superiority of the self-revelation of God given by the Son to the mediated revelation given by the Old Testament prophets. Then the author lists some personal qualities of the Son that demonstrate that assertion. That He is "appointed heir of all things" does not mean He stands to gain an inheritance one day, as the English term "heir" might imply. That He is "appointed" means He is authorized, "recognized and deserving of," this status by right. That He is "heir" is a title of dignity and authority. He has a position before God of primacy (see Heb. 1:6 "the firstborn"; Greek *prototokos*); He is the one and only heir.

It was He "through whom also He [God] made the world" (see John 1:1–3; Col. 1:15–17). Of course, the Father (Gen. 1:1; Mal. 2:10) and the Spirit (Gen. 1:2; Ps. 104:30; Job 33:4) were also involved in creation. And so too, the Son is involved as the Agent of creation—"through the Son." The Greek term translated **world** here is not *cosmos* but *aionas*, which is often rendered "ages." The idea is He made the whole "time-space continuum"—the universe—and all that's in it!

He (the Son) is the radiance of His (God the Father's) glory. The term *radiance* (used only here in the NT) can have either a passive (hence: "reflection") or active (hence: "effulgence") meaning. The image is of "extreme brightness" and likely would have reminded the readers of instances of "brightness" in the Old Testament such as the burning bush (Ex. 33:21–22) or the pillar of cloud-fire (Exo. 40:34–38; see Num. 9:15–23). Perhaps the author had in mind the experience of the disciples at the transfiguration (see Matt. 17:1–8). Just as the rays of sunlight are what one sees when one sees the sun, just so the Son gives forth the "effulgence" of God's glory. In short, just as the sun and sunlight are one and the same and yet distinct, so the Father and the Son are one yet distinct.

He (the Son) is "the exact representation" (Greek *character*) of His (God's) nature. The term exact representation (used only here in the NT) refers to the impression made by a die or an engraving. The term *nature* (Greek *hypostaseos*) came to be used in the debates of the early church to mean "person" (so distinguishing the three persons of the Godhead and the one person of Christ in whom were two "natures"—divine and human. It is important not to import the meanings of the terms that were used in later debates in history back into the meanings of the terms as they were used in the New Testament). Here the term is meant to refer to God's "essence"—His divine nature as God. The Son was and is "essentially" God!

He is the Sustainer of the created order—He upholds all things by the word of His power. The term *upholds* is not the idea that He has the world on His shoulders (like Atlas), but has the idea of "carries" or "conducts along." He is carrying the world toward a goal or purpose.

The phrase "When He had made purification of sins" makes it clear that the author has in mind Jesus Christ (see 3:6; 10:10–12). The final phrase, "He sat down at the right hand of the Majesty on high," conveys the sense of honor and authority invested in the Son. When Jesus ascended and sat at the Father's right hand, it meant that His sacrifice for sinners was accepted, that the purposes of His incarnation were accomplished (see John 17:4–5), and that He held a position that was appropriate only for one who is Himself God.

HEBREWS 1:8–9

But of the Son *He says*,

"YOUR THRONE, O GOD, IS FOREVER AND EVER,

AND THE RIGHTEOUS SCEPTER IS THE SCEPTER OF HIS KINGDOM.

⁹ YOU HAVE LOVED RIGHTEOUSNESS AND HATED LAWLESSNESS;

THEREFORE GOD, YOUR GOD, HAS ANOINTED YOU

WITH THE OIL OF GLADNESS ABOVE YOUR COMPANIONS."

The author of Hebrews quotes Psalm 45:6–7 and applies these verses to the Son (Jesus Christ). What is most significant is that here the Father is speaking of the Son and addresses Him as "God." For the Son to be given a throne and a scepter is to be given a kingdom. For Him to be "anointed" by God is to be authorized as the anointed one, that is the Messiah, the messianic king. This can be nothing other than the Davidic Kingdom, the millennial kingdom, the kingdom promised to David in 2 Samuel 7 (see Ps. 89).

2 PETER 1:1

Simon Peter, a bond-servant and apostle of Jesus Christ,

To those who have received a faith of the same kind as ours, by the righteousness of our God and Savior, Jesus Christ.

In this simple epistolary greeting, Peter makes a striking declaration of the deity of Jesus Christ; however, it requires the application of a rule of Greek grammar to fully appreciate it. The rule is called the Grandville Sharp Rule* after the grammarian who most clearly articulated it. The rule has several parts. First, it must be noted that in the Greek the New Testament nouns, even proper nouns, would most often have an article ("the"). However, when two nouns appeared connected by the conjunction "and" (Greek *kai*) and only the first noun had an article, then both nouns were to be taken as referring to the same person (or thing). This is what is found here in Peter's greeting: article—God—and (no article) Savior. This means Peter thought that both "God" and "Savior" referred to the same person. Now, one more bit of grammar is necessary. In the English there is a comma after Savior and then another noun (actually two nouns but virtually one name)—Jesus Christ. This is a feature of grammar called "apposition." (In the Greek this apposition is understood by other details in the text.) In this construction it is to be understood that the two nouns in apposition are referring to the same person. Taken altogether, in this statement Peter is saying God and Savior are the same person and that person is Jesus Christ. Peter is to be understood as calling Jesus Christ, Savior and God. (*It should be noted that the details of Sharp's rule have been questioned by some recent Greek grammarians; nevertheless, the debate has not undermined the point at hand—Peter's expression is to be understood as an affirmation of the deity of Jesus Christ.)[10]

His Divine Abilities

LIFE

> **JOHN 1:4**
> In Him was life, and the life was the Light of men.

> **JOHN 5:21**
> "For just as the Father raises the dead and gives them life, even so the Son also gives life to whom He wishes."

> **JOHN 5:26**
> "For just as the Father has life in Himself, even so He gave to the Son also to have life in Himself."

Scripture declares that only God has the ability to give life (see Deut. 32:39; Job 1:21). Jesus' ability to give life affirms His deity.

CREATION

> **JOHN 1:3**
> All things came into being through Him, and apart from Him nothing came into being that has come into being.

> **COLOSSIANS 1:16**
> For by Him all things were created, *both* in the heavens and on earth, visible and invisible, whether thrones or dominions or rulers or authorities—all things have been created through Him and for Him.

> **HEBREWS 1:2**
> In these last days has spoken to us in His Son, whom He appointed heir of all things, through whom also He made the world.

Creation (speaking of the creation of the universe), like life itself, is a capacity that belongs to God alone. John, Paul, and the author of Hebrews each avers that Jesus Christ has the power of creation and this is an unequivocal affirmation of His deity.

His Miracles

POWER OVER NATURE

> **MATTHEW 14:18–21 (SEE 15:32–39)**
> And He said, "Bring them here to Me." [19] Ordering the people to sit down on the grass, He took the five loaves and the two fish, and looking up toward heaven, He blessed *the food*, and breaking the loaves He gave them to the disciples, and the disciples *gave them* to the crowds, [20] and they all ate and were satisfied. They picked up what was left over of the broken pieces, twelve full baskets. [21] There were about five thousand men who ate, besides women and children.

> **MARK 4:38–41 (SEE MARK 6:49–51)**
> Jesus Himself was in the stern, asleep on the cushion; and they woke Him and said to Him, "Teacher, do You not care that we are perishing?" [39] And He got up and rebuked the wind and said to the sea, "Hush, be still." And the wind died down and it became perfectly calm. [40] And He said to them, "Why are you afraid? Do you still have no faith?" [41] They became very much afraid and said to one another, "Who then is this, that even the wind and the sea obey Him?"

> **MARK 6:49–51**
> But when they saw Him walking on the sea, they supposed that it was a ghost, and cried out; [50] for they all saw Him and were terrified. But immediately He spoke with them and said to them, "Take courage; it is I, do not be afraid." [51] Then He got into the boat with them, and the wind stopped; and they were utterly astonished.

Jesus' demonstrations of His authority over nature were never naked displays of power but most often occurred in instances of provision and of protection. For instance, He produced an abundant supply of food for hungry thousands from just a few fish and loaves of bread. He stilled the storm in order to preserve the disciples whose lives were in danger. Even when He walked on the water, it was no mere display of miraculous ability but He used the occasion to assure and encourage them. Furthermore, in this incident it was not only His ability to walk on water that proved His deity but it was in His words of assurance to them. When Jesus identified Himself, He said "it is I." He used the emphatic expression *ego eimi*—I am. On the lips of Jesus this was significant, for it identified Him with the covenant name of God—Yahweh ("I AM"; see Ex. 3:14).

POWER OVER ILLNESS AND DISEASE

MATTHEW 4:23
Jesus was going throughout all Galilee, teaching in their synagogues and proclaiming the gospel of the kingdom, and healing every kind of disease and every kind of sickness among the people.

MATTHEW 8:13 (SEE VV. 16–17)
And Jesus said to the centurion, "Go; it shall be done for you as you have believed." And the servant was healed that *very* moment.

MATTHEW 14:35–36
And when the men of that place recognized Him, they sent *word* into all that surrounding district and brought to Him all who were sick; [36] and they implored Him that they might just touch the fringe of His cloak; and as many as touched *it* were cured.

Christ's power over disease is proof of His Messiahship and His deity. The variety in the healing accounts are meant to highlight the extent of that power. He healed every kind of disease; He healed by His touch (see Matt. 8:2–3, a leper; Mark 7:32–35, a deaf and mute man); He healed by His word (see Matt. 9:6, the paralytic; Mark 3:5, the man with a withered hand); He healed at a distance (see Matt. 8:7–8, 13); and He healed some who asked (see Matt. 9:27–30, two blind men) and some who did not ask (John 9:6–7, one blind man; Luke 8:44, a woman with an issue of blood). "Those physical healings were vivid displays of both Jesus' power and His compassion. They were proof of His deity and living demonstrations of His divine authority."[11]

POWER OVER DEMONS

MATTHEW 8:16–17

When evening came, they brought to Him many who were demon-possessed; and He cast out the spirits with a word, and healed all who were ill. [17] *This was* to fulfill what was spoken through Isaiah the prophet: "HE HIMSELF TOOK OUR INFIRMITIES AND CARRIED AWAY OUR DISEASES."

MATTHEW 8:31–32

The demons *began* to entreat Him, saying, "If You *are going to* cast us out, send us into the herd of swine." [32] And He said to them, "Go!" And they came out and went into the swine, and the whole herd rushed down the steep bank into the sea and perished in the waters.

MATTHEW 17:18

And Jesus rebuked him, and the demon came out of him, and the boy was cured at once.

LUKE 4:33–35

In the synagogue there was a man possessed by the spirit of an unclean demon, and he cried out with a loud voice, [34] "Let us alone! What business do we have with each other, Jesus of Nazareth? Have You come to destroy us? I know who You are—the Holy One of God!" [35] But Jesus rebuked him, saying, "Be quiet and come out of him!" And when the demon had thrown him down in the midst *of the people*, he came out of him without doing him any harm.

Jesus' power over demons, like His power over disease (see above), was proof of His deity. Indeed, the demons He dealt with gave unwelcome testimony to this truth.

POWER OF LIFE (OVER DEATH)

MATTHEW 9:24–25 (SEE MARK 5:4–42)

He said, "Leave; for the girl has not died, but is asleep." And they *began* laughing at Him. 25 But when the crowd had been sent out, He entered and took her by the hand, and the girl got up.

LUKE 7:14–15

And He came up and touched the coffin; and the bearers came to a halt. And He said, "Young man, I say to you, arise!" 15 The dead man sat up and began to speak. And *Jesus* gave him back to his mother.

JOHN 11:43–44

When He had said these things, He cried out with a loud voice, "Lazarus, come forth." 44 The man who had died came forth, bound hand and foot with wrappings, and his face was wrapped around with a cloth. Jesus said to them, "Unbind him, and let him go."

Jesus raised three persons from the dead—a widow's son, a synagogue official's daughter, and the brother of two sisters. His power to raise the dead is like His power to give life—it is a power that belongs to God alone. Since He has that power, He is God. "Jesus' miracles were the verification of His divine might which He would reveal some day to reverse the curse and to restore righteousness, harmony, and peace in all of His creation. . . . He performed those miracles to demonstrate His deity and to establish His credentials as the Messiah predicted by the Old Testament prophets (see Matt. 8:16–17; 9:35; 11:5)."[12]

THE HUMANITY OF CHRIST

His Human Birth

LUKE 2:7

And she gave birth to her firstborn son; and she wrapped Him in cloths, and laid Him in a manger, because there was no room for them in the inn.

> **GALATIANS 4:4**
> But when the fullness of the time came, God sent forth His Son, born of a woman, born under the Law.

His birth was a completely normal human birth. Mary would have experienced everything any other expectant mother would have experienced. Jesus as an infant needed the same care as any newborn baby (e.g., "she wrapped Him in cloths").

His Human Development

> **LUKE 2:52**
> And Jesus kept increasing in wisdom and stature, and in favor with God and men.

Jesus experienced a completely normal human development; indeed, He was made like us "in all things" (see Heb. 2:17). He developed mentally ("in wisdom"), physically ("in stature"), spiritually ("in favor with God"), and socially ("[in favor with] men"). His sinlessness may have (and surely must have) set Him apart from all the other children of Nazareth. Other than the single incident recorded in Luke 2:41–51, nothing was so remarkable that it needed to be included in the gospel record. His life and development as a child were entirely normal.

His Human Flesh

> **JOHN 1:14A**
> And the Word became flesh, and dwelt among us.

> **HEBREWS 2:14A**
> Therefore, since the children share in flesh and blood, He Himself likewise also partook of the same.

> **1 JOHN 1:1–2**
> What was from the beginning, what we have heard, what we have seen with our eyes, what we have looked at and touched with our hands,

concerning the Word of Life— [2] and the life was manifested, and we have seen and testify and proclaim to you the eternal life, which was with the Father and was manifested to us.

The body ("flesh") of Jesus was that of a normal human being. In the early centuries of the church there were those who taught that Christ was a divine being but His body was not "real," but only seemed to be a real human body. The heresy was called Docetism (from Greek *dokein*, "to seem"). It seems likely that the apostle John had such a false teaching in mind when he wrote the first words of his first letter.

Human (Sinless) Frailties

HUNGER

MATTHEW 4:1–2

Then Jesus was led up by the Spirit into the wilderness to be tempted by the devil. [2] And after He had fasted forty days and forty nights, He then became hungry.

FATIGUE

MATTHEW 8:24

And behold, there arose a great storm on the sea, so that the boat was being covered with the waves; but Jesus Himself was asleep.

JOHN 4:5–6

So He came to a city of Samaria called Sychar, near the parcel of ground that Jacob gave to his son Joseph; [6] and Jacob's well was there. So Jesus, being wearied from His journey, was sitting thus by the well. It was about the sixth hour.

THIRST

JOHN 19:28

After this, Jesus, knowing that all things had already been accomplished, to fulfill the Scripture, said, "I am thirsty."

These verses plainly affirm that the humanity of Jesus Christ was a real bodily existence and not a mere appearance (like a hologram) or a phantasm (ghost). Docetism was an early heresy that suggested that Christ only seemed to be a man (from Greek *dokeo* "to think or seem"). This heresy explained away these texts by arguing that His hunger, fatigue, and thirst were simply instances of His "play-acting" to conceal His true heavenly identity. However, if Jesus did not have a real human body, then his sufferings on the cross would also be an instance of "play-acting." Furthermore, if He did not have a real human nature, then the affirmation of the author of Hebrews—"For we do not have a high priest who cannot sympathize with our weaknesses, but One who has been tempted in all things as we are, yet without sin"—would not be true.

Human Emotions

GRIEF

JOHN 11:35
Jesus wept.

ANGER

MARK 3:5
After looking around at them with anger, grieved at their hardness of heart, He said to the man, "Stretch out your hand." And he stretched it out, and his hand was restored.

COMPASSION

MATTHEW 14:14
When He went ashore, He saw a large crowd, and felt compassion for them and healed their sick.

JOY

HEBREWS 12:2
Fixing our eyes on Jesus, the author and perfecter of faith, who for the joy

set before Him endured the cross, despising the shame, and has sat down at the right hand of the throne of God.

Two Questions about His Humanity

HIS SINLESSNESS

2 CORINTHIANS 5:21
He made Him who knew no sin *to be* sin on our behalf, so that we might become the righteousness of God in Him.

HEBREWS 7:26
For it was fitting for us to have such a high priest, holy, innocent, undefiled, separated from sinners and exalted above the heavens.

1 PETER 2:21–22
For you have been called for this purpose, since Christ also suffered for you, leaving you an example for you to follow in His steps, [22] WHO COMMITTED NO SIN, NOR WAS ANY DECEIT FOUND IN HIS MOUTH.

No effort to charge Jesus with sin has ever been successful, nor could it be. The New Testament texts which affirm His sinlessness are clear and unequivocal. It has been suggested by a number of skeptics over the centuries that this claim is incredible and evidence that the gospel records about Jesus are more myth than fact. After all, "to err is human." However, that aphorism is not true. Adam and Eve were not created sinful nor prone to err. They were created in the image of God and that image before the fall was "very good" (see Gen. 1:31) as was the whole of God's creation before the fall in Genesis 3. Jesus was fully human but without sin.

Still, theologians continue to debate whether Jesus could have sinned. The question is put in two Latin phrases: some say Jesus was *posse non peccare*, which is a Latin expression meaning "able to not sin." Others employ another Latin expression, *non posse peccare*, which means "not able to sin." Another way to say this is: some say he was *peccable*, that is, "able to sin, but did not" and others say he was *impeccable*. Among other reasons, those who argue for His *peccability* are trying to preserve His true humanity. They feel that if He could not sin, He just would not be human (nor could He sympathize with us since humans are *non posse non peccare* "not able to not sin"). But those who hold that Jesus was *impeccable* have the better view. Jesus could not have sinned, even though He was fully human, because in the incarnation He was also fully God (see **Excursus: The Hypostatic Union**). His divine nature made it impossible for Him, the person, to sin.

HIS TEMPTATION

> **HEBREWS 4:15 (SEE MATT. 4:1–11)**
>
> For we do not have a high priest who cannot sympathize with our weaknesses, but One who has been tempted in all things as *we are, yet* without sin.

Another question that comes (after the conclusion that Jesus was *non posse peccare* "not able to sin" or impeccable) concerns His temptations. Could His temptations be real if He were not able to sin? The argument would be that if He was prevented by His divine nature from actually sinning, then His temptations would not be as real for Him as ours are for us. However, Jesus was not prevented from sinning by the intervention of His divine nature. In His human nature He knew the full weight of those temptations (probably more so than us who so often have succumbed to the temptation before the full weight of it is felt by us). Jesus experienced the temptation in His human nature and overcame those temptations by the means available to anyone with faith and confidence in the Word of God—He quoted Scripture (to the devil and to Himself). "So it was with Jesus: every temptation he faced, he faced to the end, and triumphed over it. The temptations were real, even though he did not give in to them. In fact, they were most real *because* he did not give in to them."[13]

EXCURSUS: The Hypostatic Union

The Scriptures clearly reveal that Jesus Christ was fully, truly God and fully, truly man. However, it took many years, in fact centuries, for the church to express that truth in the doctrine of the hypostatic union. This doctrine states that the one person (Greek *hypostasis*) of Christ has two natures (Greek *physis*). The definitive statement of this was delivered at the Council of Chalcedon (AD 451). The key portions of that statement (or "Definition") say the following:

> The same Son, our Lord Jesus Christ, [is] at once complete in Godhead and complete in manhood, truly God and truly man, consisting also of a reasonable soul and body; of one substance with the Father as regards his Godhead, and at the same time of one substance with us as regards his manhood . . . we all with one voice confess our Lord Jesus Christ one and the same Son, the same perfect in Godhood, the same perfect in manhood, truly God and truly man, the same consisting of a reasonable soul and a body, of one substance with the Father as touching the Godhead, the same of one substance with us as touching the manhood, like us in all things apart from sin; begotten of the Father before the ages as touching the Godhead, the same in the last days, for us and for our salvation, born from the Virgin Mary, the *Theotokos, as touching the manhood, one and the same Christ, Son, Lord, Only-begotten, to be acknowledged in two natures, without confusion, without change, without division, without separation; the distinction of natures being in no way abolished because of the union.[14] (*This Greek term means "God bearer.")

The question is: "How did that union actually work during the incarnation?" Some theologians have suggested that Christ "gave up" His deity for the duration of the incarnation. This is based on: 1) the seeming absolute difference between the nature of deity and the nature of humanity; 2) certain texts that seem to suggest He did not have divine powers (e.g., Matt. 24:36); and 3) Philippians 2:7 which reads He "emptied (Greek *ekenōsen*) Himself." Others have suggested Christ did not give up deity, but gave up the independent exercise of the powers of His deity. Neither of these suggestions is acceptable. He could not give up His deity, for if He had, the Trinity would be nullified, and He could not have given sacrifice sufficient to save sinners. He could not have given up "the independent exercise of the powers of His deity" for then His miracles would not prove that He was God (see John 20:30–31). Furthermore, to give up "the independent exercise of the powers of His deity" would be a giving up of His sovereignty, which is virtually giving up His deity. Also, the Greek term *ekenōsen* in Philippians 2:7 "is being used in a metaphorical rather than a literal sense,"[15] which means that Paul did not mean Christ literally "gave up" anything. The context indicates that *ekenōsen* should be understood in terms of what He "took on" (namely, "the form of a bondservant") rather than in terms of what He left off.[16]

Actually, a robust understanding of the hypostatic union, with a careful and accurate understanding of the texts that describe Christ's life and ministry in the Gospels, does not present the expositor and theologian with a problem, but with the answer to the question, "How did that union work?" Jesus never ceased to be the one person He was (and is). That one person at times revealed that He was God and at times revealed He was man. He lived in this world as was appropriate for one who was a God-man. In certain circumstances the person of Christ revealed His divine nature because that was most appropriate in that circumstance. In other circumstances the person of Christ revealed His human nature because that was most appropriate in that circumstance. Any attempt on our part to second guess how or why the circumstances called forth a response appropriate to one nature as over the other is pointless because we only have one (human) nature and could not possibly understand the complexity of how the two natures of Christ actually functioned. All we have is the *description* of how the two natures functioned in the one person. We do not have, and should not seek, an *explanation* of "how it worked." In short, in providing the details of Christ's life the text of Scripture is telling us, *"This is* how the hypostatic union works."

THE WORK OF CHRIST

His Offices

PROPHET

> **DEUTERONOMY 18:15, 18 (SEE ACTS 3:22–23)**
> "The LORD your God will raise up for you a prophet like me from among you, from your countrymen, you shall listen to him.". . .
> [18] "'I will raise up a prophet from among their countrymen like you, and I will put My words in his mouth, and he shall speak to them all that I command him.'"

> **MATTHEW 13:57**
> And they took offense at Him. But Jesus said to them, "A prophet is not without honor except in his hometown and in his *own* household."

The prophet's task was to be a spokesman for God, to speak His word, to reveal God and His ways to men. Jesus fulfilled the prophecy of Moses and was the long-expected prophet. But, like so many of the Old Testament prophets, He was rejected by those to whom He was sent.

He Revealed God

> **JOHN 1:18**
> No one has seen God at any time; the only begotten God who is in the bosom of the Father, He has explained *Him*.

He Spoke for God

> **JOHN 7:16**
> So Jesus answered them and said, "My teaching is not Mine, but His who sent Me."

> **JOHN 8:28**
> So Jesus said, "When you lift up the Son of Man, then you will know that I am *He*, and I do nothing on My own initiative, but I speak these things as the Father taught Me."

He Revealed the Future

> **MATTHEW 24:1–4**
>
> Jesus came out from the temple and was going away when His disciples came up to point out the temple buildings to Him. ² And He said to them, "Do you not see all these things? Truly I say to you, not one stone here will be left upon another, which will not be torn down." ³ As He was sitting on the Mount of Olives, the disciples came to Him privately, saying, "Tell us, when will these things happen, and what *will be* the sign of Your coming, and of the end of the age?" ⁴ And Jesus answered and said to them, "See to it that no one misleads you."

The rest of Matthew 24 and 25 is called the Olivet Discourse (because it was delivered on the Mount of Olives; see Matt. 24:3). In this discourse Jesus gives His version of the events of the tribulation (see Matt. 24:5–25), the rise of the Antichrist (see Matt. 24:15), and His own second coming (see Matt. 25:26–31). With this sermon Jesus confirms that He is one with the great apocalyptic prophets like Daniel and Zechariah.

PRIEST

Intercession

> **JOHN 17:9, 20**
>
> "I ask on their behalf; I do not ask on behalf of the world, but of those whom You have given Me; for they are Yours." . . .
> ²⁰ "I do not ask on behalf of these alone, but for those also who believe in Me through their word."

> **ROMANS 8:34**
>
> Who is the one who condemns? Christ Jesus is He who died, yes, rather who was raised, who is at the right hand of God, who also intercedes for us.

> **HEBREWS 7:25**
>
> Therefore He is able also to save forever those who draw near to God through Him, since He always lives to make intercession for them.

Sacrifice

HEBREWS 2:17 (SEE HEB. 9:26–27; 10:12)

Therefore, He had to be made like His brethren in all things, so that He might become a merciful and faithful high priest in things pertaining to God, to make propitiation for the sins of the people.

HEBREWS 4:14

Therefore, since we have a great high priest who has passed through the heavens, Jesus the Son of God, let us hold fast our confession.

HEBREWS 9:11–12

But when Christ appeared *as* a high priest of the good things to come, *He entered* through the greater and more perfect tabernacle, not made with hands, that is to say, not of this creation; ¹² and not through the blood of goats and calves, but through His own blood, He entered the holy place once for all, having obtained eternal redemption.

HEBREWS 10:12

But He, having offered one sacrifice for sins for all time, SAT DOWN AT THE RIGHT HAND OF GOD.

The work of a priest is twofold: to offer sacrifices and to intercede before God on behalf of the people. Christ as high priest has made the offering for His people (see **His Atonement**) and He "makes intercession" (offers up prayers) for His own. His intercessory work began while He was still on earth (see John 17) and continues in heaven.

KING

MATTHEW 2:2

"Where is He who has been born King of the Jews? For we saw His star in the east and have come to worship Him."

MATTHEW 27:11

Now Jesus stood before the governor, and the governor questioned Him, saying, "Are You the King of the Jews?" And Jesus said to him, "*It is as you say.*"

> **REVELATION 19:16**
> And on His robe and on His thigh He has a name written, "KING OF KINGS, AND LORD OF LORDS."

Jesus was the King from the moment of His birth, but He was rejected by His people. In His first coming He did not come to establish the Davidic, messianic kingdom, which is what the Jews were expecting. He will establish that kingdom at His second coming.

His Teaching

> **MATTHEW 4:23**
> Jesus was going throughout all Galilee, teaching in their synagogues and proclaiming the gospel of the kingdom, and healing every kind of disease and every kind of sickness among the people.

> **MATTHEW 7:28–29**
> When Jesus had finished these words, the crowds were amazed at His teaching; [29] for He was teaching them as *one* having authority, and not as their scribes.

Jesus' teaching was a significant part of His earthly ministry and was itself proof of His messiahship (see Luke 4:21) and His messianic authority. "Authority (Greek *exousia*) has to do with power and privilege, and is a key word in Matthew's presentation of Jesus' kingship (9:1–8; 21:23–27; 28:18). In the New Testament it is used for the power that proves and reflects the sovereignty of Jesus."[17]

His Atonement

HIS LIFE OF OBEDIENCE

> **MATTHEW 3:15**
> But Jesus answering said to him, "Permit *it* at this time; for in this way it is fitting for us to fulfill all righteousness." Then he permitted Him.

1 CORINTHIANS 1:30

But by His doing you are in Christ Jesus, who became to us wisdom from God, and righteousness and sanctification, and redemption.

ROMANS 5:19

For as through the one man's disobedience the many were made sinners, even so through the obedience of the One the many will be made righteous.

HEBREWS 5:8–9

Although He was a Son, He learned obedience from the things which He suffered. [9] And having been made perfect, He became to all those who obey Him the source of eternal salvation.

When Jesus came to John the Baptist to be baptized and inaugurate His ministry, John objected. But Jesus persuaded him by assuring him that this was "fitting . . . to fulfill all righteousness." Paul asserts that for those who are in Christ, He is our righteousness, and in Him we are "made (better, declared—see **Justification**) righteous." (Note: This "made righteous" "must be interpreted in the light of Paul's typical forensic [legal] categories. To be 'righteous' does not mean to be morally upright, but to be judged acquitted, cleared of all charges, in the heavenly judgment . . . 'righteous' itself is a legal, not a moral, term in this context."[18])

The righteousness sinners need in order to stand before God can never be achieved by themselves (see Rom. 3:20; Gal. 2:16) but can only be theirs by faith in Christ (see Rom. 3:21–28; Phil. 3:9; see **Justification**). What sinners need is a full and complete (100 percent) righteousness before God. The sinner's deficient moral standing before God is double-sided. On the one hand is the guilt of sin (presence of the negative) and on the other hand is the lack of righteousness (absence of the positive). Christ's atoning sacrifice completely takes away the negative (unrighteousness and guilt). But this is only one side of the problem; the sinner needs to overcome the lack of positive righteousness. The righteousness sinners need can be theirs only by Christ's full atonement for their sins (see **His Death Described**) and by the positive imputation (see **Imputation**) of His righteousness in life. His suffering and death are called His "passive obedience," and His life of perfect righteousness is called His "active obedience." Both are imputed to the sinner by faith in Christ.

"In other words, he took care of the guilt of sin and perfectly fulfilled the demands of righteousness. He perfectly met both the penal and the preceptive requirements of God's law. The passive obedience refers to the former and the active obedience to the latter. Christ's obedience was vicarious in the bearing of the full judgment of God upon sin, and it was vicarious in the full discharge of the demands of righteousness. His obedience becomes the ground of the remission of sin and of actual justification."[19]

HIS DEATH DESCRIBED

His Death a Penal Substitution

ISAIAH 53:3–12

³ He was despised and forsaken of men,
A man of sorrows and acquainted with grief;
And like one from whom men hide their face
He was despised, and we did not esteem Him.
⁴ Surely our griefs He Himself bore,
And our sorrows He carried;
Yet we ourselves esteemed Him stricken,
Smitten of God, and afflicted.
⁵ But He was pierced through for our transgressions,
He was crushed for our iniquities;
The chastening for our well-being *fell* upon Him,
And by His scourging we are healed.
⁶ All of us like sheep have gone astray,
Each of us has turned to his own way;
But the LORD has caused the iniquity of us all
To fall on Him.
⁷ He was oppressed and He was afflicted,
Yet He did not open His mouth;
Like a lamb that is led to slaughter,
And like a sheep that is silent before its shearers,
So He did not open His mouth.
⁸ By oppression and judgment He was taken away;

And as for His generation, who considered
That He was cut off out of the land of the living
For the transgression of my people, to whom the stroke *was due*?
[9] His grave was assigned with wicked men,
Yet He was with a rich man in His death,
Because He had done no violence,
Nor was there any deceit in His mouth.
[10] But the LORD was pleased
To crush Him, putting *Him* to grief;
If He would render Himself *as* a guilt offering,
He will see *His* offspring,
He will prolong *His* days,
And the good pleasure of the LORD will prosper in His hand.
[11] As a result of the anguish of His soul,
He will see *it and* be satisfied;
By His knowledge the Righteous One,
My Servant, will justify the many,
As He will bear their iniquities.
[12] Therefore, I will allot Him a portion with the great,
And He will divide the booty with the strong;
Because He poured out Himself to death,
And was numbered with the transgressors;
Yet He Himself bore the sin of many,
And interceded for the transgressors.

There are a few chapters in Scripture which need little further comment because the truth revealed in the very words is transparent, profound, and compelling on its own. Isaiah 53 is one of those chapters. This chapter (actually from Isa. 52:13 to 53:12), along with Isaiah 42:1–9, Isaiah 49:1–13, and Isaiah 50:4–11, is one of the so-called Servant Songs. The "Servant" is the Messiah and these songs indicate that the Servant is called by the Lord (Yahweh), empowered by the Spirit (see Isa. 49:1–3; Matt. 12:18–20); He will restore the nation of Israel and be the light of salvation to the nations (see Isa. 49:6–7; Luke 2:30–32; John 8:12); He will suffer humiliation (see Isa. 50:6; Matt. 26:67–68; 27:30; John 19:1–3); and He will be "despised and forsaken by men" (see Isa. 53:3; Matt. 12:14; John 11:53; Matt. 26:56). These descriptions of the Suffering Servant can refer to none other than Jesus Christ. The experience of Jesus Christ that lies behind the descriptions of Isaiah 53 can be nothing other than His crucifixion.

The basic theological fact of the crucifixion highlighted by this chapter is "penal substitution" and this chapter is the clearest exposition of "penal substitution" in the Bible. More clearly and compellingly than even the gospel narrative or allusions to the cross in the New Testament epistles, Isaiah 53 lays out the meaning of, or theory of, the atonement accomplished at the cross of Jesus Christ.

The doctrine of "penal substitution" is predicated on the fact of man's sin and guilt (see **Sin**) and God's righteous wrath against sin. There is a penalty for sin—punishment and death. The Suffering Servant endured that punishment and death; He was "stricken, smitten of God, and afflicted," "pierced through," "crushed," chastened, oppressed, and afflicted, "cut off" (i.e., killed), crushed and put to grief, and He suffered anguish of soul. He suffered all of that as a substitute for others. He Himself bore our griefs and carried our sorrows; He did this for our transgressions, for our iniquities, and to realize our well-being. The penalty for "the iniquity of us all" fell upon Him. Even though He was innocent as a lamb, and He "had done no violence, nor was there any deceit in His mouth," yet He took the penalty for "the transgression of my people" who deserved it. He was guiltless, yet He was rendered "a guilt offering" for others. He bore their iniquities; He bore the sin of many. The recurring theme of substitution in these verses is unmistakable.

> **GALATIANS 3:13**
> Christ redeemed us from the curse of the Law, having become a curse for us—for it is written, "CURSED IS EVERYONE WHO HANGS ON A TREE."

> **1 PETER 2:24**
> And He Himself bore our sins in His body on the cross, so that we might die to sin and live to righteousness; for by His wounds you were healed.

> **1 PETER 3:18**
>
> For Christ also died for sins once for all, *the* just for *the* unjust, so that He might bring us to God, having been put to death in the flesh, but made alive in the spirit.

The apostles Paul and Peter echo the themes of penal substitution that are presented so starkly in Isaiah 53. In Galatians 3:13, Paul cites the Law from Deuteronomy 21:23 which states that those who are executed on "a tree" are cursed, and so Christ was cursed by being executed on the cross. However, the point not to be missed is the fact that the reason for becoming so accursed is that He might take the sinners' curse as a substitute. He took the curse "for us" (Greek *hyper hēmōn*; see Rom. 5:6). The Greek preposition *hyper* could be rendered "on behalf of," making the substitutionary sense more clearly.

In 1 Peter 2:24 Peter virtually quotes Isaiah 53:4 and 5 where the notion of penal substitution is unmistakable (see above). Later in his epistle the theme of substitution is noted again when he affirms "Christ also died for sins once for all, the just for the unjust."

> I define penal substitution as follows: The Father, because of his love for human beings, sent his Son (who offered himself willingly and gladly) to satisfy his justice, so that Christ took the place of sinners. The punishment and penalty we deserved was laid on Jesus Christ instead of us, so that in the cross both God's holiness and love are manifested.
>
> The riches of what God has accomplished in Christ for his people are not exhausted by penal substitution. The multifaceted character of the atonement must be recognized to do justice to the canonical witness. God's people are impoverished if Christ's triumph over evil powers at the cross is slighted, or Christ's exemplary love is shoved to the side, or the healing bestowed on believers by Christ's cross and resurrection is downplayed. While not denying the wide-ranging character of Christ's atonement, I am arguing that penal substitution is foundational and the heart of the atonement.[20]

His Death a Sacrifice

JOHN 10:14–15, 17–18

"I am the good shepherd, and I know My own and My own know Me, [15] even as the Father knows Me and I know the Father; and I lay down My life for the sheep. . . . [17] For this reason the Father loves Me, because I lay down My life so that I may take it again. [18] No one has taken it away from Me, but I lay it down on My own initiative. I have authority to lay it down, and I have authority to take it up again. This commandment I received from My Father."

HEBREWS 9:11–12

But when Christ appeared *as* a high priest of the good things to come, *He entered* through the greater and more perfect tabernacle, not made with hands, that is to say, not of this creation; [12] and not through the blood of goats and calves, but through His own blood, He entered the holy place once for all, having obtained eternal redemption.

HEBREWS 10:4–7

For it is impossible for the blood of bulls and goats to take away sins. [5] Therefore, when He comes into the world, He says,
"SACRIFICE AND OFFERING YOU HAVE NOT DESIRED,
BUT A BODY YOU HAVE PREPARED FOR ME;
[6] IN WHOLE BURNT OFFERINGS AND *sacrifices* FOR SIN YOU HAVE TAKEN NO PLEASURE.
[7] "THEN I SAID, 'BEHOLD, I HAVE COME
(IN THE SCROLL OF THE BOOK IT IS WRITTEN OF ME)
TO DO YOUR WILL, O GOD.'"

HEBREWS 10:12

But He, having offered one sacrifice for sins for all time, SAT DOWN AT THE RIGHT HAND OF GOD.

To understand Jesus' work on the cross it is necessary to understand the biblical meaning of sacrifice. There are several key terms that define the notion of sacrifice. The first is "expiation"—which has the idea of the removal of the liability of guilt. The second is "propitiation"—which has the twin ideas of "satisfaction" and "appeasement." The sacrifice of Christ both satisfied the justice of God and appeased—turned away—His wrath. The third term is "satisfaction"—which has in the view the honor of God, which must be acknowledged and respected. The fourth term is "substitution"—which means putting one in the place of another (see 2 Cor. 5:21). The fifth term is "redemption"—which is the payment of a price in exchange for a debt. The sixth term is "reconciliation"—which points to the goal of the sacrifice, which is to bring an end to enmity and estrangement between God and the sinner. All this has been accomplished for the believer by the sacrifice of Christ.

His Death a Ransom

MATTHEW 20:28 (SEE MARK 10:45)
"Just as the Son of Man did not come to be served, but to serve, and to give His life a ransom for many."

His Death a Propitiation

LEVITICUS 16:2, 13–15
The LORD said to Moses:
"Tell your brother Aaron that he shall not enter at any time into the holy place inside the veil, before the mercy seat which is on the ark, or he will die; for I will appear in the cloud over the mercy seat. . . .
13 He shall put the incense on the fire before the LORD, that the cloud of incense may cover the mercy seat that is on *the ark of* the testimony, otherwise he will die. 14 Moreover, he shall take some of the blood of the bull and sprinkle *it* with his finger on the mercy seat on the east *side*; also in front of the mercy seat he shall sprinkle some of the blood with his finger seven times.
15 "Then he shall slaughter the goat of the sin offering which is for the people, and bring its blood inside the veil and do with its blood as he did with the blood of the bull, and sprinkle it on the mercy seat and in front of the mercy seat."

ROMANS 3:25

Whom God displayed publicly as a propitiation in His blood through faith. *This was* to demonstrate His righteousness, because in the forbearance of God He passed over the sins previously committed.

HEBREWS 2:17

Therefore, He had to be made like His brethren in all things, so that He might become a merciful and faithful high priest in things pertaining to God, to make propitiation for the sins of the people.

1 JOHN 2:2

And He Himself is the propitiation for our sins; and not for ours only, but also for *those of* the whole world.

1 JOHN 4:10

In this is love, not that we loved God, but that He loved us and sent His Son *to be* the propitiation for our sins.

The basic idea of propitiation is "satisfaction." Propitiation is often confused with "expiation." While these are related, they are not equivalent concepts. Expiation has to do with the removal or atoning of the guilt of sin, the cancelling of sin. Propitiation has to do with satisfying or appeasing the righteous wrath of God. The Greek term for propitiation is *hilasmos* (Greek verb *hilaskomai*), and a form of this word is used in the Septuagint (the Greek version of the Old Testament; the LXX) for the "mercy-seat," the covering of the Ark of the Covenant (see Ex. 25:22; 26:34; 30:6; Lev. 16:2, 14–15).

Although there is considerable debate about what exactly Paul had in view when he used the term "propitiation" (Greek *hilastērion*) in Romans 3:25, "the conclusion that *hilastērion* includes reference to the turning away of God's wrath is inescapable."[21] The term translated "to make propitiation" in Hebrews 2:17 is the verb *hilaskesthai* (see Luke 18:13). While other versions translate the term here as "to make atonement," the translation "to make propitiation" is preferable because this "understanding of the word agrees with the meaning of the verb elsewhere and with the teaching of Hebrews as a whole."[22] Its significance is the removal of the wrath of God. In 1 John 2:2 and 4:10 the term translated "propitiation" is *hilasmos*. In both instances the translation "propitiation" is preferable and the sense "to turn aside God's wrath" fits the context.

Part of the aversion to the notion of appeasement is that modern people do not like the notion that God is wrathful and must be appeased or satisfied. "But the wrath of God is real and the writers of the New Testament books no less than the Old make this clear. We must reckon with that wrath. Unpalatable though it may be, our sins, my sins, are the object of that wrath. If we are taking our Bible seriously we must realize that every sin is displeasing to God and that unless something is done about the evil we have committed we face ultimately nothing less than the divine anger."[23] The good news is, of course, Christ "Himself is the propitiation for our sins" and so that wrath has been appeased; God is satisfied.

His Bodily Resurrection

MATTHEW 28:9
And behold, Jesus met them and greeted them. And they came up and took hold of His feet and worshiped Him.

LUKE 24:2–8 (SEE JOHN 20:5)
And they found the stone rolled away from the tomb, [3] but when they entered, they did not find the body of the Lord Jesus. [4] While they were perplexed about this, behold, two men suddenly stood near them in dazzling clothing; [5] and as *the women* were terrified and bowed their faces to the ground, *the men* said to them, "Why do you seek the living One among the dead? [6] He is not here, but He has risen. Remember how He spoke to you while He was still in Galilee, [7] saying that the Son of Man must be delivered into the hands of sinful men, and be crucified, and the third day rise again." [8] And they remembered His words.

LUKE 24:12
But Peter got up and ran to the tomb; stooping and looking in, he saw the linen wrappings only; and he went away to his home, marveling at what had happened.

LUKE 24:36–39

While they were telling these things, He Himself stood in their midst and said to them, "Peace be to you." [37] But they were startled and frightened and thought that they were seeing a spirit. [38] And He said to them, "Why are you troubled, and why do doubts arise in your hearts? [39] See My hands and My feet, that it is I Myself; touch Me and see, for a spirit does not have flesh and bones as you see that I have."

JOHN 20:20

And when He had said this, He showed them both His hands and His side. The disciples then rejoiced when they saw the Lord.

Jesus's resurrection was literal and bodily. The gospel records are unequivocal that the tomb was empty. When Jesus appeared to His disciples, He placed special emphasis on His hands, feet, and side in order to show them the bodily wounds He had suffered on the cross to prove to them that it was really Him and that He, not a mere spirit, was present with them.

THE IMPORTANCE OF THE RESURRECTION

ROMANS 1:3–4

Concerning His Son, who was born of a descendant of David according to the flesh, [4] who was declared the Son of God with power by the resurrection from the dead, according to the Spirit of holiness, Jesus Christ our Lord.

1 CORINTHIANS 15:3–8

For I delivered to you as of first importance what I also received, that Christ died for our sins according to the Scriptures, [4] and that He was buried, and that He was raised on the third day according to the Scriptures, [5] and that He appeared to Cephas, then to the twelve. [6] After that He appeared to more than five hundred brethren at one time, most of whom remain until now, but some have fallen asleep; [7] then He appeared to James, then to all the apostles; [8] and last of all, as to one untimely born, He appeared to me also.

1 CORINTHIANS 15:20–22

But now Christ has been raised from the dead, the first fruits of those who are asleep. [21] For since by a man *came* death, by a man also *came* the resurrection of the dead. [22] For as in Adam all die, so also in Christ all will be made alive.

EPHESIANS 1:19–20

And what is the surpassing greatness of His power toward us who believe. *These are* in accordance with the working of the strength of His might [20] which He brought about in Christ, when He raised Him from the dead and seated Him at His right hand in the heavenly *places*.

It is impossible to exaggerate the importance of the resurrection of Jesus Christ. The resurrection is the assurance that He is the Son of God. It is the assurance that He is the Messiah. Jesus had repeatedly told His disciples that He would be taken, beaten, crucified, and rise again (Matt. 16:21; 17:22–23; 20:17–19; Mark 8:31; 9:30–32; 10:32–34; Luke 9:22, 43–45; 18:31–34; 24:7, 26, 46; see John 2:19–22; 3:14; 7:6, 8, 30, 33–36; 8:20, 21; 10:11, 15; 12:7, 23; 15:24–25), and so when He rose from the dead, His words and all His claims were verified. The resurrection is the assurance that He will come again—to judge (see Acts 10:40–42; 17:31; 2 Tim. 4:1) and to reign (see Rev. 1:5–7, 18). The resurrection is the assurance that our sins are forgiven and that all who are in Christ will be raised with Him (see 1 Cor. 15:20–22).

His Ascension

ACTS 1:9–11 (SEE V. 2)

And after He had said these things, He was lifted up while they were looking on, and a cloud received Him out of their sight. [10] And as they were gazing intently into the sky while He was going, behold, two men in white clothing stood beside them. [11] They also said, "Men of Galilee, why do you stand looking into the sky? This Jesus, who has been taken up from you into heaven, will come in just the same way as you have watched Him go into heaven."

ACTS 2:32–33A

This Jesus God raised up again, to which we are all witnesses. [33] Therefore having been exalted to the right hand of God,

HEBREWS 4:14

Therefore, since we have a great high priest who has passed through the heavens, Jesus the Son of God, let us hold fast our confession.

HEBREWS 7:26

For it was fitting for us to have such a high priest, holy, innocent, undefiled, separated from sinners and exalted above the heavens.

HEBREWS 9:24

For Christ did not enter a holy place made with hands, a *mere* copy of the true one, but into heaven itself, now to appear in the presence of God for us.

The ascension of Christ is significant because it describes in actual, temporal terms the first step of the exaltation of Christ that Paul refers to in Philippians 2:8–11. The ascension is the visible transition of Christ to His heavenly position as high priest and intercessor for His people (see Ps. 110:4). "Jesus' ascension is linked to a promise of his return (Acts 1:11)," and so the ascension "underscores the certainty of Jesus' return."[24]

His Return

MATTHEW 24:30

And then the sign of the Son of Man will appear in the sky, and then all the tribes of the earth will mourn, and they will see the SON OF MAN COMING ON THE CLOUDS OF THE SKY with power and great glory.

REVELATION 19:11–12, 16

And I saw heaven opened, and behold, a white horse, and He who sat on it *is* called Faithful and True, and in righteousness He judges and wages war. [12] His eyes *are* a flame of fire, and on His head *are* many diadems; and He has a name written *on Him* which no one knows except Himself. . . . [16] And on His robe and on His thigh He has a name written, "KING OF KINGS, AND LORD OF LORDS."

It is often overlooked that His return and the establishment of His kingdom is properly to be understood as a vital part of the work of Christ and the culmination of His office as king.

---

1. Douglas McCready, *He Came Down from Heaven: The Preexistence of Christ and The Christian Faith* (Downers Grove, IL: InterVarsity Press, 2005), 9.

2. See John MacArthur, *The MacArthur New Testament Commentary: Matthew 16–23* (Chicago: Moody Publishers, 1988), 250.

3. James Montgomery Boice, *The Gospel of Matthew, Vol. I; The King and His Kingdom: Matthew 1–17* (Grand Rapids, MI: Baker Books, 2001), 24–25.

4. These comments are drawn from Kevin D. Zuber, "Zechariah 9:9–10: Rejoice, Your King Is Coming," in Michael Rydelnik and Edwin Blum, eds., *The Moody Handbook of Messianic Prophecy: Studies and Expositions of the Messiah in the Old Testament* (Chicago: Moody Publishers, 2019), 1261–70.

5. Moo, *Romans*, 567.

6. Ibid., 568.

7. Peter T. O'Brien notes that "ἐν μορφῇ θεοῦ ('in the form of God') is a key phrase in the entire hymn. It stands at the head of the paragraph, and one's exegesis of it has a bearing on the interpretation of the whole passage." *The Epistle to the Philippians* (Grand Rapids, MI: William B. Eerdmans Publishing Company, 1991), 206.

8. Gordon D. Fee, *Pauline Christology: An Exegetical-Theological Study* (Peabody, MA: Hendrickson Publishers, 2007), 379.

9. Ibid., 381.

10. See Daniel B. Wallace, *Granville Sharp's Canon and Its Kin: Semantics and Significance* (New York: Peter Lang Publishing, 2009).

11. John MacArthur, *None Other: Discovering the God of the Bible* (Orlando, FL: Reformation Trust Publishing, 2017), 119.

12. John MacArthur, *The MacArthur New Testament Commentary: Matthew 8–15* (Chicago: Moody Publishers, 1987), 75.

13. Grudem, *Systematic Theology*, 539.

14. Davis, *The First Seven Ecumenical Councils (325–787)*, 186.

15. O'Brien, *Philippians*, 218.

16. See Gordon D. Fee, *Paul's Letter to the Philippians* (Grand Rapids, MI: William B. Eerdmans Publishing Company, 1995), 211. Fee confirms Paul is explaining "the *nature* of Christ's emptying himself" was "by taking on the 'form' of a slave."

17. John MacArthur, *The MacArthur New Testament Commentary: Matthew 1–7* (Chicago: Moody Publishers, 1985), 488.

18. Moo, *Romans*, 345.

19. John Murray, *Redemption Accomplished and Applied* (1955; repr., Grand Rapids, MI: William B. Eerdmans Publishing Company, 2015), 21–22.

20. Thomas R. Schreiner, "Penal Substitution View," in *The Nature of the Atonement: Four Views*, eds. James Beilby and Paul R. Eddy (Downers Grove, IL: InterVarsity Press, 2006), 67.

21. Moo, *Romans*, 235.

22. Leon Morris, *The Atonement: Its Meaning and Significance* (Downers Grove, IL: InterVarsity Press, 1983), 171.

23. ibid., 176.

24. M. Ovey, "Ascension [and Heavenly Session of Christ]," in Davie, *New Dictionary of Theology*, 67.

CHAPTER 5

GOD THE HOLY SPIRIT

Pneumatology

Pneumatology is the study of the personhood, deity, and ministries of the Holy Spirit.

HIS PERSONHOOD

The Spirit Has Life

ROMANS 8:2

For the law of the Spirit of life in Christ Jesus has set you free from the law of sin and of death.

The Spirit Has Intellect

ROMANS 8:27

And He who searches the hearts knows what the mind of the Spirit is, because He intercedes for the saints according to *the will of* God.

1 CORINTHIANS 2:10–11

For to us God revealed *them* through the Spirit; for the Spirit searches all things, even the depths of God. [11] For who among men knows the *thoughts* of a man except the spirit of the man which is in him? Even so the *thoughts* of God no one knows except the Spirit of God.

The Spirit Has Emotions

ROMANS 15:30
Now I urge you, brethren, by our Lord Jesus Christ and by the love of the Spirit, to strive together with me in your prayers to God for me.

EPHESIANS 4:30
Do not grieve the Holy Spirit of God, by whom you were sealed for the day of redemption.

The Spirit Has Will

ACTS 13:2
While they were ministering to the Lord and fasting, the Holy Spirit said, "Set apart for Me Barnabas and Saul for the work to which I have called them."

1 CORINTHIANS 12:11
But one and the same Spirit works all these things, distributing to each one individually just as He wills.

The Spirit Has Personal Relationships

... with Apostles

ACTS 15:28
"For it seemed good to the Holy Spirit and to us to lay upon you no greater burden than these essentials.

... with Unbelievers

JOHN 16:8
"And He, when He comes, will convict the world concerning sin and righteousness and judgment."

... *with Believers*

1 CORINTHIANS 6:19–20

Or do you not know that your body is a temple of the Holy Spirit who is in you, whom you have from God, and that you are not your own? [20] For you have been bought with a price: therefore glorify God in your body.

1 CORINTHIANS 12:7

But to each one is given the manifestation of the Spirit for the common good.

EPHESIANS 4:3–4

Being diligent to preserve the unity of the Spirit in the bond of peace. [4] *There is* one body and one Spirit, just as also you were called in one hope of your calling.

HIS DEITY

Assertions of His Deity

MATTHEW 12:31–32

"Therefore I say to you, any sin and blasphemy shall be forgiven people, but blasphemy against the Spirit shall not be forgiven. [32] Whoever speaks a word against the Son of Man, it shall be forgiven him; but whoever speaks against the Holy Spirit, it shall not be forgiven him, either in this age or in the *age* to come."

Blasphemy is a sin that can only be committed against God. "Blasphemy (Greek *bleptein*, 'to injure', and Greek *pheme*, 'reputation') denotes evil, slanderous or defamatory speech about God. It draws on the Hebrew verbs *na-kob* and *qillel*, which mean to pronounce a curse on God."[1]

ACTS 5:3, 4B

But Peter said, "Ananias, why has Satan filled your heart to lie to the Holy Spirit and to keep back *some* of the price of the land?... [4b] You have not lied to men but to God."

At first, when Peter rebuked Ananias for his duplicity, he accused Ananias of lying to the Holy Spirit, and then in reiterating this indictment, he asserted that Ananias had lied to God. Peter was not accusing Ananias of two lies but one. Peter's intention was not to make a theological point but to emphasize the seriousness of Ananias's actions: to lie to the Holy Spirit is to lie to God.

> **1 CORINTHIANS 2:10–11**
>
> For to us God revealed *them* through the Spirit; for the Spirit searches all things, even the depths of God. [11] For who among men knows the *thoughts* of a man except the spirit of the man which is in him? Even so the *thoughts* of God no one knows except the Spirit of God.

> **1 CORINTHIANS 3:16**
>
> Do you not know that you are a temple of God and *that* the Spirit of God dwells in you?

Just as a man knows his own inner thoughts, as only he can, just so the Spirit knows the inner thoughts of God. Paul's comparison would make no sense if the Spirit were not both a person (a "force," or "influence" does not have thoughts) and deity. Paul is explaining why the wise men of the world (see 1 Cor. 1:26–27), and natural men (see 1 Cor. 2:14) with natural capacities (1 Cor. 2:9), cannot understand the wisdom of God (namely the gospel message of the cross; see 1 Cor. 1:18). Only those who have the Spirit of God can know the things of God, because the Spirit is the one who knows the thoughts of God and He reveals them to believers.

Attributes of His Deity

The Scriptures ascribe the major attributes of perfection of God to the Holy Spirit. This argues that the several authors where this occurs considered the Holy Spirit to be God.

OMNISCIENCE

1 CORINTHIANS 2:13

Which things we also speak, not in words taught by human wisdom, but in those taught by the Spirit, combining spiritual *thoughts* with spiritual *words*.

OMNIPRESENCE

PSALM 139:7

Where can I go from Your Spirit?
Or where can I flee from Your presence?

JOHN 14:17

That is the Spirit of truth, whom the world cannot receive, because it does not see Him or know Him, *but* you know Him because He abides with you and will be in you.

OMNIPOTENCE

JOB 33:4

The Spirit of God has made me,
And the breath of the Almighty gives me life.

ZECHARIAH 4:6

Then he said to me, "This is the word of the Lord to Zerubbabel saying, 'Not by might nor by power, but by My Spirit,' says the Lord of hosts."

TRUTH

JOHN 14:17

That is the Spirit of truth, whom the world cannot receive, because it does not see Him or know Him, *but* you know Him because He abides with you and will be in you.

1 JOHN 5:6B

It is the Spirit who testifies, because the Spirit is the truth.

HOLINESS

MATTHEW 12:32

Whoever speaks a word against the Son of Man, it shall be forgiven him; but whoever speaks against the Holy Spirit, it shall not be forgiven him, either in this age or in the *age* to come.

ETERNITY

HEBREWS 9:14A

How much more will the blood of Christ, who through the eternal Spirit offered Himself without blemish to God.

Works of Deity

The Scriptures ascribe a number of the works of God to the Holy Spirit. This argues that the several authors where this occurs considered the Holy Spirit to be God.

CREATION

GENESIS 1:2

The earth was formless and void, and darkness was over the surface of the deep, and the Spirit of God was moving over the surface of the waters.

INSPIRATION

2 PETER 1:21

For no prophecy was ever made by an act of human will, but men moved by the Holy Spirit spoke from God.

REGENERATION

TITUS 3:5

He saved us, not on the basis of deeds which we have done in righteousness, but according to His mercy, by the washing of regeneration and renewing by the Holy Spirit.

THE MINISTRY OF THE SPIRIT TO THE SON

The Ministry of the Spirit at the Birth/Conception of the Son

MATTHEW 1:20B
"For the Child who has been conceived in her is of the Holy Spirit."

LUKE 1:35
The angel answered and said to her, "The Holy Spirit will come upon you, and the power of the Most High will overshadow you; and for that reason the holy Child shall be called the Son of God."

The Ministry of the Spirit during the Ministry of the Son

MARK 1:12
Immediately the Spirit impelled Him *to go* out into the wilderness.

LUKE 4:1–2A
Jesus, full of the Holy Spirit, returned from the Jordan and was led around by the Spirit in the wilderness [2a] for forty days, being tempted by the devil.

The Ministry of the Spirit at the Death of the Son

HEBREWS 9:14A
How much more will the blood of Christ, who through the eternal Spirit offered Himself without blemish to God?

HIS MINISTRIES IN THE OLD TESTAMENT

Creation

JOB 33:4 (SEE 32:8; GEN. 1:2)
The Spirit of God has made me,
And the breath of the Almighty gives me life.

Empowerment for Service

The instances of Spirit empowerment in the Old Testament are not to be contrasted to the indwelling ministry of the Spirit as that is indicated in the New Testament. The empowering work of the Spirit in the Old Testament can be contrasted to the gifting ministry of the Spirit in the New. Empowerment in the Old Testament was often temporary and often selectively given to the leaders of the nation of Israel such as judges, prophets, and kings. At times it was given to craftsmen for specific tasks (see Ex. 31:3). In the New Testament the Spirit distributes giftedness to every member of the body of Christ (see 1 Cor. 12:7), and that giftedness is not temporary but ongoing for the growth and benefit of the body (see Eph. 4:12).

EMPOWERMENT OF CRAFTSMEN

EXODUS 31:2–3

"See, I have called by name Bezalel, the son of Uri, the son of Hur, of the tribe of Judah. ³ I have filled him with the Spirit of God in wisdom, in understanding, in knowledge, and in all *kinds of* craftsmanship.

EMPOWERMENT OF JUDGES

JUDGES 3:9–10A

When the sons of Israel cried to the LORD, the LORD raised up a deliverer for the sons of Israel to deliver them, Othniel the son of Kenaz, Caleb's younger brother. ¹⁰ The Spirit of the LORD came upon him, and he judged Israel.

JUDGES 6:34

So the Spirit of the LORD came upon Gideon; and he blew a trumpet, and the Abiezrites were called together to follow him.

JUDGES 14:19A

Then the Spirit of the LORD came upon him mightily, and he went down to Ashkelon and killed thirty of them and took their spoil.

EMPOWERMENT OF KINGS

1 SAMUEL 10:10

When they came to the hill there, behold, a group of prophets met him; and the Spirit of God came upon him mightily, so that he prophesied among them.

1 SAMUEL 11:6

Then the Spirit of God came upon Saul mightily when he heard these words, and he became very angry.

1 SAMUEL 16:13

Then Samuel took the horn of oil and anointed him in the midst of his brothers; and the Spirit of the LORD came mightily upon David from that day forward. And Samuel arose and went to Ramah.

1 SAMUEL 19:23

He proceeded there to Naioth in Ramah; and the Spirit of God came upon him also, so that he went along prophesying continually until he came to Naioth in Ramah.

EMPOWERMENT OF PROPHETS

EZEKIEL 2:2 (SEE 8:3; 11:1, 24)

As He spoke to me the Spirit entered me and set me on my feet; and I heard *Him* speaking to me.

MICAH 3:8

On the other hand I am filled with power—
With the Spirit of the LORD—
And with justice and courage
To make known to Jacob his rebellious act,
Even to Israel his sin.

HIS MINISTRIES IN RELATION TO SALVATION
AND THE CHRISTIAN LIFE

Regeneration

JOHN 3:5–6

Jesus answered, "Truly, truly, I say to you, unless one is born of water and the Spirit he cannot enter into the kingdom of God. [6] That which is born of the flesh is flesh, and that which is born of the Spirit is spirit."

TITUS 3:5

He saved us, not on the basis of deeds which we have done in righteousness, but according to His mercy, by the washing of regeneration and renewing by the Holy Spirit.

Indwelling

ROMANS 8:11

But if the Spirit of Him who raised Jesus from the dead dwells in you, He who raised Christ Jesus from the dead will also give life to your mortal bodies through His Spirit who dwells in you.

1 CORINTHIANS 3:16

Do you not know that you are a temple of God and *that* the Spirit of God dwells in you?

2 TIMOTHY 1:14

Guard, through the Holy Spirit who dwells in us, the treasure which has been entrusted to *you*.

Sealing

EPHESIANS 4:30

Do not grieve the Holy Spirit of God, by whom you were sealed for the day of redemption.

Testifying

ROMANS 8:16

The Spirit Himself testifies with our spirit that we are children of God.

Filling

EPHESIANS 5:18

And do not get drunk with wine, for that is dissipation, but be filled with the Spirit.

This is the only text where Paul speaks of the filling of the Spirit. The idea of filling here is a yielding of control to the Spirit for ministry or special service. The contrast drawn is the yielding of personal control that happens when one becomes drunk, in distinction to the yielding of personal control that happens when one is filled (Greek *pleroō*) by the Spirit. Thus, "Spirit filling is both God's sovereign empowering of us by the Spirit for special activity and the Spirit's filling us with His own character."[2] In this sense filling is a command that a believer obeys by yielding to the Spirit's influence, mainly by knowing and obeying the Word of God.

In other places, such as Luke 1:15, 41, 67 (in each the Greek term is *pimplēmi*) and Acts (Acts 2:4; 4:8, 31; 9:17; 13:9 Greek *pimplēmi*; 13:52 Greek *pleroō*), the filling seems to be associated with an ability to speak, either in praise, or a prophetic utterance, or, in the case of the apostles on the day of Pentecost, in tongues (see Acts 2:4). In these cases the filling is a sovereign act of God and the individuals who are filled simply receive the blessing of being filled.[3]

Teaching

JOHN 14:26

"But the Helper, the Holy Spirit, whom the Father will send in My name, He will teach you all things, and bring to your remembrance all that I said to you."

JOHN 15:26

When the Helper comes, whom I will send to you from the Father, *that is* the Spirit of truth who proceeds from the Father, He will testify about Me.

Guiding/Leading

JOHN 16:13–14

But when He, the Spirit of truth, comes, He will guide you into all the truth; for He will not speak on His own initiative, but whatever He hears, He will speak; and He will disclose to you what is to come. [14] He will glorify Me, for He will take of Mine and will disclose *it* to you.

ROMANS 8:14

For all who are being led by the Spirit of God, these are sons of God.

Convicting

JOHN 16:8

"And He, when He comes, will convict the world concerning sin and righteousness and judgment."

Interceding

ROMANS 8:26

In the same way the Spirit also helps our weakness; for we do not know how to pray as we should, but the Spirit Himself intercedes for *us* with groanings too deep for words.

MINISTRIES IN RELATION TO THE CHURCH

Baptizing

1 CORINTHIANS 12:13

For by one Spirit we were all baptized into one body, whether Jews or Greeks, whether slaves or free, and we were all made to drink of one Spirit.

In common use the phrase "baptism of the Spirit" is often (incorrectly) used to refer to the gift of tongues, at other times it is used to refer to other (supposed) ecstatic manifestations of the Spirit, and yet at other times it is used loosely for the Spirit's enabling or empowering of an individual in a special way (see **Empowerment for Service**). It is remarkable that a phrase found just seven times in the Bible is used in such diverse ways in common and even theological use.

The phrase "baptism of the Spirit" is never found in the Old Testament. The first reference to the baptism of the Spirit comes from John the Baptist. In a prophecy found in all four gospels (see Matt. 3:11; Mark 1:8; Luke 3:16; John 1:33), John the Baptist compares his ministry to that of the Messiah to come. In Matthew's version John announces: "As for me, I baptize you with water for repentance, but He who is coming after me is mightier than I, and I am not fit to remove His sandals; He will baptize you with (Greek *en*; "in, with, by") the Holy Spirit and fire." John does not specify what the "baptism of the Holy Spirit" will entail but he does indicate that it is yet future.

Furthermore, in the comparison John is making, it seems that what John intends by this statement is this: just as he did something in/with water, so the Messiah will do something in/with the Spirit. The baptism of John was a baptism of repentance, which "required a radical break with the past by repenting and becoming part of the messianic community."[4] Those baptized by John repented from sin and all the identifications associated with it and in turn identified themselves with the "messianic community." John's baptism was essentially "ecclesiastical" in nature. It was not primarily a personal experience performed in splendid isolation for the individual but a corporate rite that involved becoming part of the community awaiting the promised Messiah.[5] This appears to be part of the significance of Jesus' own submission to John's baptism: He too makes a break, not from sin but from His obscurity and is now identified with the emergent messianic community.[6] Thus, the baptism by the Spirit, whatever else it might entail, is like John's baptism in that it accomplishes an "identity with a community."

The next use of the phrase is by Jesus Himself in Acts 1:5. In His instructions to the apostles, Jesus reminded them of the "Father's promise" (see Acts

1:4), which in some fashion will be realized soon. Specifically, He recalled John's words: "for John baptized with water, but you will be baptized with the Holy Spirit not many days from now" (Acts 1:5). At this point the baptism of the Spirit is still future, and it is apparent that Jesus is referring to the events of Acts 2 and the inauguration of the church (see **Inaugurated at Pentecost**). This is confirmed by the next use of the phrase (the sixth of the seven times) in Acts 11. In his report to the church in Jerusalem of the events at the house of Cornelius, the Gentile centurion (see Acts 10:1ff), Peter noted that "the Holy Spirit fell upon" the Gentiles, "just as *He did* upon us at the beginning." In this he was making an obvious reference to Acts 2 and the Day of Pentecost (Acts 11:15). Here Peter once more recalls what has been promised: "And I remembered the word of the Lord, how He used to say, 'John baptized with water, but you will be baptized with the Holy Spirit'" (Acts 11:16). Here the baptism is no longer something that will happen in the future but is both a past and a recurring event. Even Peter does not explicitly explain what this baptism entailed, but it is clearly associated with the inauguration of the new community, the church, begun in Acts 2.

The final occurrence of this phrase is found in 1 Corinthians 12:13. This is the only occasion where the phrase is actually defined. This verse then is to be accepted as "the major passage, which may be taken as the basis of interpretation of the other passages."[7] This use is a "Pauline retrospective interpretation of what it meant to be baptized with the Holy Spirit." Whatever else it may involve, the main idea of the baptism of the Spirit indicates "the oneness of the body of Christ."[8] "The purpose of our common experience of the Spirit is that we be formed into one body. . . .This phrase ('into one body') expresses the reason for this sentence in the first place."[9] It seems clear that Paul's intent here is *to define* what baptism of the Spirit is, namely the formation of the body of Christ. The baptism of the Spirit work of Christ, which forms the body of Christ, is in effect the new community of those who are one in Christ.

Gifting

1 CORINTHIANS 12:7

But to each one is given the manifestation of the Spirit for the common good.

The word for spiritual gifts (Greek *charisma*), obviously related to the word for grace (Greek *charis*), means something that is given due to the grace of God. A spiritual gift is a God-given ability for service to/in the church. Every member of the body—that is, every believer—has one or a combination of gifts (see 1 Peter 4:10). The list of spiritual gifts in 1 Corinthians 12 and Romans 12 is not meant to be exhaustive but is intended to be representative of the kinds of Spirit-empowered service the members of the body of Christ, the church, are to perform for one another. These gifts are to be exercised in love (see 1 Cor. 13:8, 13).

Some gifts, or areas of giftedness, were given for the unique circumstances of the early church (see Heb. 2:3–4). For instance, the gifts of tongues and the interpretation of tongues which was a "divine enablement to speak in [and understand] a real, human language that had not been previously learned"[10] were for the purpose of preaching the gospel to unbelievers in their own language (see Acts 2:5–11) and as a sign to unbelieving Israel (see 1 Cor. 14:20–22). The miraculous gifts were given to confirm the work and ministry of the apostles (see 2 Cor. 12:12). Once the circumstances of the apostolic era were past, and with the completion of the New Testament, these gifts ceased.

1. L. Bretherton, "Blasphemy," in Davie, *New Dictionary of Theology*, 125.
2. Ryrie, *Basic Theology*, 435.
3. See Andreas J. Köstenberger, "What Does it Mean to Be Filled with the Spirit?," *Journal of the Evangelical Theological Society* (June 1997): 229–40.
4. Robert H. Stein, *Jesus the Messiah: A Survey of the Life of Christ* (Downers Grove, IL: InterVarsity Press, 1996), 97.
5. Ibid., 93.
6. Ibid., 97.

7. John F. Walvoord, *The Holy Spirit* (Grand Rapids, MI: Zondervan, 1966), 139.

8. Walter C. Kaiser, "The Baptism in the Holy Spirit as the Promise of the Father: A Reformed Perspective," in *Perspectives on Spirit Baptism: Five Views*, ed. Chad Owen Brand (Nashville, TN: B&H Books, 2004), 20.

9. Gordon D. Fee, *The First Epistle to the Corinthians* (Grand Rapids, MI: William B. Eerdmans Publishing Company, 1987), 606.

10. MacArthur and Mayhue, *Biblical Doctrine*, 385.

CHAPTER 6

MAN AND SIN

Biblical Anthropology and Hamartiology

Biblical anthropology is the study of man's origins and nature. Hamartiology is the study of man's fall and sin.

CREATION OF MAN

GENESIS 1:26–27

Then God said, "Let Us make man in Our image, according to Our likeness; and let them rule over the fish of the sea and over the birds of the sky and over the cattle and over all the earth, and over every creeping thing that creeps on the earth." [27] God created man in His own image, in the image of God He created him; male and female He created them.

ACTS 17:26

And He made from one *man* every nation of mankind to live on all the face of the earth, having determined *their* appointed times and the boundaries of their habitation.

The Bible teaches that man, the human race, along with the entire creation, is the product of the creative hand of God. Man is not the product of an evolutionary process that took millions of years and millions of deaths of man and animals, the mutation and adaptation of species in a blind, mindless, meaningless process that just happened to produce human beings. Man was created by a personal, self-conscious, all powerful God (see **Attributes of God**), in the image of God, in order to have relationship with God, for the glory of God.

EXCURSUS: Sudden Creation in Six Literal Days

The creation depicted in Genesis 1 and 2 and elsewhere in the Bible (e.g., Ps. 104) was *ex nihilo* (Latin for "out of nothing"), that is, using no pre-existing materials. That creation was "supernatural" in the sense that it did not happen according to natural laws and processes but was the direct, divine action of God. As such, creation is quite beyond the capacity of finite humans to fully grasp or explain, quite beyond the capacity of finite humans to confirm or refute by natural means (e.g., science), but not beyond the capacity of finite humans to know and understand what God has revealed about that creation. "Supernatural" means just that, and the natural mind, unaided by the revelation of the only eyewitness to creation—namely, God Himself—cannot understand how it happened (see 1 Cor. 2:14).

This creation was "sudden," that is, it was instantaneous with no gradual development but with the superficial appearance of age. That is, Adam, for instance, did not go through the natural processes of gestation, birth, infancy, and growth to adulthood. He appeared instantaneously as a fully grown man, as did Eve when she was made from Adam's rib.

That the creation of the universe, and everything on earth, was accomplished in six literal days is the plain teaching of Genesis chapter 1. First, the word for "day" (Gen. 1:5, 8, 13, 19, 23, 31) (Hebrew *yom*), when used with a numerical adjective, always means a literal day (see Num. 7:12–78). Second, the phrase "evening and morning" is best understood in the way that phrase is commonly used, that is, a summary of a single twenty-four-hour day, and is not used of "long periods of uncharted time." Third, a creation of one week of literal days fits with the cycle of work and rest set forth by Moses for the nation of Israel in Exodus 20:11 and 31:16–17. Fourth, the note of the times ("seasons and days and years") in Genesis 1:14 is tied to the heavenly bodies, the greater lights (i.e., the sun and moon, Gen. 1:16–18) that were to govern the day and the night. This defines "day" and "night" as the cycle of time between when the sun shines and when the moon is visible (which we know is determined by the earth turning one full revolution on its axis). We know this as one twenty-four-hour period of time—a day. The period of time indicated by the term *years* is likewise governed by these heavenly bodies and refers to the annual cycle of the earth moving around the sun, or approximately the time it takes for the moon to go through its phases twelve times. In none of these time references are there indications of "symbolic" numbers or mythic references. In short, in Genesis 1:14 "day" means daytime, "night" means nighttime, together they make one twenty-four-hour day, and "year" means a year.[1] "To stretch the days into long ages or to insert long ages between the days is biblically illegitimate. The traditional Judeo-Christian understanding is thus confirmed by biblical exegesis: *the universe was created by God within one literal week of days.*"[2]

Adam and Eve as Historical Persons

GENESIS 2:15

Then the LORD God took the man and put him into the garden of Eden to cultivate it and keep it.

GENESIS 3:20

Now the man called his wife's name Eve, because she was the mother of all *the* living.

GENESIS 5:1, 5

This is the book of the generations of Adam. In the day when God created man, He made him in the likeness of God. . . . [5] So all the days that Adam lived were nine hundred and thirty years, and he died.

ROMANS 5:14

Nevertheless death reigned from Adam until Moses, even over those who had not sinned in the likeness of the offense of Adam, who is a type of Him who was to come.

1 CORINTHIANS 15:21–23

For since by a man *came* death, by a man also *came* the resurrection of the dead. [22] For as in Adam all die, so also in Christ all will be made alive. [23] But each in his own order: Christ the first fruits, after that those who are Christ's at His coming.

The biblical accounts in Genesis must be taken literally and should be understood as depicting actual historical events and persons. In addition to arguments for historicity of the early chapters of Genesis from biblical creationism[3] and studies that compare the biblical accounts with ancient Near Eastern literature,[4] there are several arguments from the biblical and theological perspective.[5] The narratives that tell the story of Adam and Eve (i.e., especially Gen. 1–3) seem to be intending to convey literal history, even if there is a theological perspective as well. Furthermore, the narratives of the early chapters of Genesis appear very much like the later chapters that tell the stories of Abraham and Joseph, which themselves appear to intend to be describing literal historical events about literal historical persons. Most tellingly, the apostle Paul refers to Adam in contexts where he also refers to Christ, and his very argument turns on the literal history of each one. "If a historical Adam did not represent all mankind in sinfulness, a historical Christ could not represent all mankind in righteousness. If all men did not fall with the first Adam, all men could not be saved by Christ, the second and last Adam (see 1 Cor. 15:20–22, 45)."[6]

THE INSTITUTION OF MARRIAGE

GENESIS 2:18, 22–24

Then the LORD God said, "It is not good for the man to be alone; I will make him a helper suitable for him.". . .
[22] The LORD God fashioned into a woman the rib which He had taken from the man, and brought her to the man. [23] The man said,
"This is now bone of my bones,
And flesh of my flesh;
She shall be called Woman,
Because she was taken out of Man."
[24] For this reason a man shall leave his father and his mother, and be joined to his wife; and they shall become one flesh.

The institution of marriage is not the result of the process of human evolution, nor is it an invention of human society. It was created and established by God. Marriage was given as the basis of the family, and the family was given as the basis of human society.

In the biblical sense marriage is defined as one man and one woman in an exclusive, lifelong commitment of fidelity, devotion, care, and love.

THE IMAGE OF GOD IN MAN

GENESIS 1:26–27

Then God said, "Let Us make man in Our image, according to Our likeness; and let them rule over the fish of the sea and over the birds of the sky and over the cattle and over all the earth, and over every creeping thing that creeps on the earth." [27] God created man in His own image, in the image of God He created him; male and female He created them.

GENESIS 5:2

He created them male and female, and He blessed them and named them Man in the day when they were created.

Scripture teaches that man is a unique creation of God. Man is not the measure of all things, but a creature, dependent upon and beholden to the Creator; nor is he an accident but a purposeful and valuable being made "in the image and likeness of God." "The creation of man is unique among all God's creative works. He was created for God Himself (Isa. 43:7), for fellowship in the truth and glory of God (John 17:22–24)."[7] This would seem to indicate that man is given the endowments necessary for a relationship with God. Unlike the other creatures in his world, man has the ability for conscious self-reflection (intellect); man has the ability of mutual interpersonal affection (emotions); and man has the capacity for personal choice (will).

The key terms in Genesis 1:26–27 are "image" (Hebrew *ṣelem*) and "likeness" (Hebrew *demût*). In Latin the equivalent terms are *imago* and *similitude* and the equivalent New Testament Greek words are *eikon* and *homoiousia*. The two terms are mostly synonymous with only slight nuances of difference in meaning. The term *image* (Hebrew *ṣelem*) is used of "carved images" that are representative in a more concrete way, like a statue; the term *likeness* (Hebrew *demût*) conveys something more abstract, like a literary description of a character in a novel. If the word *şelem* was used alone, we might tend to think of the image as a concrete or physical representation. If the word *demût* was used alone, we might think of the image as abstract, unreal, or "mere" representation. But in using them together the Scriptures teach that the image is not an incidental or extrinsic likeness or a mere abstraction but that it is "real"—substantial yet not physical.

This text also indicates that gender "male-ness" and "female-ness" is a part of the image of God in mankind. Gender is not a social construct but intrinsic to each person being made in the image of God. "Gender is not vague, flexible, or personally determined by preference, nor does it occur by accident or through an evolutionary process." "Gender is deeply embedded in human identity and is established at conception."[8] All attempts to twist or alter the basic God-given design of two genders—male and female—is not only an attack on objective (biological) reality, but it is an attack on God, on His creative sovereignty.

> **GENESIS 5:1B, 3**
>
> In the day when God created man, He made him in the likeness of God. . . .
> [3] When Adam had lived one hundred and thirty years, he became the father of *a son* in his own likeness, according to his image, and named him Seth.

The genealogy of the godly line through Adam's third son, Seth, begins by hearkening back to Genesis 1:26–27. In Genesis 5:1 and 3 the term "likeness" (Hebrew *demût*) is used twice: once of Adam's likeness to God, and once of Seth's likeness to Adam. While it may seem obvious that a son (Seth) should resemble his father (Adam), it is clear "that the purpose of reference to likeness and image in v. 3, in connection with the begetting of Seth, is to show that Adam's progeny was to be defined in the same terms as those of Adam himself; in other words, that the identity characterized by the image of God was maintained in Adam's offspring."[9] The key point to observe here is that this is after the fall of man (see Gen. 3) and that even after the fall the image of God in man is retained and passed on to Adam's descendants.

An interesting feature of this note concerning the image and likeness of God is the use of the terms/prepositions used. In Genesis 1:26–27 the prepositions used were "in" (with the image [*ṣelem*] of God, three times) and "according to" (for the likeness [*demût*]). In Genesis 5:1 and 3 the same prepositions are used but here "in" (Hebrew *ki*) is used for the likeness (two times) and "according to" (Hebrew *bin*) is used for the image. Probably this interchange of prepositions with the two terms *ṣelem* and *demût* is meant to reiterate the point that the image is real and something more than merely physical.

> **GENESIS 9:6 (SEE 1 COR. 11:7; JAMES 3:9)**
> "Whoever sheds man's blood,
> By man his blood shall be shed,
> For in the image of God
> He made man."

This text reiterates the fact that the image of God in man is in every descendant of Adam, in every human being. It also indicates that an attack on any one image bearer is ultimately an attack on God Himself.

> **EPHESIANS 4:24**
> And put on the new self, which in *the likeness of* God has been created in righteousness and holiness of the truth.

> **COLOSSIANS 3:10**
> And have put on the new self who is being renewed to a true knowledge according to the image of the One who created him.

Most commentators agree that in these two texts Paul is referencing Genesis 1:26–27 and that he has in mind the fact that man was made in the image and likeness of God. Literally the text of Ephesians 4:24 reads "and put on the new man, the according-to-God-[one] created in righteous and holiness of the truth." The Greek uses the preposition *kata* which means (in this grammatical arrangement) "according to" and recalls the careful uses of the Hebrew prepositions in Genesis 5:1–3 (noted above). In Colossians 3:10 Paul uses "image" (Greek *eikon*) again with the Greek preposition *kata* ("according to"). In both of these texts Paul is addressing believers and encouraging them in practical sanctification ("lay aside the old self," Eph. 4:22; see Col. 3:10; "put on the new self"). This involves being "renewed in the spirit of your mind" (Eph. 4:23) and "being renewed to a true knowledge" (Col. 3:10). This "renewal" is, in some sense, back to the "likeness of God," back to the "image of the One who created him." A "renewal" indicates something was lost and needed to be restored or retrieved, and in these verses that something seems to be cognitive, personal, and relating to the mind.

In summary, restricting the focus to what these rich texts indicate about the image of God in man, these two texts indicate that something of the image was lost and what was lost is being restored in believers who are experiencing sanctification that leads to greater likeness to Christ. That sanctification is principally a "renewal of the mind." "In Rom. 12:2 Paul says the Christians are to be 'transformed by the renewing of your minds,' and in Titus 3:5 this is all chalked up to the work of the Holy Spirit. But the Spirit's work of renewal is christologically defined: each person, because of the regenerating work of the Spirit, is being renewed into the image of God, which is Christ himself, which means the renewal is into Christoformity. The template for our renewal is the image of God born by Christ (Col. 1:5)."[10]

THE CONSTITUTION AND NATURE OF MAN

There Is a Material Part to Man's Nature

GENESIS 2:7
Then the LORD God formed man of dust from the ground, and breathed into his nostrils the breath of life; and man became a living being.

MATTHEW 10:28
"Do not fear those who kill the body but are unable to kill the soul; but rather fear Him who is able to destroy both soul and body in hell."

There Is an Immaterial Part to Man's Nature

ISAIAH 26:9

At night my soul longs for You,
Indeed, my spirit within me seeks You diligently;
For when the earth experiences Your judgments
The inhabitants of the world learn righteousness.

LUKE 1:46–47

And Mary said:
"My soul exalts the Lord,
And my spirit has rejoiced in God my Savior."

1 THESSALONIANS 5:23

Now may the God of peace Himself sanctify you entirely; and may your spirit and soul and body be preserved complete, without blame at the coming of our Lord Jesus Christ.

HEBREWS 4:12

For the word of God is living and active and sharper than any two-edged sword, and piercing as far as the division of soul and spirit, of both joints and marrow, and able to judge the thoughts and intentions of the heart.

Some theologians see a distinction between the spirit (Hebrew, *rûach*; Greek, *pneuma*) and the soul (Hebrew, *nepheš* [lit. "life"]; Greek, *psyche*) and suggest that this indicates the two facets of man's immaterial being. Man's material being, his body [Greek, *sōma*], would constitute a third facet making man a tri-partite being (trichotomy). However, the term *soul* is used often to refer to the whole person (see Acts 2:41) as well as to man's immaterial being (see Matt. 10:28), while the term *spirit* is used only for the immaterial being of man. It is therefore doubtful to suggest that the immaterial being man is made of two parts. However, man's constitution is not simply two parts (dichotomy) because the Scriptures identify man's immaterial being with a variety of terms beside "soul" and "spirit" such as "heart" (see Matt. 15:19–20; Rom. 10:9–10) and "mind" (see Rom. 12:2; Eph. 4:23). It seems better to affirm that man's being is multifaceted in both his material and immaterial being.

THE FALL OF MAN

Genesis 3 is unquestionably one of the most important chapters in God's revealed Word. Without this historical record the plight of man, and indeed all the trouble in the world caused by sin, would be an unfathomable mystery. And without this chapter the redemption accomplished by Christ would be an indecipherable riddle. Nothing in the text suggests this is a myth or that Adam and Eve are fictitious characters. The events recorded here must be understood as genuinely historical and Adam and Eve as real historical persons.

The Event

GENESIS 3:1–7

Now the serpent was more crafty than any beast of the field which the LORD God had made. And he said to the woman, "Indeed, has God said, 'You shall not eat from any tree of the garden'?" [2] The woman said to the serpent, "From the fruit of the trees of the garden we may eat; [3] but from the fruit of the tree which is in the middle of the garden, God has said, 'You shall not eat from it or touch it, or you will die.'" [4] The serpent said to the woman, "You surely will not die! [5] For God knows that in the day you eat from it your eyes will be opened, and you will be like God, knowing good and evil." [6] When the woman saw that the tree was good for food, and that it was a delight to the eyes, and that the tree was desirable to make *one* wise, she took from its fruit and ate; and she gave also to her husband with her, and he ate. [7] Then the eyes of both of them were opened, and they knew that they were naked; and they sewed fig leaves together and made themselves loin coverings.

The serpent was a real animal which was in some sense used as the instrument of Satan to tempt the original couple (see **Satan**). His tactics were simple but effective. First, he spoke to Eve alone without the protecting influence of her husband, thus subverting God's order in marriage. Second, he questioned God's word and then he boldly contradicted God's word. His explanation was intended to suggest that God's restriction (of the tree of the knowledge of good and evil) was not fair, and he attributed a hostile and petty motive for this restriction. It is at this point, when Eve begins to contemplate the serpent's words, that the precipice of the fall is reached. When Eve began to weigh the merits of the fruit—it looked tasty, it looked good, the prospect of "knowing good and evil" was desirable—she assumed that she, a creature of God, had the criteria to judge the word of the Creator, between God's word and Satan's word. By reasoning in this way she was already implicitly guilty of denying the authority of the word of God. (Any reasoning that places the Word of God under the criteria of man's own thinking will lead to an implicit denial, and ultimately rejection, of the authority of the Word of God [see **Theology and the Biblical Worldview**]).

Eve gave the fruit to her husband and he ate. Whereas she had been deceived, Adam's sin was blatant disobedience and rebellion. His sin had serious consequences for his posterity.

The Consequences of the Fall

SEPARATION FROM GOD

> **GENESIS 3:8–10**
>
> They heard the sound of the LORD God walking in the garden in the cool of the day, and the man and his wife hid themselves from the presence of the LORD God among the trees of the garden. [9] Then the LORD God called to the man, and said to him, "Where are you?" [10] He said, "I heard the sound of You in the garden, and I was afraid because I was naked; so I hid myself."

Whereas Adam and Eve had enjoyed fellowship with God in the garden, they now hid themselves in fear and shame.

DEATH

Fact of Death (see Personal Eschatology, Death; Bodily)

> **GENESIS 2:16–17**
>
> The LORD God commanded the man, saying, "From any tree of the garden you may eat freely; [17] but from the tree of the knowledge of

good and evil you shall not eat, for in the day that you eat from it you
will surely die."

GENESIS 3:19
By the sweat of your face
You will eat bread,
Till you return to the ground,
Because from it you were taken;
For you are dust,
And to dust you shall return.

ROMANS 5:12, 14
Therefore, just as through one man sin entered into the world, and
death through sin, and so death spread to all men, because all
sinned. . . .
[14] Nevertheless death reigned from Adam until Moses, even over those
who had not sinned in the likeness of the offense of Adam, who is a
type of Him who was to come.

The stark fact that (with a couple of arguable exceptions) every single
human being who has ever lived has died demands an explanation. That
reason is sin.

SIN

Original Sin

ROMANS 5:12
Therefore, just as through one man sin entered into the world, and
death through sin, and so death spread to all men, because all sinned.

ROMANS 5:18–19
So then as through one transgression there resulted condemnation to
all men, even so through one act of righteousness there resulted justification of life to all men. [19] For as through the one man's disobedience
the many were made sinners, even so through the obedience of the
One the many will be made righteous.

PSALM 51:5

Behold, I was brought forth in iniquity,

And in sin my mother conceived me.

PSALM 58:3

The wicked are estranged from the womb;

These who speak lies go astray from birth.

1 CORINTHIANS 15:22A

For as in Adam all die.

EPHESIANS 2:3

Among them we too all formerly lived in the lusts of our flesh, in-

dulging the desires of the flesh and of the mind, and were by nature

children of wrath, even as the rest.

The great Dutch theologian Herman Bavinck has observed, "The doctrine of original sin is one of the weightiest but also one of the most difficult subjects in the field of dogmatics."[11] It is a difficult doctrine because
it takes very careful study to follow the subtle teaching of the Bible (especially that of the apostle Paul in Romans 5) and it is difficult to understand. However, the doctrine is especially difficult for individualistically
minded human beings to accept after it is understood! Romans 5:12 is
the key text; this verse lists four facts about sin and death: the source of
sin, "through one man sin entered into the world"; the connection between sin and death, "and death through sin"; the result of the connection, "and so death spread to all men"; and the explanation of that result,
"because all sinned."

The source of sin, "through one man sin entered into the world," refers to the sin of Adam in the garden (see **The Fall of Man, The Event**
above). The connection between sin and death, "and death through
sin" was made clear to the original couple in (see **Death, Fact of Death**
above; see Gen. 2:16–17; 3:19). The result of the connection, "and so
death spread to all men," is the reality for which the account in Genesis
3 is the explanation. "As [Romans] 5:12b depicts the *entrance* of death as

the consequence of sin, [Romans 5:]12c makes it explicit that this death has *spread* to every single person."[12] Why death is universal is explained in the last fact, namely, "because all sinned."

In what sense have "all sinned"? Some have suggested that Paul means "all have committed sins" so that "the death of each person ([Rom. 5:]12c) is directly caused by that person's own, individual sinning."[13] However, this is simply not what the phrase means and does not accord with the parallel expression in verse 18. "In other words, how can we logically relate the assertions 'each person dies because *each person* sins [in the course of history]' and '*one man's* trespass led to condemnation for all people' (v. 18a)?"[14] Furthermore, this phrase has to have something to do with Adam. The "death [that] spread to all men" is not the result of a string of individual sins but expressly "by the transgression of the one, death reigned through the one" (see Rom. 5:17a). Five times (Rom. 5:15, 16, 17, 18, 19) Paul makes the point that for "one man's sin" death reigned, and that "one man" can be none other than Adam.

Some have taken the view that in some sense all men were "really there in Adam" and is called by many "the realistic view" or "seminal view." This view says all men were in Adam in the sense that, say, Levi was in Abraham, according to the argument of the author of Hebrews in Hebrews 7:9–10. Thus, in some sense all men sinned with Adam in his first sin. However, this view seems somewhat foreign to the point of the passage which, again, emphasizes the source of sin is through "one man," not the many in the one man. And this view breaks the parallel between Adam and Christ.

The preferable view, called the "representative view" by many, understands Paul to be teaching the immediate imputation of Adam's sin to his posterity. That is, he stood as a representative of all those born of and after him and when he fell, his act of sin was "imputed" or "reckoned" to all. Douglas Moo explains, "If, then, we are to read [Rom. 5:]12d in light of vv. 5:18–19—and since the comparative clauses in these verses repeat the substance of v. 12, this seems to be a legitimate procedure—'all sinned' must be given some kind of 'corporate' meaning: 'sinning' not as voluntary acts of sin in 'one's own person,' but sinning 'in and with' Adam. . . . [Thus,] the sin here [Rom. 5:12d] attributed to the 'all' is to be understood, in the light of vv. 5:12a–c and 15–19, as a sin that is in some manner is identical to the sin committed by Adam. . . . All people, therefore, stand condemned 'in Adam,' guilty by reason of the sin all committed 'in him.'"[15] This view preserves the parallel between Adam and Christ in Romans 5 and 1 Corinthians 15 and accords with the doctrine of the imputation of Christ's righteousness to those who have faith in Him (see **Justification**).

Personal Sin

> Question 14: What is sin?
>
> Answer: Sin is any want of conformity unto, or transgression of, the law of God.[16]

PROVERBS 20:9

Who can say, "I have cleansed my heart,
I am pure from my sin"?

ROMANS 3:23

For all have sinned and fall short of the glory of God.

1 JOHN 1:8

If we say that we have no sin, we are deceiving ourselves and the truth is not in us.

THE DEPRAVITY AND INABILITY OF MAN

GENESIS 6:5

Then the LORD saw that the wickedness of man was great on the earth, and that every intent of the thoughts of his heart was only evil continually.

PROVERBS 22:15A

Foolishness is bound up in the heart of a child.

JEREMIAH 17:9

The heart is more deceitful than all else

And is desperately sick;
Who can understand it?

ROMANS 3:10–18

As it is written,

"THERE IS NONE RIGHTEOUS, NOT EVEN ONE;

[11] THERE IS NONE WHO UNDERSTANDS,

THERE IS NONE WHO SEEKS FOR GOD;

[12] ALL HAVE TURNED ASIDE, TOGETHER THEY HAVE BECOME USELESS;

THERE IS NONE WHO DOES GOOD,

THERE IS NOT EVEN ONE."

[13] "THEIR THROAT IS AN OPEN GRAVE,

WITH THEIR TONGUES THEY KEEP DECEIVING,"

"THE POISON OF ASPS IS UNDER THEIR LIPS";

[14] "WHOSE MOUTH IS FULL OF CURSING AND BITTERNESS";

[15] "THEIR FEET ARE SWIFT TO SHED BLOOD,

[16] DESTRUCTION AND MISERY ARE IN THEIR PATHS,

[17] AND THE PATH OF PEACE THEY HAVE NOT KNOWN."

[18] "THERE IS NO FEAR OF GOD BEFORE THEIR EYES."

ROMANS 6:17A

But thanks be to God that though you were slaves of sin.

GALATIANS 5:19–21A

Now the deeds of the flesh are evident, which are: immorality, impurity, sensuality, [20] idolatry, sorcery, enmities, strife, jealousy, outbursts of anger, disputes, dissensions, factions, [21] envying, drunkenness, carousing, and things like these.

EPHESIANS 2:1–3

And you were dead in your trespasses and sins, [2] in which you formerly walked according to the course of this world, according to the prince of the power of the air, of the spirit that is now working in the sons of disobedience. [3] Among them we too all formerly lived in the lusts of our flesh, indulging the desires of the flesh and of the mind, and were by nature children of wrath, even as the rest.

> **EPHESIANS 4:17–19**
>
> So this I say, and affirm together with the Lord, that you walk no longer just as the Gentiles also walk, in the futility of their mind, [18] being darkened in their understanding, excluded from the life of God because of the ignorance that is in them, because of the hardness of their heart; [19] and they, having become callous, have given themselves over to sensuality for the practice of every kind of impurity with greediness.

The Scriptures teach the "total depravity," or more accurately the "total inability," of man. This doctrine affirms that men are utterly unable to keep God's Law (see **The Elements of the Gospel, The Law is Unattainable**); their hearts are "desperately wicked"; they are under the sway of Satan ("the prince of the power of the air, of the spirit that is now working in the sons of disobedience"); they live lives of disobedience, "immorality, impurity, sensuality, idolatry," etc.; they are dead (separated from God; see **Personal Eschatology, Spiritual Death**) in transgressions and sins and are in fact "slaves of sin." The only hope for salvation is God's grace (see Eph. 2:8–9).

---

1. This discussion draws on material from John C. Whitcomb, *The Early Earth: An Introduction to Biblical Creationism* (Grand Rapids, MI: Baker Book House, 1986), 28–32.

2. Ibid., 32. Emphasis in the original.

3. See Whitcomb, *The Early Earth.*

4. See John Oswalt, *The Bible Among the Myths: Unique Revelation or Just Ancient Literature?* (Grand Rapids, MI: Zondervan, 2009).

5. See Abner Chou, "'Did God Really Say?'—Hermeneutics and History in Genesis 3," in *What Happened in the Garden: The Reality and Ramifications of the Creation and Fall of Man*, ed. Abner Chou (Grand Rapids, MI: Kregel Academic, 2016) 19–46.

6. John MacArthur, *The MacArthur New Testament Commentary: Romans 1–8* (Chicago, IL: Moody Publishers, 1991), 294. See also MacArthur and Mayhue, *Biblical Doctrine*, 405–07.

7. Harold G. Stigers, *A Commentary on Genesis* (Grand Rapids, MI: Zondervan Publishing House, 1979), 61.

8. MacArthur and Mayhue, *Biblical Doctrine*, 426.

9. John Murray, "Man in the Image of God," in *Collected Writings of John Murray, Vol. 2: Select Lectures in Systematic Theology* (Edinburgh: Banner of Truth, 1977), 35.

10. Scot McKnight, *The Letter to the Colossians* (Grand Rapids, MI: William B. Eerdmans Publishing Company, 2018), 311.

11. Herman Bavinck, *Reformed Dogmatics: Sin and Salvation in Christ*, ed. John Bolt, trans. John Vriend (Grand Rapids, MI: Baker Academic, 2006), 3:100.

12. Moo, *Romans*, 320.
13. Ibid., 323.
14. Ibid., 323
15. Ibid., 326.
16. Williamson, *Westminster Shorter Catechism*, 54.

CHAPTER 7

SALVATION

Soteriology

Soteriology is the doctrine of salvation (Greek *sōtēria* "deliverance, salvation"). Perhaps more accurately it is the doctrine of redemption because it deals with "the *application of the work of redemption*"[1] by God, the outcome of which is the salvation of the elect.

DIVINE ELECTION AND PREDESTINATION

The Fact of Divine Election and Predestination

JOHN 15:16

You did not choose Me but I chose you, and appointed you that you would go and bear fruit, and *that* your fruit would remain, so that whatever you ask of the Father in My name He may give to you.

ROMANS 8:28–29

And we know that God causes all things to work together for good to those who love God, to those who are called according to *His* purpose. [29] For those whom He foreknew, He also predestined *to become* conformed to the image of His Son, so that He would be the firstborn among many brethren.

ROMANS 9:10–14

And not only this, but there was Rebekah also, when she had conceived *twins* by one man, our father Isaac; ¹¹ for though *the twins* were not yet born and had not done anything good or bad, so that God's purpose according to *His* choice would stand, not because of works but because of Him who calls, ¹² it was said to her, "THE OLDER WILL SERVE THE YOUNGER." ¹³ Just as it is written, "JACOB I LOVED, BUT ESAU I HATED." ¹⁴ What shall we say then? There is no injustice with God, is there? May it never be!

1 CORINTHIANS 1:26–28

For consider your calling, brethren, that there were not many wise according to the flesh, not many mighty, not many noble; ²⁷ but God has chosen the foolish things of the world to shame the wise, and God has chosen the weak things of the world to shame the things which are strong, ²⁸ and the base things of the world and the despised God has chosen, the things that are not, so that He may nullify the things that are.

EPHESIANS 1:4–5, 9

Just as He chose us in Him before the foundation of the world, that we would be holy and blameless before Him. In love ⁵ He predestined us to adoption as sons through Jesus Christ to Himself, according to the kind intention of His will. . . . ⁹ He made known to us the mystery of His will, according to His kind intention which He purposed in Him.

2 THESSALONIANS 2:13

But we should always give thanks to God for you, brethren beloved by the Lord, because God has chosen you from the beginning for salvation through sanctification by the Spirit and faith in the truth.

Although the doctrines of election and predestination have occasioned no small amount of consternation and even controversy, they are clearly taught in Scripture. In order to appreciate these doctrines, closer attention should be made to the texts of Scripture and less attention to philosophical and psychological problems created by those who object to what Scripture plainly teaches. God's sovereign choice of the elect was not made with cold indifference, nor in an arbitrary manner. Indeed, God did not elect or predestine any on the basis of anything inherently or presciently seen in man. That is, God did not look down the corridors of time to see who would have faith and then elect them. He chose for His own good purposes.

God's Own Reasons for Election and Predestination

In Ephesians 1 and Romans 9 Paul explains that election ("He chose"; Greek *eklegomai*) was intended to display God's mercy, God's love, God's "kind intention," and to make known "to us the mystery of His will." God wants His creatures to know His mercy, love, and goodness; so rather than leave all of them to the sad condition brought on the race by Adam's sin (see **The Fall of Man**, and **Original Sin**), He lovingly and kindly chose those who would be saved. Anyone who objects that the choice of some and not all is "unfair" is substituting a human standard of "fairness" for God's standard, which is simply untenable (see Rom. 9:20 "On the contrary, who are you, O man, who answers back to God? The thing molded will not say to the molder, 'Why did you make me like this,' will it?"). God's choice of the elect was not designed to satisfy human criteria for evenhandedness but to display His own glory (see Rom. 9:23 "And He did so to make known the riches of His glory upon vessels of mercy, which He prepared beforehand for glory."). Furthermore, this choice was "in Christ" ("in Him"); that is, it was made for the sake of Christ, in light of the believer's union with Christ (see **Union with Christ**).

The Purpose of Election and Predestination for the Redeemed

The election of God was purposeful for the elect themselves. Jesus made it clear that they are elect to a life of fruitfulness ("I chose you, and appointed you that you would go and bear fruit"). They are "predestined to become conformed to the image of His Son," that is, they are elect to a life of increasing Christlikeness. They are elect to a life of "salvation through sanctification by the Spirit and faith in the truth." This election was to the end that the elect "would be holy and blameless before Him." They are predestined to adoption as sons, that is, they are brought into a filial relationship with God (see

Adoption). Further, this relationship brings them into a relationship "among many brethren," that is, since all the elect are adopted as sons "in Christ," they are brothers "in Christ." Finally, Paul taught election as a comfort to the elect: those who are "the called," and who "love God" can know that the same God who chose them "in Him before the foundation of the world" will cause "all things to work together for (their) good."

> The doctrine of election tells us that I am a Christian simply because God in eternity past decided to set his love on me. But why did he decide to set his love on me? Not for anything good in me, but simply because he decided to love me. There is no more ultimate reason than that. It humbles us before God to think in this way. It makes us realize that we have no claim on God's grace whatsoever. Our salvation is due to grace alone. Our only response is to give God eternal praise.[2]

THE EXTENT OF CHRIST'S REDEMPTION

Particular Redemption

This is the belief that Christ died to pay for the sins of a particular group of people, namely the elect. These verses speak directly to the question of "for whom did Christ die?"

CHRIST DIED FOR HIS SHEEP

> **JOHN 10:11**
> "I am the good shepherd; the good shepherd lays down His life for the sheep."

> **JOHN 10:14–15**
> "I am the good shepherd, and I know My own and My own know Me, [15] even as the Father knows Me and I know the Father; and I lay down My life for the sheep."

The wonderful image of a shepherd who diligently and selflessly cares for his sheep was a well-known biblical metaphor in the Old Testament (see Ps. 23:1; 79:13; 80:1; Ezek. 34:14). Jesus employs that metaphor for His relationship to His disciples and for those other sheep of which He said "I must bring them also" (see John 10:16). As a good shepherd Jesus knows His sheep (see John 10:27) and He knows those who are not His sheep (see John 10:26). This context makes it very clear that not everyone is one of His sheep. And Jesus' statement could not be more definite: He laid down His life for His sheep.

CHRIST DIED FOR THE CHURCH

> **ACTS 20:28**
>
> "Be on guard for yourselves and for all the flock, among which the Holy Spirit has made you overseers, to shepherd the church of God which He purchased with His own blood."

> **EPHESIANS 5:25**
>
> Husbands, love your wives, just as Christ also loved the church and gave Himself up for her.

Paul's admonishment to the elders of the church at Ephesus (see Acts 20:17) picks up the metaphor of shepherding the flock, only here the shepherding is to be done by the elders. Paul reminded these elders that Christ purchased the church at a tremendous cost, namely "with His own blood." That last phrase is obviously a reference to Christ's sacrifice on the cross. This was not a sacrifice to provide for a potential transaction, but an actual transaction, accomplished at the time He shed His blood. This is evident by Jesus' cry from the cross "*Tetelestai!*" which is a Greek term that literally means "it has been accomplished."

The comparison Paul makes in Ephesians 5 bears out that it was for the church, and none else, that Jesus died. Husbands are "to love their own wives" (see Eph. 5:28) with an exclusive and sacrificial love. The pattern of that exclusive and sacrificial love is Christ, "who loved the church and gave Himself up for her." To suggest that Christ's death was anything less than as exclusive as the relationship between a man and his own wife would ruin the point Paul is making here.

CHRIST DIED FOR THE ELECT

ROMANS 8:32–33

He who did not spare His own Son, but delivered Him over for us all, how will He not also with Him freely give us all things? [33] Who will bring a charge against God's elect? God is the one who justifies.

While Paul does use the word *all* in Romans 8:32, it is in fact a limited "all." It is "us all" and in the context the "us" is "God's elect." "This is not universalism, for *us* means 'us Christians,' 'us of whom we have been speaking.'"[3]

Summary: This doctrine does not teach that the value of Christ's death was limited in any way. His death was of infinite value and certainly sufficient to pay for the sins of all humankind. But the question of the intent, the design, of Christ's death is another matter. The texts noted above, and indeed all the texts that speak of actual vicarious atonement (e.g., 1 Cor. 15:3 "Christ died *for our sins*"; 1 Thess. 5:10 Christ "died *for us*"), indicate that the intent and design of Christ's work on the cross was for a particular group, namely the elect.[4]

> What does redemption mean? It does not mean redeemability, that we are placed in a redeemable position. It means that Christ purchased and procured redemption. This is the triumphant note of the New Testament whenever it plays on the redemptive chord. Christ redeemed us to God by his blood (Rev. 5:9). He obtained eternal redemption (Heb. 9:12) . . . It is to beggar the concept of redemption as an effective securement of release by price and by power to construe it as anything less than the effectual accomplishment which secures the salvation of those who are its objects.[5]

General Redemption

This is the view that Christ died to pay for the sins of everyone who ever lived in the world. Two types of verses are usually appealed to here: those that say Christ died for the *world* and those that say He died for *all*.

CHRIST DIED FOR THE WORLD

JOHN 1:29

The next day he saw Jesus coming to him and said, "Behold, the Lamb of God who takes away the sin of the world!"

JOHN 3:16–17

"For God so loved the world, that He gave His only begotten Son, that whoever believes in Him shall not perish, but have eternal life. [17] For God did not send the Son into the world to judge the world, but that the world might be saved through Him."

The problem with using these verses to argue for general redemption is that they only make the case for general redemption inferentially. In John 1:29 this statement by John the Baptist is meant to identify Jesus; it is not meant to directly argue for general redemption. Likewise, the well-known, and widely quoted John 3:16 is meant to express the extent of God's love (i.e., it extends to the world). It is an inference to suggest that the giving of the Son (the expression of God's love) was for the redemption of the whole world. Furthermore, the meaning of "world" is not "every person who ever lived" but the sphere where humanity lives, the system by which it operates (see John 3:19). He made this "world" (see John 1:10) but it has come under the sway of evil (see John 12:31; 16:11) and now does not know Him (see John 1:10). It is this world into which God sent His Son to redeem it. "The world is the place where God has come to do his redeeming and transforming work."[6] Jesus' mission, in salvation and judgment (which is what "the Lamb of God" will do; see 1 Cor. 5:7 and Rev. 5:6–10; 6:1–17) will "take away (remove) sin" from the world sphere and system. He does this because, despite the opposition of the world (see John 1:9–11; 7:7), He loves the world and the humanity in it.

CHRIST DIED FOR ALL

2 CORINTHIANS 5:14–15

For the love of Christ controls us, having concluded this, that one died for all, therefore all died; ¹⁵ and He died for all, so that they who live might no longer live for themselves, but for Him who died and rose again on their behalf.

1 TIMOTHY 2:6

Who gave Himself as a ransom for all, the testimony *given* at the proper time.

2 PETER 3:9

The Lord is not slow about His promise, as some count slowness, but is patient toward you, not wishing for any to perish but for all to come to repentance.

In each instance, the use of the word *all* must be understood by the context. In 2 Corinthians 5 it is clear that the "all" for whom Christ died are also "that they who live might no longer live for themselves," and this cannot be every person who has ever lived. Paul is speaking to the believers in Corinth and the "all" refers to "all" of them, as believers. In the context of 1 Timothy 2, Paul encouraged Timothy to pray "on behalf of all men" and he gives the example of "kings and all who are in authority" (1 Tim. 2:1–2). Here "all" cannot be every person who has ever lived but means something like "all kinds of men, even kings" etc. That rendering fits better for 1 Timothy 2:6 as well, which may be rendered "gave Himself for all kinds of men." In 2 Peter the apostle is writing to encourage believers in a time of trial. These believers had endured for a long time and there was no end in sight. Peter wanted them to know that their relief would come in due time (see 2 Peter 3:1–8, 10). He also assured them that the delay was for their benefit in that it gave ample time for them to "come to repentance." In short, the "all" is to be understood as "all of you." Thus, the verse means "but is patient toward you, not wishing for any *of you* to perish but for all *of you* to come to repentance."

THE ELEMENTS OF THE GOSPEL

The Requirement of the Law

THE LAW IS GOOD

ROMANS 7:12
So then, the Law is holy, and the commandment is holy and righteous and good.

1 TIMOTHY 1:8
But we know that the Law is good, if one uses it lawfully.

THE LAW IS UNATTAINABLE

GALATIANS 3:10–12
For as many as are of the works of the Law are under a curse; for it is written, "CURSED IS EVERYONE WHO DOES NOT ABIDE BY ALL THINGS WRITTEN IN THE BOOK OF THE LAW, TO PERFORM THEM." [11] Now that no one is justified by the Law before God is evident; for, "THE RIGHTEOUS MAN SHALL LIVE BY FAITH." [12] However, the Law is not of faith; on the contrary, "HE WHO PRACTICES THEM SHALL LIVE BY THEM."

GALATIANS 3:19
Why the Law then? It was added because of transgressions, having been ordained through angels by the agency of a mediator, until the seed would come to whom the promise had been made.

GALATIANS 3:23–25
But before faith came, we were kept in custody under the law, being shut up to the faith which was later to be revealed. [24] Therefore the Law has become our tutor *to lead us* to Christ, so that we may be justified by faith. [25] But now that faith has come, we are no longer under a tutor.

The Provision of Sovereign Grace

ROMANS 3:23–24

For all have sinned and fall short of the glory of God, [24] being justified as a gift by His grace through the redemption which is in Christ Jesus.

ROMANS 5:15

But the free gift is not like the transgression. For if by the transgression of the one the many died, much more did the grace of God and the gift by the grace of the one Man, Jesus Christ, abound to the many.

ROMANS 5:20–21

The Law came in so that the transgression would increase; but where sin increased, grace abounded all the more, [21] so that, as sin reigned in death, even so grace would reign through righteousness to eternal life through Jesus Christ our Lord.

EPHESIANS 2:8–9

For by grace you have been saved through faith; and that not of your-selves, *it is* the gift of God; [9] not as a result of works, so that no one may boast.

The Message of the Death, Burial, and Resurrection of Jesus Christ

ROMANS 6:23

For the wages of sin is death, but the free gift of God is eternal life in Christ Jesus our Lord.

1 CORINTHIANS 15:3–4

For I delivered to you as of first importance what I also received, that Christ died for our sins according to the Scriptures, [4] and that He was buried, and that He was raised on the third day according to the Scriptures.

1 PETER 2:24

And He Himself bore our sins in His body on the cross, so that we might die to sin and live to righteousness; for by His wounds you were healed.

ORDO SALUTIS, THE ORDER OF SALVATION

"The ordo salutis describes the process by which the work of salvation, wrought in Christ, is subjectively realized in the hearts and lives of sinners. It aims at describing in their logical order, and also in their interrelations, the various movements of the Holy Spirit in the application of the work of redemption."[7]

The Golden Chain

ROMANS 8:30

And these whom He predestined, He also called; and these whom He called, He also justified; and these whom He justified, He also glorified.

Calling

GENERAL CALL

ISAIAH 55:1, 6–7

"Ho! Every one who thirsts, come to the waters;
And you who have no money come, buy and eat.
Come, buy wine and milk
Without money and without cost."...
[6] Seek the LORD while He may be found;
Call upon Him while He is near.
[7] Let the wicked forsake his way
And the unrighteous man his thoughts;
And let him return to the LORD,
And He will have compassion on him,
And to our God,
For He will abundantly pardon.

MATTHEW 11:28

"Come to Me, all who are weary and heavy-laden, and I will give you rest."

LUKE 14:23

"And the master said to the slave, 'Go out into the highways and along the hedges, and compel *them* to come in, so that my house may be filled.'"

ACTS 2:38

Peter *said* to them, "Repent, and each of you be baptized in the name of Jesus Christ for the forgiveness of your sins; and you will receive the gift of the Holy Spirit."

ACTS 16:31

They said, "Believe in the Lord Jesus, and you will be saved, you and your household."

ACTS 17:30

Therefore having overlooked the times of ignorance, God is now declaring to men that all *people* everywhere should repent.

The general call is the message of the gospel (sometimes referred to as the gospel call; see **The Elements of the Gospel**) that is to be preached by believers to all people. It is a freely offered, and indiscriminately presented, message about Jesus Christ in order that all may know the facts of the gospel. It includes a command to believe, and a command to repent, and a command to come to Christ.

The admonition to "come!" is a command. The admonitions to "repent," "be baptized," and "believe," are all in the imperative (command) mood. In the parable of the "big dinner" (Luke 14:16–24), Jesus illustrates the various excuses men have for not accepting God's invitation to come to Him (and by extension the excuses men use for not responding to the gospel). After being rejected several times, the lord giving the dinner instructed his slaves to go to those on the fringes of society and "compel them to come in." The term compel (Greek *anankason*) is a strong term indicating "constraint," or even the use of force. This is not to suggest that in making the general call, or gospel call, preachers or evangelists should use force to get converts. However, it does suggest that the notion of giving "invitations" (something never found in the New Testament) is too weak to capture the sense and method of this call. The lost must be approached with compassion and the style of presentation may be meek or bold, but the call should be framed as a command from the Sovereign God, who is gracious to provide the capacity (see **Regeneration**) and the faith (see Eph. 2:8–9) to obey the command. The General Call also offers the promise of the forgiveness of sins.

EFFECTUAL CALL/EFFICACIOUS GRACE

JOHN 6:44

No one can come to Me unless the Father who sent Me draws him; and I will raise him up on the last day.

ROMANS 1:1, 6–7A

Paul, a bond-servant of Christ Jesus, called *as* an apostle, set apart for the gospel of God. . . . [6] among whom you also are the called of Jesus Christ; [7] to all who are beloved of God in Rome, called *as* saints: Grace to you and peace from God our Father and the Lord Jesus Christ.

ROMANS 8:28–30

And we know that God causes all things to work together for good to those who love God, to those who are called according to *His* purpose. [29] For those whom He foreknew, He also predestined *to become* conformed to the image of His Son, so that He would be the firstborn among many brethren; [30] and these whom He predestined, He also called; and these whom He called, He also justified; and these whom He justified, He also glorified.

ROMANS 9:23–24

And *He did so* to make known the riches of His glory upon vessels of mercy, which He prepared beforehand for glory, [24] *even* us, whom He also called, not from among Jews only, but also from among Gentiles.

1 CORINTHIANS 1:9, 23–24

God is faithful, through whom you were called into fellowship with His Son, Jesus Christ our Lord. . . .
[23] but we preach Christ crucified, to Jews a stumbling block and to Gentiles foolishness, [24] but to those who are the called, both Jews and Greeks, Christ the power of God and the wisdom of God.

EPHESIANS 1:18

I pray that the eyes of your heart may be enlightened, so that you will know what is the hope of His calling, what are the riches of the glory of His inheritance in the saints.

EPHESIANS 4:1, 4–5

Therefore I, the prisoner of the Lord, implore you to walk in a manner worthy of the calling with which you have been called. . . . [4] *There is* one body and one Spirit, just as also you were called in one hope of your calling; [5] one Lord, one faith, one baptism.

2 TIMOTHY 1:9

Who has saved us and called us with a holy calling, not according to our works, but according to His own purpose and grace which was granted us in Christ Jesus from all eternity.

1 PETER 2:9

But you are A CHOSEN RACE, A royal PRIESTHOOD, A HOLY NATION, A PEOPLE FOR *God's* OWN POSSESSION, so that you may proclaim the excellencies of Him who has called you out of darkness into His marvelous light.

The effectual call is the work of God in grace and mercy, when He uses the gospel call (see 2 Thess. 2:14), and by the power of the Word (see Rom. 10:17), and with the drawing work of the Father (see John 6:44; see Acts 16:14 "the Lord opened her heart") to bring a person—willingly and effectively—to saving faith in Christ.

REGENERATION

JOHN 1:12–13

But as many as received Him, to them He gave the right to become children of God, *even* to those who believe in His name, [13] who were born, not of blood nor of the will of the flesh nor of the will of man, but of God.

JOHN 3:3–7

Jesus answered and said to him, "Truly, truly, I say to you, unless one is born again he cannot see the kingdom of God." [4] Nicodemus said to Him, "How can a man be born when he is old? He cannot enter a second time

into his mother's womb and be born, can he?" [5] Jesus answered, "Truly,
truly, I say to you, unless one is born of water and the Spirit he cannot
enter into the kingdom of God. [6] That which is born of the flesh is flesh,
and that which is born of the Spirit is spirit. [7] Do not be amazed that I said
to you, 'You must be born again.'"

2 CORINTHIANS 5:17
Therefore if anyone is in Christ, *he is* a new creature; the old things passed
away; behold, new things have come.

EPHESIANS 2:5
Even when we were dead in our transgressions, made us alive together
with Christ (by grace you have been saved).

TITUS 3:5
He saved us, not on the basis of deeds which we have done in righteousness, but according to His mercy, by the washing of regeneration and
renewing by the Holy Spirit.

1 PETER 1:23
For you have been born again not of seed which is perishable but imperishable, *that is*, through the living and enduring word of God.

1 JOHN 5:1
Whoever believes that Jesus is the Christ is born of God, and whoever
loves the Father loves the *child* born of Him.

Regeneration (Greek *palingenesia*) refers to the doctrine of the "new birth." In
John 3:3 the expression "born again" (Greek *gennēthē anōthen*) means "born
from above," which conveys the idea of a second birth ("born again") as well
as the fact that this is a birth "from above," that is, not of an earthly cause; it
has a supernatural cause—God Himself. The new birth is not something initiated, aided, or accomplished by human effort. Like natural birth, it is a work
initiated and accomplished by another which has effects for the one who is
born, namely life. This is why Jesus likened the new birth to the movement of
the wind. This new birth, however, inexorably leads to life and growth with all
its attendant experiences. Regeneration is instantaneous, happens below the

level of conscious experience, but is a radical change with eventually discernible effects. One who is "born again" is a "new creature." "Regeneration is the
implanting of the *principle* of the new spiritual life in a man."[8]

EXCURSUS: Regeneration Precedes Conversion

The texts that refer to regeneration make it clear (as does the very metaphor of "birth") that the work of regeneration is a monergistic work (a
work of one) of God. This accords with the truth of the "total depravity" of
man, that is, that man is utterly unable to save himself (see **The Depravity
and Inability of Man**). In regeneration God is the One who makes the sinner alive (see Eph. 2:5). Conversion is the act of God turning the sinner so
that the sinner turns to God and trusts Christ in repentance and faith (see 1
Thess. 1:9) (see **Conversion, Repentance, and Faith/Belief**).

Several texts in 1 John make it clear that the new birth comes before
faith (belief). These texts are: 1 John 2:29 ("you know that everyone also who
practices righteousness is born of Him"); 1 John 3:9 ("No one who is born
of God practices sin, because His seed abides in him; and he cannot sin,
because he is born of God"); 1 John 4:7 ("Beloved, let us love one another,
for love is from God; and everyone who loves is born of God and knows
God"); and 1 John 5:1 ("Whoever believes that Jesus is the Christ is born
of God, and whoever loves the Father loves the *child* born of Him"). In each
of these texts the verb "born" (Greek *gennaô*) is in the Greek perfect tense.
This tense is sometimes translated into the English simple present tense.
However, the Greek perfect tense denotes an action that precedes another
action (which is indicated by a verb in the immediate context). Hence a more
accurate translation in each of the first three cases would be "everyone also
who practices righteousness *has been* born of Him," "and he cannot sin,
because he *has been* born of God," "everyone who loves *has been* born
of God." This makes sense since no evangelical would claim that a sinner
is born again *because* he practiced righteousness, or *because* he stopped
sinning, or *because* he loves God. Those good things are the effects or re-
sults of being born again. So, in the final text, the more accurate rendering is

"Whoever believes that Jesus is the Christ *has been* born of God" because belief (faith) is the effect or result of being born from above. In other words, regeneration precedes faith (belief).

CONVERSION

> **1 THESSALONIANS 1:9**
>
> For they themselves report about us what kind of a reception we had with you, and how you turned to God from idols to serve a living and true God.

Conversion is a two-sided concept that involves repentance on one side and faith on the other. In 1 Thessalonians 1:9 Paul's commendation of the Thessalonians captures the "turning from" idea of repentance and the "turning to" idea of faith. Conversion happens when God turns (gives the gifts of faith and repentance to) a sinner to Himself in such a way that the sinner does indeed turn.

REPENTANCE

> **MATTHEW 3:1–2**
>
> Now in those days John the Baptist came, preaching in the wilderness of Judea, saying, ² "Repent, for the kingdom of heaven is at hand."

> **LUKE 5:32**
>
> I have not come to call the righteous but sinners to repentance.

> **ACTS 2:38**
>
> Peter *said* to them, "Repent, and each of you be baptized in the name of Jesus Christ for the forgiveness of your sins; and you will receive the gift of the Holy Spirit."

> **ACTS 3:19**
>
> Therefore repent and return, so that your sins may be wiped away, in order that times of refreshing may come from the presence of the Lord.

ACTS 26:19–20

So, King Agrippa, I did not prove disobedient to the heavenly vision, [20] but *kept* declaring both to those of Damascus first, and *also* at Jerusalem and *then* throughout all the region of Judea, and *even* to the Gentiles, that they should repent and turn to God, performing deeds appropriate to repentance.

2 TIMOTHY 2:25

With gentleness correcting those who are in opposition, if perhaps God may grant them repentance leading to the knowledge of the truth.

The importance of repentance (and the preaching of repentance) is seen in the many passages that speak of repentance and the record of those in the narratives of the New Testament who preached repentance—John the Baptist, Jesus, Peter, Paul, and others. The two Greek terms for repentance are *metanoia* and *epistrephō*. The term *metanoia* has the notion of a "change of mind," and *epistrephō* has the notion of a "change of behavior."[9] In Acts 3:19 Peter uses both terms in the same sentence—"repent [Greek *metanoēsate*] and return [Greek *epistrepsate*]." Also, in Acts 26:20, in the same sentence, Paul uses both terms: "repent [Greek *metanoein*] and turn [Greek *epistrephein*] to God." Thus, it seems, "the meanings of these two words . . . overlap."[10] Thus, true repentance is both a change of mind and a change of behavior. God is the One who grants or gives repentance.

> Repentance is not merely shame or sorrow for sin, although genuine repentance always involves an element of remorse. It is a redirection of the human will, a purposeful decision to forsake all unrighteousness and pursue righteousness instead.[11]

FAITH/BELIEF

JOHN 3:36

"He who believes in the Son has eternal life; but he who does not obey the Son will not see life, but the wrath of God abides on him."

ACTS 16:30–31

And after he brought them out, he said, "Sirs, what must I do to be saved?"

[31] They said, "Believe in the Lord Jesus, and you will be saved, you and your household."

ROMANS 3:22

Even *the* righteousness of God through faith in Jesus Christ for all those who believe; for there is no distinction.

ROMANS 10:9

That if you confess with your mouth Jesus *as* Lord, and believe in your heart that God raised Him from the dead, you will be saved.

EPHESIANS 2:8–10

For by grace you have been saved through faith; and that not of yourselves, *it is* the gift of God; [9] not as a result of works, so that no one may boast. [10] For we are His workmanship, created in Christ Jesus for good works, which God prepared beforehand so that we would walk in them.

HEBREWS 11:1, 8A

Now faith is the assurance of *things* hoped for, the conviction of things not seen. . . .

[8] By faith Abraham, when he was called, obeyed.

The Greek noun for "faith" is *pistis* and the Greek verb "to believe" is *pisteuein*. Thus, "to believe" is essentially "to have, or exercise faith." Faith is not mere intellectual assent, nor a subjective aspiration (a "blind leap") but involves understanding (see Heb.11:1), personal appropriation (see the metaphors of drinking and eating in John 4:14; 6:51), and commitment (e.g., the example of Abraham, Heb. 11:8). In John 3:36, the apostle John contrasts those who believe (and have eternal life) and those who "do not obey" (and so "will not see life"). Clearly faith includes the obedience the unbelievers lack. "Obedience is the inevitable manifestation of true faith."[12]

This faith is a gift ("it is the gift of God"), as Paul makes clear to the Philippians ("For to you *it has been granted* for Christ's sake, not only *to believe* in Him, but also to suffer for His sake" Phil. 1:29, emphasis added), and Peter makes clear to his readers ("To those who *have received a faith* of the same kind as ours" 2 Peter1:1b, emphasis added).

EXCURSUS: The Elements of Faith

Typically theologians see three elements to faith. The first is *knowledge*. There is an inescapable intellectual or cognitive element to saving faith, for one must hear and understand the very words of the gospel call (see Rom. 10:13–17). Beyond this there must be an intellectual grasp of the meaning and truth content of those words. In short, coming to faith in Christ involves overcoming ignorance (see John 4:22; Acts 17:23), but more it involves a genuine comprehension of the facts of the gospel and the truth of those facts. For instance, in 1 Thessalonians 2:13 Paul is commending the Thessalonian believers for their faith (note: "you who believe" at the end of the verse). That faith came, Paul tells them, "when you received the word of God which you heard from us." That is, they had heard, and in that sense had come to an awareness, a knowledge of the gospel message. But Paul goes on and notes that this knowledge became a deeper intellectual perception when "you accepted it not as the word of men, but for what it really is, the word of God." Both aspects of knowledge are necessary for saving faith. Faith requires one to know what the words mean, in the sense of their dictionary definitions, and what they *really* mean, that is, in the sense of the truth content that those words express.

The second element is *assent*. This goes beyond an intellectual grasp or cognitive comprehension of the facts but a personal acceptance of the facts as having personal significance.

The third element is *trust*. This goes beyond even the personal assent to what is intellectually comprehended. It involves a personal appropriation of the promise of forgiveness and personal commitment to the truth of the gospel message. This commitment includes submission to Christ as Lord and the obedience appropriate to His Lordship.[13]

These three elements are often identified respectively by the Latin terms *notitia, assensus,* and *fiducia.*

JUSTIFICATION

The biblical doctrine of justification deals with the fundamental issue of how guilty sinners can be acquitted and restored to favor with
an infinitely righteous and just God.[14]

GENESIS 15:6

Then he believed in the LORD; and He reckoned it to him as righteousness.

DEUTERONOMY 25:1

"If there is a dispute between men and they go to court, and the judges
decide their case, and they justify the righteous and condemn the wicked."

JOB 25:4

"How then can a man be just with God?
Or how can he be clean who is born of woman?"

PROVERBS 17:15

He who justifies the wicked and he who condemns the righteous,
Both of them alike are an abomination to the LORD.

LUKE 18:14

"I tell you, this man went to his house justified rather than the other; for
everyone who exalts himself will be humbled, but he who humbles himself
will be exalted."

The point of citing these texts is not so much to articulate the doctrine of justification but to understand the notion of the term *justify*. In Deuteronomy
25:1 the Law is instructing judges to decide the cases that come before them
in such a way that they declare the righteous to be righteous or just, and they
declare the wicked to be condemned. In Proverbs 17:15 the point is that
to do the reverse—that is, to declare the wicked to be righteous or just and
declare the righteous to be condemned—is a perversion of justice and "an
abomination to the LORD." For the purpose of understanding the doctrine of
"Justification by Faith," these texts make the point that the actions of a judge
are legal declarations that do not actually make the righteous to be righteous,

nor do they make the wicked to be wicked. Such declarations should be true to the actual character of the persons being adjudicated, but sadly in human courts it is possible that such declarations are not true about the persons being adjudicated. Nevertheless, the legal declaration is what matters. In the doctrine of "Justification by Faith" this legal declaration is a key feature.

In what is possibly the most important single paragraph ever written (Romans 3:21–26), Paul brings out something of the grandeur of Christ's saving work.[15]

The Key Text

ROMANS 3:21–28

But now apart from the Law *the* righteousness of God has been manifested, being witnessed by the Law and the Prophets, [22] even *the* righteousness of God through faith in Jesus Christ for all those who believe; for there is no distinction; [23] for all have sinned and fall short of the glory of God, [24] being justified as a gift by His grace through the redemption which is in Christ Jesus; [25] whom God displayed publicly as a propitiation in His blood through faith. *This was* to demonstrate His righteousness, because in the forbearance of God He passed over the sins previously committed; [26] for the demonstration, *I say,* of His righteousness at the present time, so that He would be just and the justifier of the one who has faith in Jesus. [27] Where then is boasting? It is excluded. By what kind of law? Of works? No, but by a law of faith. [28] For we maintain that a man is justified by faith apart from works of the Law.

This is the *locus classicus* of the essential doctrine of "Justification by Faith Alone." Perhaps the best way to understand this vital text of Romans (3:21ff) is a series of questions that in effect follows Paul's flow of thought.

The underlying question behind this text is, "How can a man be just before God?" (see Job 9:2 "But how can a man be in the right before God?"). This question arises because of Paul's conclusion in Rom. 3:20, "by the works of the Law no flesh will be justified in His (God's) sight." In the first two and a half chapters of Romans Paul has methodically argued that the pagan, idolatrous Gentile (see Rom. 1:18–32) and the moralistic, Law-honoring (but Law-breaking) Jew (see Rom. 2:1–3:9), indeed, "all the world" (see Rom. 3:10–19) are "under sin" (Rom. 3:9) and "accountable to God" (Rom. 3:19; see v. 23). The answer to the question is: a man needs to be righteous (or just) before God, but on his own he cannot be (see Rom. 3:10). However, there is hope, namely the gospel Paul preached (see Rom. 1:15–16). It is in this gospel that "the righteousness of God is revealed" (Rom. 1:17). In Romans 3:21ff Paul is about to show how a man may have the righteousness that he must have before God. (Note: The terms righteous, righteousness, just, and justification all come from the same Greek root *dik-* and the way Paul uses those terms is based on the Hebrew terms *ṣādeq* (verb: "to be just or righteous"), *ṣedāqâ* (noun: "righteous"), and *ṣāddiq* (adjective: "righteous").

What is the "righteousness of God" Paul has in mind here in Romans 3:21 (see Rom. 1:17)? To answer that question, in this paragraph Paul gives nine facts about the righteousness of God.

One: this righteousness is "apart from the Law." As Paul has already demonstrated, this righteousness is not attained by keeping the Old Testament Law because one would need to keep every point of the Law perfectly (see James 2:10). Furthermore, this righteousness is not attained by *any* system of human law or personal morality. This is the righteousness God gives, not a righteousness one earns by works (see Eph. 2:9).

Two: this righteousness "has been manifested." The gospel of Jesus Christ and the provision of righteousness has appeared, is available, and is being preached by Paul and the apostles. This term also indicates that this gospel was no human invention. It is revealed by God.

Three: this righteousness is "witnessed by the Law and the Prophets." These terms reflect the customary division of the Old Testament and are meant to indicate the whole of the Old Testament. Paul's point here is that this means of justification is not something new or a change from how one was made right with God in the Old Testament. Indeed, in Romans 4 Paul makes it clear that this was the experience of both Abraham (see Rom. 4:1–3, 9–25) and David (see 4:5–8).

Four: this righteousness is "through faith in Jesus Christ for all who believe." This is the key fact of this essential doctrine. This is "justification by faith" (see Rom. 3:28). This faith is not the cause or ground of justification (i.e., being declared righteous, see below). It is not an exchange for or instead of righteousness. It is not taken "as righteousness" in the sense of as a replacement for or substitute for righteousness. It is not a condition for righteousness. Faith is the means by which the sinner receives the gift of righteousness. Faith is an instrument, the "hand that receives the gift" and is itself a gift (see Eph. 2:8–9). It is not "faith in faith," but "faith in Christ!" The object of the faith makes the faith effective; the faith itself is powerless. This faith is not mere intellectual assent but an intellectual understanding (Latin *notitia*), personal, heartfelt agreement (Latin *assensus*), and personal, volitional commitment (Latin *fiducia*).

Five: this righteousness is "for all those who believe; for there is no distinction." The righteousness in view here is available for any repentant sinner who believes the gospel of Jesus Christ. Paul has made clear that the problem was comprehensive (see Rom. 3:10ff); this fact means that the "solution" is as comprehensive as the "problem." In other words, since everyone has the *same* problem (sin), this solution is applicable to "all." This also indicates that the cross work of Christ that accomplished redemption (see vv. 24–25) was sufficient for all.

Six: this righteousness of God is necessary, "For all have sinned and fall short of the glory of God." Paul has already demonstrated this in Romans 3:10–19.

Seven: this righteousness of God is a gift of God's grace ("being justified as a gift by His grace"). This righteousness is given as a gift. The term *justified* means "to be declared right." The idea is forensic or legal. This "justification" is a legal pronouncement made by God in which He declares that the alien righteousness of Christ is imputed (reckoned, counted) to the one who has put faith in Christ. The basis of this declaration is only on the basis of grace—the unmerited favor of God.

Eight: this righteousness is "through the redemption which is in Christ Jesus" made available because of the "propitiation in His blood"—in other words, by His sacrificial death on the cross. It is on the basis of Christ's perfect (law-obedient, sinless) life and His sacrificial (penal-substitutionary) death that this righteousness is manifested and available. The term *propitiation* has the twin notions of "satisfaction" and "appeasement." The sacrifice of Christ both appeases, turns away God's wrath, and satisfies God's justice.

Nine: this righteousness is a demonstration of God's righteousness and His rightness (He is just) "so that He would be just and the justifier of the one who has faith in Jesus." The unspoken question Paul is answering here is, "How can God be just to save sinners in this way?"

> Justification is a legal pronouncement made by God in the present, prior to the day of judgment, declaring sinners to be not guilty and therefore to be acquitted, by pardoning all their sins and reckoning them to be righteous in His sight, on the basis of Christ as their representative and substitute, whose righteousness in life and death is put to their account when in self-despairing trust they look to Him alone for salvation.[16]

Justification Is . . .
. . . by faith.

ROMANS 5:1
Therefore, having been justified by faith, we have peace with God through our Lord Jesus Christ.

GALATIANS 3:24
Therefore the Law has become our tutor *to lead us* to Christ, so that we may be justified by faith.

. . . in the name of Jesus Christ.

1 CORINTHIANS 6:11
Such were some of you; but you were washed, but you were sanctified, but you were justified in the name of the Lord Jesus Christ and in the Spirit of our God.

. . . not by works.

GALATIANS 2:16

Nevertheless knowing that a man is not justified by the works of the Law but through faith in Christ Jesus, even we have believed in Christ Jesus, so that we may be justified by faith in Christ and not by the works of the Law; since by the works of the Law no flesh will be justified.

. . . by the grace of God.

TITUS 3:7

So that being justified by His grace we would be made heirs according to *the* hope of eternal life.

. . . demonstrated by works.

JAMES 2:21–24

Was not Abraham our father justified by works when he offered up Isaac his son on the altar? ²² You see that faith was working with his works, and as a result of the works, faith was perfected; ²³ and the Scripture was fulfilled which says, "AND ABRAHAM BELIEVED GOD, AND IT WAS RECKONED TO HIM AS RIGHTEOUSNESS," and he was called the friend of God. ²⁴ You see that a man is justified by works and not by faith alone.

James's view of justification is not in conflict with that of the apostle Paul. Paul uses the term *justification* in the legal, declarative sense, whereas James uses the term *justification* in the "demonstrative" sense. In other words, James is saying Abraham's works demonstrated his rightness (righteousness, justification) before God. The (almost!) sacrifice of Isaac took place years after Abraham had "believed in the LORD; and He reckoned it to him as righteousness" (Gen. 15:6). "James is teaching, then, that Abraham's willingness to offer Isaac vindicates his faith before men—a teaching with which the apostle Paul was in wholehearted agreement (Eph. 2:10). There is thus no conflict between the two inspired writers."[17]

IMPUTATION

ROMANS 4:3–4 (SEE GEN. 15:6)

For what does the Scripture say? "ABRAHAM BELIEVED GOD, AND IT WAS CREDITED TO HIM AS RIGHTEOUSNESS." [4] Now to the one who works, his wage is not credited as a favor, but as what is due.

ROMANS 4:22–24

Therefore IT WAS ALSO CREDITED TO HIM AS RIGHTEOUSNESS. [23] Now not for his sake only was it written that it was credited to him, [24] but for our sake also, to whom it will be credited, as those who believe in Him who raised Jesus our Lord from the dead.

2 CORINTHIANS 5:21

He made Him who knew no sin *to be* sin on our behalf, so that we might become the righteousness of God in Him.

Faith is the means by which the righteousness of Christ is "credited," or "counted," or "reckoned" to the believer. This is known as "imputation." Just as Adam's sin was imputed to his posterity (see Rom. 5:12, 18–19; see **Original Sin**), so Christ's righteousness is imputed to those who have faith in Him.

REDEMPTION

1 CORINTHIANS 6:20

For you have been bought with a price: therefore glorify God in your body.

1 CORINTHIANS 7:23

You were bought with a price; do not become slaves of men.

GALATIANS 3:13

Christ redeemed us from the curse of the Law, having become a curse for us—for it is written, "CURSED IS EVERYONE WHO HANGS ON A TREE."

1 PETER 1:18–19

Knowing that you were not redeemed with perishable things like silver or gold from your futile way of life inherited from your forefathers, [19] but with precious blood, as of a lamb unblemished and spotless, *the blood* of Christ.

When Paul reminded the Corinthian believers of their redemption—"you have been bought with a price"—they would have recognized the phrase *you have been bought* (Greek *ēgorasthēte*) as a term normally associated with something from the Greco-Roman culture of day, namely the practice of slavery. The term Paul uses refers to the purchase of slaves from a marketplace. Paul is reminding them of the fact that they have been purchased from bondage to sin (see Rom. 6:17–18, 22). The price of this purchase was "the blood of Christ."

When Paul says "Christ redeemed us from the curse of the Law," he has a different metaphor in mind. Here Paul has in mind the Old Testament Law, specifically Deuteronomy 21:23, which pronounced a curse on anyone who was hung on a tree as a guilty criminal. "Paul is saying that Christ's death on the cross meant that he bore the curse that would otherwise have rested on us . . . He bore the curse that sinners incurred and this is viewed as paying the price of a price, an act of redemption."[18]

> Christ has become our Redeemer. Jesus told us himself that this was the reason for his coming to earth: "For even the Son of Man did not come to be served, but to serve, and to give his life as a ransom for many" (Mk. 10:45). His word "ransom" is the technical term used of the money paid to release a prisoner of war or a slave. To release the slaves of sin he paid the price. We were in captivity. We were in the strong grip of evil. We could not break free. But the price was paid and the result is that we go free. "Sin shall not be your master" (Rom. 6:14).[19]

UNION WITH CHRIST

Union with Christ is really the central truth of the whole doctrine of salvation.[20]

Union with Christ Declared

ROMANS 6:3–5
Or do you not know that all of us who have been baptized into Christ Jesus have been baptized into His death? [4] Therefore we have been

buried with Him through baptism into death, so that as Christ was raised from the dead through the glory of the Father, so we too might walk in newness of life. [5] For if we have become united with *Him* in the likeness of His death, certainly we shall also be *in the likeness* of His resurrection.

1 CORINTHIANS 15:22

For as in Adam all die, so also in Christ all will be made alive.

GALATIANS 2:20

I have been crucified with Christ; and it is no longer I who live, but Christ lives in me; and the *life* which I now live in the flesh I live by faith in the Son of God, who loved me and gave Himself up for me.

GALATIANS 3:27

For all of you who were baptized into Christ have clothed yourselves with Christ.

EPHESIANS 1:3–4A

Blessed *be* the God and Father of our Lord Jesus Christ, who has blessed us with every spiritual blessing in the heavenly *places* in Christ, [4] just as He chose us in Him before the foundation of the world, that we would be holy and blameless before Him.

EPHESIANS 2:5

Even when we were dead in our transgressions, made us alive together with Christ (by grace you have been saved).

EPHESIANS 2:10

For we are His workmanship, created in Christ Jesus for good works, which God prepared beforehand so that we would walk in them.

COLOSSIANS 3:1–4

Therefore if you have been raised up with Christ, keep seeking the things above, where Christ is, seated at the right hand of God. [2] Set your mind on the things above, not on the things that are on earth. [3] For you have died and your life is hidden with Christ in God. [4] When Christ, who is our life, is revealed, then you also will be revealed with Him in glory.

The believer's union with Christ simply means the experiences of Christ— His life of righteousness, His death, His resurrection, His heavenly presence—are spiritually the experiences of the one who has faith in Christ. This union is described in two ways in the New Testament: many passages affirm *Christ is in us* (Gal. 2:20; see Rom. 8:10; 2 Cor. 13:5; Eph. 3:17; Col. 1:27) and many passages affirm *we are in Christ* (2 Cor. 5:17; see John 15:4, 5, 7; 1 Cor. 15:22; 2 Cor. 12:2; Gal. 3:28; Eph. 1:4; 2:10; Phil. 3:9; 1 Thess. 4:16; 1 John 4:13). This union began with the believer's election before the foundation of the world. This union is the basis for the believer's new life and good works in the present. This union is the basis for the believer's hope of glory.

The significance of this union is that all the blessings and benefits of Christ's life, death, and resurrection belong to the Christian.

Union with Christ Illustrated

JOHN 15:4–5

Abide in Me, and I in you. As the branch cannot bear fruit of itself unless it abides in the vine, so neither *can* you unless you abide in Me. [5] I am the vine, you are the branches; he who abides in Me and I in him, he bears much fruit, for apart from Me you can do nothing.

The metaphor of the vine and the branches in John 15 illustrates the fact of, and some of the key features of, the believer's union with Christ. As the vine is the source of life, of nourishment, of growth, of productivity for the branches, so Christ is the source of the believer's life, sanctification, and spiritual fruitfulness.

ADOPTION

Adoption is an act of God, along with the other aspects of salvation, whereby He makes one who was an enemy (see Rom. 5:10) His child and a member of His household.

JOHN 1:12

But as many as received Him, to them He gave the right to become children of God, *even* to those who believe in His name.

ROMANS 8:15

For you have not received a spirit of slavery leading to fear again, but you have received a spirit of adoption as sons by which we cry out, "Abba! Father!"

ROMANS 8:23 (SEE ROM. 9:4)

And not only this, but also we ourselves, having the first fruits of the Spirit, even we ourselves groan within ourselves, waiting eagerly for *our* adoption as sons, the redemption of our body.

GALATIANS 4:5

So that He might redeem those who were under the Law, that we might receive the adoption as sons.

EPHESIANS 1:5

He predestined us to adoption as sons through Jesus Christ to Himself, according to the kind intention of His will.

The privileges of adoption are: a new and intimate familial relationship with God as a loving Father; the right to address Him as "Abba, Father"; the care and compassion of God as Father (see Matt. 7:11); the loving discipline of our Father (see Heb. 12:5–6; see Prov. 3:11–12); and the joy of a new family relationship with other brothers and sisters in Christ (see Rom. 1:13; 1 Cor. 1:10; James 1:2). This adoption is our present legal standing, but the full experience of this adoption will be realized when we experience full and final redemption and the resurrection of our bodies. As those who are adopted, we are His "children, heirs also, heirs of God and fellow heirs with Christ." We may "suffer with Him" but that is "so that we may also be glorified with *Him*" (see Rom. 8:17).

RECONCILIATION

ROMANS 5:8–11

But God demonstrates His own love toward us, in that while we were yet sinners, Christ died for us. [9] Much more then, having now been justified by His blood, we shall be saved from the wrath *of God* through Him. [10] For if while we were enemies we were reconciled to God through the death of His Son, much more, having been reconciled, we shall be saved by His life. [11] And not only this, but we also exult in God through our Lord Jesus Christ, through whom we have now received the reconciliation.

2 CORINTHIANS 5:18–20

Now all *these* things are from God, who reconciled us to Himself through Christ and gave us the ministry of reconciliation, [19] namely, that God was in Christ reconciling the world to Himself, not counting their trespasses against them, and He has committed to us the word of reconciliation. [20] Therefore, we are ambassadors for Christ, as though God were making an appeal through us; we beg you on behalf of Christ, be reconciled to God.

EPHESIANS 2:16

And might reconcile them both in one body to God through the cross, by it having put to death the enmity.

COLOSSIANS 1:20–21

And through Him to reconcile all things to Himself, having made peace through the blood of His cross; through Him, *I say*, whether things on earth or things in heaven. [21] And although you were formerly alienated and hostile in mind, *engaged* in evil deeds.

The notion of reconciliation is predicated on the reality that men are at enmity with God (see Rom. 8:7; James 4:4). By faith in Christ's work on the cross this enmity is removed. The Greek term for reconciliation is *katallassó* and has the notion of "effecting a change." Reconciliation is a work of God and it is something believers receive. Because they have this provision, believers are admonished to "be reconciled to God." This reconciliation is available to the world, so believers are "ambassadors for Christ" and they call unbelievers to come in faith and "be reconciled to God." There will be an ultimate reconciliation of all things "on earth or things in heaven."

SANCTIFICATION

Necessity

> **HEBREWS 12:14**
> Pursue peace with all men, and the sanctification without which no one will see the Lord.

> **1 PETER 1:15–16**
> But like the Holy One who called you, be holy yourselves also in all *your* behavior; [16] because it is written, "YOU SHALL BE HOLY, FOR I AM HOLY."

Justification is the legal declaration that the one who has faith in Christ stands in the righteousness of Christ before God. Sanctification concerns the practical righteousness in which the believer in Christ is to live and grow. This sanctification is not optional. A genuine believer, one who is truly in union with Christ, will demonstrate that union by increasing lifelong practical holiness.

God Sanctifies

> **EPHESIANS 5:25–26**
> Husbands, love your wives, just as Christ also loved the church and gave Himself up for her, [26] so that He might sanctify her, having cleansed her by the washing of water with the word.

> **PHILIPPIANS 2:13**
> For it is God who is at work in you, both to will and to work for *His* good pleasure.

> **1 THESSALONIANS 5:23**
> Now may the God of peace Himself sanctify you entirely; and may your spirit and soul and body be preserved complete, without blame at the coming of our Lord Jesus Christ.

HEBREWS 12:9–10

Furthermore, we had earthly fathers to discipline us, and we respected them; shall we not much rather be subject to the Father of spirits, and live? [10] For they disciplined us for a short time as seemed best to them, but He *disciplines us* for *our* good, so that we may share His holiness.

1 PETER 1:2

According to the foreknowledge of God the Father, by the sanctifying work of the Spirit, to obey Jesus Christ and be sprinkled with His blood: May grace and peace be yours in the fullest measure.

Sanctification is a work of God. It is a work of the Father ("the Father of spirits"), it is a work of the Son (who sanctifies and cleanses His church), and it is a work of the Holy Spirit. Paul expresses this without reference to one particular person of the Trinity: "Now may the God of peace sanctify you entirely."

Man Participates in Sanctification

ROMANS 8:13

For if you are living according to the flesh, you must die; but if by the Spirit you are putting to death the deeds of the body, you will live.

2 CORINTHIANS 7:1

Therefore, having these promises, beloved, let us cleanse ourselves from all defilement of flesh and spirit, perfecting holiness in the fear of God.

GALATIANS 5:24

Now those who belong to Christ Jesus have crucified the flesh with its passions and desires.

PHILIPPIANS 2:12

So then, my beloved, just as you have always obeyed, not as in my presence only, but now much more in my absence, work out your salvation with fear and trembling.

EPHESIANS 2:10

For we are His workmanship, created in Christ Jesus for good works, which God prepared beforehand so that we would walk in them.

PHILIPPIANS 3:13–14

Brethren, I do not regard myself as having laid hold of *it* yet; but one thing *I do*: forgetting what *lies* behind and reaching forward to what *lies* ahead, [14] I press on toward the goal for the prize of the upward call of God in Christ Jesus.

2 PETER 1:5

Now for this very reason also, applying all diligence, in your faith supply moral excellence, and in *your* moral excellence, knowledge.

1 JOHN 1:8–9

If we say that we have no sin, we are deceiving ourselves and the truth is not in us. [9] If we confess our sins, He is faithful and righteous to forgive us our sins and to cleanse us from all unrighteousness.

1 JOHN 3:3

And everyone who has this hope *fixed* on Him purifies himself, just as He is pure.

Sanctification requires the responsible participation of the believer. It is incorrect to suggest that there is God's work and then there is man's work in sanctification as if each has a part to do. "God's working in us is not suspended because we work, nor our working suspended because God works. Neither is the relation strictly one of co-operation as if God did his part and we did ours so that the conjunction or co-ordination of both produced the required result. God works in us and we also work. But the relation is that *because* God works we work. All working out of salvation on our part is the effect of God's working in us."[21] In those terms, sanctification is God's work and the believer himself is the instrument which God uses in the work of sanctification for "we are His workmanship." God uses the means of the instructions and admonitions of Scripture (e.g., to put to death the deeds of the body, to cleanse themselves from all defilement, to crucify the flesh with its passions and desires, to work out their salvation with fear and trembling, to apply all diligence to pursue moral excellence, and to purify themselves) to motivate and accomplish the believer's sanctification.

Believers do not attain perfection in this life but they "press on" in the pursuit of greater sanctification.

ASSURANCE AND PERSEVERANCE

JOHN 6:37–39

"All that the Father gives Me will come to Me, and the one who comes to Me I will certainly not cast out. [38] For I have come down from heaven, not to do My own will, but the will of Him who sent Me. [39] This is the will of Him who sent Me, that of all that He has given Me I lose nothing, but raise it up on the last day."

JOHN 10:27–28

"My sheep hear My voice, and I know them, and they follow Me; [28] and I give eternal life to them, and they will never perish; and no one will snatch them out of My hand."

ROMANS 8:16, 31–39

The Spirit Himself testifies with our spirit that we are children of God. . . .

[31] What then shall we say to these things? If God *is* for us, who *is* against us? [32] He who did not spare His own Son, but delivered Him over for us all, how will He not also with Him freely give us all things? [33] Who will bring a charge against God's elect? God is the one who justifies; [34] who is the one who condemns? Christ Jesus is He who died, yes, rather who was raised, who is at the right hand of God, who also intercedes for us. [35] Who will separate us from the love of Christ? Will tribulation, or distress, or persecution, or famine, or nakedness, or peril, or sword? [36] Just as it is written,

"FOR YOUR SAKE WE ARE BEING PUT TO DEATH ALL DAY LONG;
WE WERE CONSIDERED AS SHEEP TO BE SLAUGHTERED."

[37] But in all these things we overwhelmingly conquer through Him who loved us. [38] For I am convinced that neither death, nor life, nor angels, nor principalities, nor things present, nor things to come, nor powers, [39] nor

height, nor depth, nor any other created thing, will be able to separate us from the love of God, which is in Christ Jesus our Lord.

PHILIPPIANS 1:6

For I am confident of this very thing, that He who began a good work in you will perfect it until the day of Christ Jesus.

2 TIMOTHY 1:12

For this reason I also suffer these things, but I am not ashamed; for I know whom I have believed and I am convinced that He is able to guard what I have entrusted to Him until that day.

1 PETER 1:3–5

Blessed be the God and Father of our Lord Jesus Christ, who according to His great mercy has caused us to be born again to a living hope through the resurrection of Jesus Christ from the dead, ⁴ to *obtain* an inheritance *which is* imperishable and undefiled and will not fade away, reserved in heaven for you, ⁵ who are protected by the power of God through faith for a salvation ready to be revealed in the last time.

The assurance of a believer is an assurance of Christ and His work on our behalf; it is confidence in the promises of Christ and the power of Christ. This is not a promise that no matter what happens after a profession of faith in Christ (i.e., life of sin or life of holiness) one may be assured of eternal life. This doctrine is the assurance that nothing can prevent a genuine believer from persevering in his or her faith and commitment to Christ.

GLORIFICATION

ROMANS 8:29

For those whom He foreknew, He also predestined *to become* conformed to the image of His Son, so that He would be the firstborn among many brethren.

1 CORINTHIANS 15:53

For this perishable must put on the imperishable, and this mortal must put on immortality.

1 JOHN 3:2

Beloved, now we are children of God, and it has not appeared as yet what we will be. We know that when He appears, we will be like Him, because we will see Him just as He is.

Glorification is the final step in the application of redemption and is a work of God entirely. It is the state of believers when their legal standing in justification and the actual holiness at which sanctification aims are fully realized. The glorified saint is fully conformed to the image of Christ and ultimately will be given an immortal body just like the resurrected body of Christ.

1. Louis Berkhof, *Systematic Theology*, 4th ed. (Grand Rapids, MI: William B. Eerdmans Publishing Company, 1939), 415.

2. Grudem, *Systematic Theology*, 686–87.

3. Morris, *Romans*, 336.

4. See David N. Steele, Curtis C. Thomas, and S. Lance Quinn, *The Five Points of Calvinism: Defined, Defended, and Documented* (Phillipsburg, NJ: P&R Publishing, 2004).

5. Murray, *Redemption*, 63.

6. Mounce, "World," *Expository Dictionary*, 808.

7. Berkhof, *Systematic Theology*, 415–16.

8. Ibid., 468.

9. Anthony A. Hoekema, *Saved by Grace* (Grand Rapids, MI: William B. Eerdmans Publishing Company, 1989), 124–27.

10. Ibid., 127.

11. John MacArthur, *The Gospel According to Jesus: What Is Authentic Faith?* (Grand Rapids, MI: Zondervan, 2008), 179.

12. Ibid., 190.

13. Ibid., 189; see Berkhof, *Systematic Theology*, 503–05.

14. Bruce Demarest, *The Cross and Salvation: The Doctrine of Salvation* (Wheaton, IL: Crossway Books, 1997), 345.

15. Morris, *Romans*, 173.

16. Philip H. Eveson, *The Great Exchange: Justification by Faith Alone* (Leominster, UK: Day One Publications, 1996), 193.

17. John MacArthur, *The MacArthur New Testament Commentary: James* (Chicago: Moody Publishers, 1998), 137.

18. Morris, *The Atonement*, 121.

19. Ibid., 120–21.

20. Murray, *Redemption*, 161.

21. Ibid., 148–49.

CHAPTER 8

ANGELS

Angelology

Angelology is the study of the existence and nature of angels, as well as Satan and demons.

GOOD ANGELS

Existence: Nature and Functions

GENESIS 3:24

So He drove the man out; and at the east of the garden of Eden He stationed the cherubim and the flaming sword which turned every direction to guard the way to the tree of life.

GENESIS 19:1A, 5A, 10, 12–13

Now the two angels came to Sodom in the evening as Lot was sitting in the gate of Sodom. . . .

⁵ And they called to Lot and said to him, "Where are the men who came to you tonight?". . .

¹⁰ But the men reached out their hands and brought Lot into the house with them, and shut the door.

¹² Then the *two* men said to Lot, "Whom else have you here? A son-in-law, and your sons, and your daughters, and whomever you have in the city, bring *them* out of the place; ¹³ for we are about to destroy this place,

because their outcry has become so great before the LORD that the LORD has sent us to destroy it."

GENESIS 28:12

He had a dream, and behold, a ladder was set on the earth with its top reaching to heaven; and behold, the angels of God were ascending and descending on it.

ISAIAH 6:1–3

In the year of King Uzziah's death I saw the Lord sitting on a throne, lofty and exalted, with the train of His robe filling the temple. [2] Seraphim stood above Him, each having six wings: with two he covered his face, and with two he covered his feet, and with two he flew. [3] And one called out to another and said,

"Holy, Holy, Holy, is the LORD of hosts,
The whole earth is full of His glory."

LUKE 1:11

And an angel of the Lord appeared to him, standing to the right of the altar of incense. (There is a conversation, see Luke 1:18–19).

LUKE 2:9–10, 13–14

And an angel of the Lord suddenly stood before them, and the glory of the Lord shone around them; and they were terribly frightened. [10] But the angel said to them, "Do not be afraid; for behold, I bring you good news of great joy which will be for all the people. . . .

[13] And suddenly there appeared with the angel a multitude of the heavenly host praising God and saying,

[14] "Glory to God in the highest,
And on earth peace among men with whom He is pleased."

ACTS 5:19–20

But during the night an angel of the Lord opened the gates of the prison, and taking them out he said, [20] "Go, stand and speak to the people in the temple the whole message of this Life."

ACTS 8:26A

But an angel of the Lord spoke to Philip saying, "Get up and go south to the road that descends from Jerusalem to Gaza."

> **ACTS 12:7**
>
> And behold, an angel of the Lord suddenly appeared and a light shone in the cell; and he struck Peter's side and woke him up, saying, "Get up quickly." And his chains fell off his hands.

> **HEBREWS 1:4, 6–7, 14**
>
> Having become as much better than the angels, as He has inherited a more excellent name than they. . . .
>
> ⁶And when He again brings the firstborn into the world, He says,
>
> "AND LET ALL THE ANGELS OF GOD WORSHIP HIM."
>
> ⁷And of the angels He says,
>
> "WHO MAKES HIS ANGELS WINDS,
>
> AND HIS MINISTERS A FLAME OF FIRE." . . .
>
> ¹⁴Are they not all ministering spirits, sent out to render service for the sake of those who will inherit salvation?

> **REVELATION 5:11**
>
> Then I looked, and I heard the voice of many angels around the throne and the living creatures and the elders; and the number of them was myriads of myriads, and thousands of thousands.

There can be little doubt that the Bible reveals the existence of angels. The Hebrew term translated for angels is *mal'akh* and appears 213 times in the Old Testament. The Greek term *angelos* occurs 176 times in the New Testament. The Greek term means "messenger," or "ambassador" and conveys something of the nature and functions of angels. The appearances of angels reveal that they have personal qualities (personhood): they can converse with humans (intellect), they express joy and praise at Jesus' birth (emotions), and they give direction and have an evident desire to worship God (will).

The angels can appear as men but have capacities and power that make it clear they are transcendent, living creatures of God. Angels serve God as messengers of judgment, they give Him praise, and they reveal significant developments in the progress of God's program (i.e., to Daniel in Daniel 9 and to Mary in Luke 1). There are at least two classes of angels: cherubim, whose main function is service, and seraphim (mentioned only in Isaiah 6; literally "burning ones") whose main function appears to be worship. The number of angels is finite but unfathomably large.

Angels are called "ministering spirits," which means they are servants of God. Angels serve God by praising Him and they provide unseen protection of believers (see Ps. 34:7; 35:5–6). "Ministering (*leitourgika*) does not convey the idea of slavery, but of official functioning. [Angels] have been duly commissioned and sent forth (*apostellomena*) with the responsibility of aiding believers. . . . Furthermore, this is true of all of them, regardless of what rank they may hold."[1]

Jesus' References to Angels

MATTHEW 18:10

"See that you do not despise one of these little ones, for I say to you that their angels in heaven continually see the face of My Father who is in heaven."

MATTHEW 22:30

"For in the resurrection they neither marry nor are given in marriage, but are like angels in heaven."

MATTHEW 24:36

"But of that day and hour no one knows, not even the angels of heaven, nor the Son, but the Father alone."

LUKE 12:8–9

"And I say to you, everyone who confesses Me before men, the Son of Man will confess him also before the angels of God; [9] but he who denies Me before men will be denied before the angels of God."

LUKE 15:10

"In the same way, I tell you, there is joy in the presence of the angels of God over one sinner who repents."

Jesus' references to angels confirm their existence and reveal several important realities about them. The angels both "see the face of God" and in some capacity serve the saints of God; "these little ones" (Matt. 18:10) is probably a reference to believers.[2] The angels do not have gender and do not marry (although they typically appear as men; see Gen. 19; the only two named angels are male, see **Named Angels**). Angels are not omniscient. Angels are interested in the testimony of believers, and they take joy in the salvation of sinners (see 1 Peter 1:12).

THE ANGELS' SERVICE TO JESUS

They Announced His Birth

> **LUKE 1:26–27**
> Now in the sixth month the angel Gabriel was sent from God to a city in Galilee called Nazareth, [27] to a virgin engaged to a man whose name was Joseph, of the descendants of David; and the virgin's name was Mary.

They Protected Him as an Infant

> **MATTHEW 2:13A**
> Now when they had gone, behold, an angel of the Lord appeared to Joseph in a dream and said, "Get up! Take the Child and His mother and flee to Egypt."

They Served Him in His Earthly Ministry

> **MATTHEW 4:11**
> Then the devil left Him; and behold, angels came and *began* to minister to Him.

They Announced His Resurrection

> **MATTHEW 28:5–6**
> The angel said to the women, "Do not be afraid; for I know that you are looking for Jesus who has been crucified. [6] He is not here, for He has risen, just as He said. Come, see the place where He was lying."

They Explained His Ascension

ACTS 1:10–11

And as they were gazing intently into the sky while He was going, behold, two men in white clothing stood beside them. [11] They also said, "Men of Galilee, why do you stand looking into the sky? This Jesus, who has been taken up from you into heaven, will come in just the same way as you have watched Him go into heaven."

They Will Accompany Him at His Second Coming

MATTHEW 25:31

"But when the Son of Man comes in His glory, and all the angels with Him, then He will sit on His glorious throne."

The angels' service to Jesus not only reveals something of the nature and function of angels but is an indication of the transcendent importance of His incarnation, His life, His ministry, and His second coming. These magnificent, powerful, heavenly beings are the obedient servants of the Son of God.

NAMED ANGELS

Michael

DANIEL 10:13

"But the prince of the kingdom of Persia was withstanding me for twenty-one days; then behold, Michael, one of the chief princes, came to help me, for I had been left there with the kings of Persia."

JUDE 9

But Michael the archangel, when he disputed with the devil and argued about the body of Moses, did not dare pronounce against him a railing judgment, but said, "The Lord rebuke you!"

REVELATION 12:7 (SEE LUKE 1:19, 26)
And there was war in heaven, Michael and his angels waging war with the dragon. The dragon and his angels waged war.

Gabriel

DANIEL 8:16
And I heard the voice of a man between *the banks of* Ulai, and he called out and said, "Gabriel, give this *man* an understanding of the vision."

DANIEL 9:21
While I was still speaking in prayer, then the man Gabriel, whom I had seen in the vision previously, came to me in *my* extreme weariness about the time of the evening offering.

SATAN

Existence/Names/Activities

GENESIS 3:1A, 2A, 14A
Now the serpent was more crafty than any beast of the field which the LORD God had made. . . .
2a The woman said to the serpent. . . .
14a The LORD God said to the serpent.

1 CHRONICLES 21:1
Then Satan stood up against Israel and moved David to number Israel.

JOB 1:6
Now there was a day when the sons of God came to present themselves before the LORD, and Satan also came among them.

ZECHARIAH 3:1–2
Then he showed me Joshua the high priest standing before the angel of the LORD, and Satan standing at his right hand to accuse him. 2 The LORD said to Satan, "The LORD rebuke you, Satan! Indeed, the LORD who has chosen Jerusalem rebuke you! Is this not a brand plucked from the fire?"

MATTHEW 4:1

Then Jesus was led up by the Spirit into the wilderness to be tempted by the devil.

MATTHEW 12:24

But when the Pharisees heard *this*, they said, "This man casts out demons only by Beelzebul the ruler of the demons."

MATTHEW 13:19A (SEE 13:39)

"When anyone hears the word of the kingdom and does not understand it, the evil *one* comes and snatches away what has been sown in his heart."

JOHN 8:44

"You are of *your* father the devil, and you want to do the desires of your father. He was a murderer from the beginning, and does not stand in the truth because there is no truth in him. Whenever he speaks a lie, he speaks from his own *nature*, for he is a liar and the father of lies."

JOHN 12:31

"Now judgment is upon this world; now the ruler of this world will be cast out."

2 CORINTHIANS 4:4

In whose case the god of this world has blinded the minds of the unbelieving so that they might not see the light of the gospel of the glory of Christ, who is the image of God.

2 CORINTHIANS 11:14

No wonder, for even Satan disguises himself as an angel of light.

EPHESIANS 2:2

In which you formerly walked according to the course of this world, according to the prince of the power of the air, of the spirit that is now working in the sons of disobedience.

JAMES 4:7

Submit therefore to God. Resist the devil and he will flee from you.

> **1 PETER 5:8**
>
> Be of sober *spirit*, be on the alert. Your adversary, the devil, prowls around like a roaring lion, seeking someone to devour.

> **REVELATION 9:11**
>
> They have as king over them, the angel of the abyss; his name in Hebrew is Abaddon, and in the Greek he has the name Apollyon.

> **REVELATION 12:9, 17**
>
> And the great dragon was thrown down, the serpent of old who is called the devil and Satan, who deceives the whole world; he was thrown down to the earth, and his angels were thrown down with him. . . .
> [17] So the dragon was enraged with the woman, and went off to make war with the rest of her children, who keep the commandments of God and hold to the testimony of Jesus.

> **REVELATION 20:10**
>
> And the devil who deceived them was thrown into the lake of fire and brimstone, where the beast and the false prophet are also; and they will be tormented day and night forever and ever.

As with the angels, there is no question that Scripture reveals the existence of Satan. That he actually has personhood can be seen in the traits of personality attributed to him in Scripture: intellect (he speaks and reasons); emotions (he has anger, Rev. 12:17); he demonstrates will (see Isaiah 14 under **The Fall of Satan**). He has several names that reveal his character: "Satan" means "adversary," and he is an adversary against God, God's plans, and God's people. "Devil" means "slanderer" or "accuser." The devil "slanders God" and "accuses" the people of God (see Job 1). The names "Abaddon" and "Apollyon" refer to his work of "destruction" or simply the "destroyer." He is quintessentially "the evil one" (see Matt. 13:19) (Greek *ponēros*), and as such he is utterly opposed to the righteousness, goodness, and justice of God. He is the "serpent of old" and "the dragon" to come, each time opposing and blaspheming God.

He is called "the father of lies" because he seeks to subvert the truth of God with lies as he did with Eve in Genesis 3. He is called "the ruler of this world," "the god of this world," and "the prince of the power of the air," not because he rules it as an independent monarch but because the world itself is in rebellion to God and is under Satan's sway. His tactics are lies, deception (coming as an "angel of light"), false teaching, promoting evil, and disobedience to God. He is as relentless as a hungry lion seeking its prey. However, Satan does not have free reign. He is under the authority of God at all times, he can be resisted, and his doom is sure (see Gen. 3:15b).

The Fall of Satan

ISAIAH 14:12–15

"How you have fallen from heaven,
O star of the morning, son of the dawn!
You have been cut down to the earth,
You who have weakened the nations!
13 "But you said in your heart,
'I will ascend to heaven;
I will raise my throne above the stars of God,
And I will sit on the mount of assembly
In the recesses of the north.
14 I will ascend above the heights of the clouds;
I will make myself like the Most High.'
15 Nevertheless you will be thrust down to Sheol,
To the recesses of the pit."

EZEKIEL 28:12–16

"Son of man, take up a lamentation over the king of Tyre and say to him,
'Thus says the Lord GOD,

"You had the seal of perfection,
Full of wisdom and perfect in beauty.
13 "You were in Eden, the garden of God;
Every precious stone was your covering:
The ruby, the topaz and the diamond;
The beryl, the onyx and the jasper;
The lapis lazuli, the turquoise and the emerald;
And the gold, the workmanship of your settings and sockets,
Was in you.

> On the day that you were created
> They were prepared.
> ¹⁴ "You were the anointed cherub who covers,
> And I placed you *there*.
> You were on the holy mountain of God;
> You walked in the midst of the stones of fire.
> ¹⁵ "You were blameless in your ways
> From the day you were created
> Until unrighteousness was found in you.
> ¹⁶ "By the abundance of your trade
> You were internally filled with violence,
> And you sinned;
> Therefore I have cast you as profane
> From the mountain of God.
> And I have destroyed you, O covering cherub,
> From the midst of the stones of fire.""'"

The fall of man is recorded in Genesis 3, but that was not the origin of evil in God's creation. Genesis 3 begins with "Now the serpent . . ." That entity was Satan (see **Satan: Existence/Names/Activities**) and he was already the malevolent archenemy of his creator God when he made his first appearance in Scripture. In Genesis there is no explanation of how Satan came to be the tempter in Genesis 3 and so the logical questions are: when did Satan fall, how did Satan fall, and what was the nature of Satan's sin?

With respect to the first question, there is very little in Scripture to pinpoint the time of Satan's fall other than to say it must have happened sometime between the end of the creation week (see Gen. 1:31 where all that God had made was still "very good") and Genesis 3:1.

With respect to question two, many have turned to Isaiah 14:12–15 and Ezekiel 28:1–19, seeing them as texts that describe the fall of Satan. Others hold that these texts are judgment taunts against Ancient Near Eastern (ANE) kings (of Babylon in Isaiah 14:14 and of Tyre in Ezekiel 28:2, 12). Several reasons argue for the former understanding. First, (as will be noted below) the language clearly exceeds any literal application to a human king, no matter how great his megalomania. Second, even if the language is taken as hyperbolic, that is, describing in hyperbolic terms the attitudes of ANE kings, the question is: What is the referent of this hyperbolic language? That is, where did these descriptions come from? It seems that these kings are being likened to some exemplar or prototype. Thus, even if the immediate referents in the mind of Isaiah and Ezekiel are ANE kings, it seems that they are regarded as mere antitypes of another entity whose attitude and actions is the inspiration their own. Third, there are other instances in Scripture where a prophecy, virtually seamlessly, refers to two persons at the same time. The prophecy of Nathan in 2 Samuel 7 is an example. In that text, the promise made to David is that he will have a son who will establish a kingdom and sit upon David's throne in Jerusalem (2 Sam. 7:12–16). Several of the descriptions in that prophecy clearly point to David's son Solomon (see 2 Sam. 7:13a and 14), but others point to a greater son—Jesus Christ, whose kingdom and throne will be established forever (see 2 Sam. 7:13b, 16). Something of the same phenomenon appears to be happening in Isaiah 14 and Ezekiel 28; within these two passages are references to an ANE king and references to Satan.

While it is true that "exaggerated and extravagant language was used in the (ANE) records when the king was being described,"[3] it seems that the language used in both of these texts describes an entity who is more than human. He was called "star of the morning, son of the dawn"; his abode, from which he has fallen, was "heaven" and "the holy mountain of God," "in the midst of the stones of fire" (probably a reference to the presence of God); he was active in "Eden, the garden of God" (a clear reference to Genesis 3); his order of being as a creature ("you were created") was angelic and lofty, indeed, he was "the anointed cherub who covers" (he was an angel with an elevated rank); his original moral state was faultless ("You had the seal of perfection"; "You were blameless in all your ways"); and he was beautiful like the beauty of many precious stones ("Every precious stone was your covering"). It seems not only arguable but preferable to take the ultimate referent in both passages as Satan.

The sin of Satan is described in terms of an inordinate aspiration. Five expressions of his overweening will ("I will ascend to heaven," "I will raise my throne above the stars of God" [possibly other angels], "I will sit on the mount of the assembly" [i.e., over the other angels]; "I will ascend to the heights of the clouds," "I will make myself like God") reveal a heart surfeited with conceit and pride (see 1 Tim. 3:6). As a result of this blasphemous pride, Satan was expelled from his lofty position ("How you have fallen from heaven," "Therefore I have cast you as profane, From the mountain of God") and he will "be thrust down to Sheol, To the recesses of the pit" (see Rev. 20:3).[4]

DEMONS

Existence/Names/Activities

1 KINGS 22:23

"Now therefore, behold, the LORD has put a deceiving spirit in the mouth of all these your prophets; and the LORD has proclaimed disaster against you."

MATTHEW 8:16

When evening came, they brought to Him many who were demon-possessed; and He cast out the spirits with a word, and healed all who were ill.

MATTHEW 8:28–29

When He came to the other side into the country of the Gadarenes, two men who were demon-possessed met Him as they were coming out of the tombs. *They were* so extremely violent that no one could pass by that way. ²⁹ And they cried out, saying, "What business do we have with each other, Son of God? Have You come here to torment us before the time?"

MATTHEW 10:1 (SEE MARK 1:27)

Jesus summoned His twelve disciples and gave them authority over unclean spirits, to cast them out, and to heal every kind of disease and every kind of sickness.

MATTHEW 25:41

Then He will also say to those on His left, "Depart from Me, accursed ones, into the eternal fire which has been prepared for the devil and his angels."

> **1 TIMOTHY 4:1**
>
> But the Spirit explicitly says that in later times some will fall away from the faith, paying attention to deceitful spirits and doctrines of demons.

> **JUDE 6**
>
> And angels who did not keep their own domain, but abandoned their proper abode, He has kept in eternal bonds under darkness for the judgment of the great day,

> **REVELATION 12:9**
>
> And the great dragon was thrown down, the serpent of old who is called the devil and Satan, who deceives the whole world; he was thrown down to the earth, and his angels were thrown down with him.

As with the holy angels and Satan, there is no question that Scripture reveals the existence of demons. They are angels who fell with Satan and cooperate with him in his opposition to God. Like their master, Satan, they are deceivers and they promote false doctrines. They are the source of misery in those over whom they gain dominance. They can exert a powerful influence on the vulnerable but, as Christ proved in His ministry, they are no match for God's power. Believers should be wary of demons but not fear them. Some demons are already incarcerated; and the end of all demons, as with Satan, is eternal punishment.

---

1. Homer A. Kent, Jr., *The Epistle to the Hebrews: A Commentary* (Winona Lake, IN: BMH Books, 1972), 46.
2. MacArthur, *Matthew 16–23*, 114.
3. Alfred Martin and John Martin, *Isaiah: The Glory of the Messiah* (Chicago: Moody Publishers, 1983), 72.
4. For further details on these verses and the fall of Satan, see C. Fred Dickason, *Angels: Elect and Evil* (Chicago: Moody Publishers, 1995), 135–45.

CHAPTER 9

THE CHURCH

Ecclesiology

Ecclesiology is the study of the nature, distinctions, and origin of the church, as well as the metaphors, order, and function of the church.

THE NATURE OF THE CHURCH

The Local Church

The local church is a body of (professed) believers who assemble in a particular location or setting, with recognized leadership, with mutual commitments (to practice marks and duties of the church; see **The Marks of the Church**, and **The Functions of the Church**), and with a recognized membership. The local church is a mixed body with those who are genuine Christians and some who may be merely professed believers (see the parable of the wheat and the tares, Matt. 13:24–30).

> **ACTS 8:1B (SEE 11:22)**
> And on that day a great persecution began against the church in Jerusalem, and they were all scattered throughout the regions of Judea and Samaria, except the apostles.

1 CORINTHIANS 1:2 (SEE 2 COR.1:1)
To the church of God which is at Corinth, to those who have been sancti-fied in Christ Jesus, saints by calling, with all who in every place call on the name of our Lord Jesus Christ, their *Lord* and ours.

GALATIANS 1:2
And all the brethren who are with me,
To the churches of Galatia.

1 THESSALONIANS 1:1B
To the church of the Thessalonians in God the Father and the Lord Jesus Christ: Grace to you and peace.

In each of these texts the geographical designations (sometimes regions and sometimes cities) indicate that the term *church* (Greek *ekklēsia*) is often used of an identifiable group of Christians in a particular geographical location. It is assumed that this group meets in some regular fashion for specific reasons and activities related to devotion to Christ (see Acts 2:42, "They were contin-ually devoting themselves to the apostles' teaching and to fellowship, to the breaking of bread and to prayer").

ROMANS 16:1, 5
I commend to you our sister Phoebe, who is a servant of the church which is at Cenchrea. . . .
⁵ also *greet* the church that is in their house. Greet Epaenetus, my beloved, who is the first convert to Christ from Asia.

Paul's reference to "the church that is in their house" indicates that the term *church* (Greek *ekklēsia*) can be used of a gathering of believers in a home or any similar setting. A "church" in a city or region need not include the entire Christian population of a city or region.

The Universal Church

The universal church is made up of all regenerate Christians, from Pentecost to the present—those who are already in heaven and those who are still liv-ing on earth. All who come to saving faith in Jesus Christ are also members of the universal church, which is "the assembly and church of the firstborn who are enrolled in heaven" (see Heb. 12:23).

> **MATTHEW 16:18**
>
> "I also say to you that you are Peter, and upon this rock I will build My church; and the gates of Hades will not overpower it."

> **EPHESIANS 1:22–23**
>
> And He put all things in subjection under His feet, and gave Him as head over all things to the church, ²³ which is His body, the fullness of Him who fills all in all.

> **EPHESIANS 4:15–16**
>
> But speaking the truth in love, we are to grow up in all *aspects* into Him who is the head, *even* Christ, ¹⁶ from whom the whole body, being fitted and held together by what every joint supplies, according to the proper working of each individual part, causes the growth of the body for the building up of itself in love.

> **COLOSSIANS 1:18**
>
> He is also head of the body, the church; and He is the beginning, the firstborn from the dead, so that He Himself will come to have first place in everything.

These uses of the term *church* (Greek *ekklēsia*) refer to the "universal church" or the entire "body of Christ" (see 1 Cor. 12:12–13; Eph. 4:4). This use of the term in such contexts does not designate a local group of Christian believers but the entire number of true Christian believers throughout the church age (see Heb. 12:23).

The Church Is Not Israel

The church is a unique institution. It is not a venue for entertainment, it is not a business, it is not a social club, it is not one ethnic people, it is not a nation— hence it is not the continuation of, nor a replacement of, the nation of Israel. The church is a body (see 1 Cor. 12:27) and the nation of Israel is just that—a nation; these are two entirely distinct institutions.

ROMANS 9:6

But *it is* not as though the word of God has failed. For they are not all Israel who are *descended* from Israel.

GALATIANS 3:7–9

Therefore, be sure that it is those who are of faith who are sons of Abraham. [8] The Scripture, foreseeing that God would justify the Gentiles by faith, preached the gospel beforehand to Abraham, *saying*, "ALL THE NATIONS WILL BE BLESSED IN YOU." [9] So then those who are of faith are blessed with Abraham, the believer.

GALATIANS 3:25–29

But now that faith has come, we are no longer under a tutor. [26] For you are all sons of God through faith in Christ Jesus. [27] For all of you who were baptized into Christ have clothed yourselves with Christ. [28] There is neither Jew nor Greek, there is neither slave nor free man, there is neither male nor female; for you are all one in Christ Jesus. [29] And if you belong to Christ, then you are Abraham's descendants, heirs according to promise.

GALATIANS 6:16

And those who will walk by this rule, peace and mercy *be* upon them, and upon the Israel of God.

EPHESIANS 3:4–6

By referring to this, when you read you can understand my insight into the mystery of Christ, [5] which in other generations was not made known to the sons of men, as it has now been revealed to His holy apostles and prophets in the Spirit; [6] *to be specific*, that the Gentiles are fellow heirs and fellow members of the body, and fellow partakers of the promise in Christ Jesus through the gospel.

These several passages have been the focus of the debate over the identity of the nation of Israel and the church. In Romans 9:6b Paul is not suggesting that the church is the true Israel. In the context he has in mind the physical descendants of Abraham (see Rom. 9:3), and he is observing the simple fact that throughout the history of the nation there were those who actually lived as true believers in Israel and those who did not. In Galatians 3 Paul is not suggesting that those who come to faith in Christ are the "real" descendants of Abraham (as if "faith" replaced physical descent and ethnic identity); he is saying those who come to faith in Christ (i.e., Gentile believers) are *also, in a sense,* "Abraham's descendants, heirs according to promise," because by faith they "belong to Christ" (and Christ is the quintessential heir to the promises of the Abrahamic Covenant). In other words, those who are in Christ (see **Union with Christ**) receive the (soteriological) blessings of the promise because they are in Christ. They do not, however, supersede or replace the nation of Israel in terms of the national promises, especially regarding the land (see **Abrahamic Covenant**; see Rom. 11:29).[1] When Paul refers to the "Israel of God" in Galatians 6:16, he means the godly remnant in national or ethnic Israel. The grammar of this expression will not allow the term *Israel* to be understood as a reference to the church.[2] In the New Testament the term *Israel* always refers to national or ethnic Israel.

In Ephesians 3 Paul refers to the "mystery of Christ." A "mystery" in New Testament terms refers to something revealed in the New Testament that was hidden in the Old Testament.[3] The "mystery of Christ" is the fact that in the era of the church, believing Jews and Gentiles now make up one body, a circumstance never envisioned, and a metaphor never used, of Israel in the Old Testament.[4] "In conclusion, the mystery is not that the Gentiles would be saved because the OT gives evidence for their salvation, but rather that believing Jews and Gentiles are together in Christ. This concept was revolutionary for Jews and Gentiles alike."[5]

THE ORIGIN OF THE CHURCH

Promised by Christ

MATTHEW 16:18

"I also say to you that you are Peter, and upon this rock I will build My church; and the gates of Hades will not overpower it."

Jesus' promise reveals at least three facts about the church. One, His promise "I will" is a future tense verb indicating that the church is not yet in existence prior to, nor during, His earthly ministry but will be inaugurated in the future. Two, that His church will be "built" indicates that it will not appear fully complete but will be progressively assembled (see Eph. 4:12). And three, this church belongs to Christ—it is "My church" which means the members of His church must function under His authority and serve for His purposes. (See the letters to the seven churches in Revelation chapters 2 and 3, as these letters reveal His authority and His purposes.)

Inaugurated at Pentecost

ACTS 2:1–3
When the day of Pentecost had come, they were all together in one place. ² And suddenly there came from heaven a noise like a violent rushing wind, and it filled the whole house where they were sitting. ³ And there appeared to them tongues as of fire distributing themselves, and they rested on each one of them.

ACTS 11:15–18
"And as I began to speak, the Holy Spirit fell upon them just as *He did* upon us at the beginning. ¹⁶ And I remembered the word of the Lord, how He used to say, 'John baptized with water, but you will be baptized with the Holy Spirit.' ¹⁷ Therefore if God gave to them the same gift as *He gave* to us also after believing in the Lord Jesus Christ, who was I that I could stand in God's way?" ¹⁸ When they heard this, they quieted down and glorified God, saying, "Well then, God has granted to the Gentiles also the repentance *that leads* to life."

The "beginning" that Peter refers to in Acts 11 is the beginning of the church which took place on the Day of Pentecost (see Acts 2:1–4) in fulfillment of the promise of Jesus from Acts 1:5b "you will be baptized with the Holy Spirit not many days from now." In 1 Corinthians 12:13a Paul describes the manner by which the church is being built—"For by one Spirit we were all baptized into one body." This is not primarily an endowment that is given to believers but a spiritual reality that happens to them, when they are brought into union with Christ and with His body, the church. This specific baptizing ministry of the Spirit was not operative in the Old Testament because there was no body of Christ, and no Old Testament believer ever was or could be in union with Christ. This baptizing work of the Spirit had been promised by John the Baptist (see Matt. 3:11; Mark 1:8; Luke 3:16; John 1:33) and that promise was still future when Jesus reminded the disciples of it in Acts 1:5. That baptizing work first occurred on the Day of Pentecost as recorded in Acts 2 and confirmed by Peter in Acts 11.

THE ORDER OF THE LOCAL CHURCH

Leadership

ELDERS

ACTS 20:17, 28
From Miletus he sent to Ephesus and called to him the elders of the church. . . .
[28] Be on guard for yourselves and for all the flock, among which the Holy Spirit has made you overseers, to shepherd the church of God which He purchased with His own blood.

EPHESIANS 4:11–12
And He gave some *as* apostles, and some *as* prophets, and some *as* evangelists, and some *as* pastors and teachers, [12] for the equipping of the saints for the work of service, to the building up of the body of Christ.

1 TIMOTHY 5:17
The elders who rule well are to be considered worthy of double honor, especially those who work hard at preaching and teaching.

1 PETER 5:1–2A
Therefore, I exhort the elders among you, as *your* fellow elder and witness of the sufferings of Christ, and a partaker also of the glory that is to be revealed, [2] shepherd the flock of God among you, exercising oversight not under compulsion.

The New Testament does not teach any one of the three commonly recognized forms of church polity—hierarchical, presbyterian, or congregational. There is no "church constitution" given in the New Testament. For the function and governance of the church the New Testament gives instructions to godly men who are charged with "shepherding the flock of God." These men are to meet certain qualifications and they must perform certain duties.

The titles of elder (Greek *presbuteros*), bishop or overseer (Greek *epískopos*), pastor or shepherd (Greek *poimēn*) all refer to essentially the same office. This can be seen by the fact that these titles appear in the same context and refer to the same individuals or office holders. For instance, in speaking to the elders from Ephesus, Paul uses the titles elders, overseers, and shepherds (i.e., pastors) of the same men. Peter exhorts the elders and admonishes them to shepherd their own flocks.

Some elders may serve more in administration ("rule well") and others in preaching and teaching.

Qualifications of Elders

1 TIMOTHY 3:1–7

It is a trustworthy statement: if any man aspires to the office of overseer, it is a fine work he desires *to do*. [2] An overseer, then, must be above reproach, the husband of one wife, temperate, prudent, respectable, hospitable, able to teach, [3] not addicted to wine or pugnacious, but gentle, peaceable, free from the love of money. [4] *He must be* one who manages his own household well, keeping his children under control with all dignity [5] (but if a man does not know how to manage his own household, how will he take care of the church of God?), [6] *and* not a new convert, so that he will not become conceited and fall into the condemnation incurred by the devil. [7] And he must have a good reputation with those outside *the church*, so that he will not fall into reproach and the snare of the devil.

TITUS 1:5–9

For this reason I left you in Crete, that you would set in order what remains and appoint elders in every city as I directed you, [6] *namely*, if any man is above reproach, the husband of one wife, having children who believe, not accused of dissipation or rebellion. [7] For the overseer must be above reproach as God's steward, not self-willed, not quick-tempered, not addicted to wine, not pugnacious, not fond of sordid gain, [8] but hospitable, loving what is good, sensible, just, devout, self-controlled, [9] holding fast the faithful word which is in accordance with the teaching, so that he will be able both to exhort in sound doctrine and to refute those who contradict.

Because the health and progress of the church depends on its leaders, those men must be proven and qualified. "Nothing is more needed in the church than the careful application of the biblical principles of leadership."[6] It is not enough for a man to simply want the office, although a leader should desire the position and not be coerced into serving. The qualifications of the elders have to do with moral character and spiritual maturity, not organizational skill, entrepreneurial ability, or personal charisma. The overall quality of elders is that they are "above reproach" (Greek *anepilēmpton*). The idea is "they cannot be laid hold of," that is, a censure or accusation cannot be successfully held against them. The pastor-elder must be a man of integrity and of impeccable morals; he must be sexually faithful to his wife. The expression "husband of one wife" is a euphemism for sexually pure[7] (i.e., not one who has mistresses or frequents brothels). His children, by their good behavior, must demonstrate his ability to lead with love and discipline. He must be a man who exhibits discretion, dignity, and hospitality. He must have a good reputation, that is, the respect and good repute of others, both inside and outside the church. He must not be controlled by pride, pleasures (such as drinking wine), or the pursuit of personal gain—either fame, power, or wealth. He must not be rash or have a quick temper but rather be a man of gentle-firmness. The term *gentle* (Greek *epieikē*) has the notion of "equitable" or "seemly."

The one skill qualification is "able to teach." This is required so that he can "lead and feed" (i.e., be a shepherd for) the flock. He does this as a "pastor-teacher" (see Eph. 4:11) and by "work[ing] hard at preaching and teaching" (see 1 Tim. 5:17). He must teach sound (Greek *hugiainō*; i.e., "wholesome, healthy") doctrine (see Titus 2:1; 1 Tim. 4:6) so that he is able to refute false teaching. Women cannot be elders (see 1 Tim. 2:12). The pastor-elders are to be mature men, not recent converts or men without training or experience.

DEACONS

Qualifications of Deacons

> **1 TIMOTHY 3:8–12**
> Deacons likewise *must be* men of dignity, not double-tongued, or addicted to much wine or fond of sordid gain, ⁹ *but* holding to the mystery of the faith with a clear conscience. ¹⁰ These men must also first be tested; then let them serve as deacons if they are beyond reproach. ¹¹ Women *must* likewise *be* dignified, not malicious gossips, but temperate, faithful in all things. ¹² Deacons must be husbands of *only* one wife, *and* good managers of *their* children and their own households.

Like the elders, deacons must be men of the highest moral standard. The women mentioned may be the wives of the deacons, or they may be deaconesses.

DUTIES OF ELDERS

To Shepherd

> **ACTS 20:28 (SEE 1 PET. 5:2A)**
> Be on guard for yourselves and for all the flock, among which the Holy Spirit has made you overseers, to shepherd the church of God which He purchased with His own blood.

To Teach

> **1 TIMOTHY 4:11**
> Prescribe and teach these things.

> **2 TIMOTHY 4:1–2**
>
> I solemnly charge *you* in the presence of God and of Christ Jesus, who is to judge the living and the dead, and by His appearing and His kingdom: [2] preach the word; be ready in season *and* out of season; reprove, rebuke, exhort, with great patience and instruction.

To Do the Work of Evangelism

> **2 TIMOTHY 4:5B**
>
> Do the work of an evangelist, fulfill your ministry.

To Care for the Flock

> **1 PETER 5:1–3**
>
> Therefore, I exhort the elders among you, as *your* fellow elder and witness of the sufferings of Christ, and a partaker also of the glory that is to be revealed, [2] shepherd the flock of God among you, exercising oversight not under compulsion, but voluntarily, according to *the will of* God; and not for sordid gain, but with eagerness; [3] nor yet as lording it over those allotted to your charge, but proving to be examples to the flock.

The main idea of Peter's admonition to the elders under his care was that they were to put the care of the flock, the church, before all personal considerations.

To Pray for the Saints

> **JAMES 5:14**
>
> Is anyone among you sick? *Then* he must call for the elders of the church and they are to pray over him, anointing him with oil in the name of the Lord.

Membership

The members of the church are described by a number of metaphors that reveal what the church is "to be" and "to do."

The Metaphors of the Church

FLOCK

JOHN 10:16

"I have other sheep, which are not of this fold; I must bring them also, and they will hear My voice; and they will become one flock *with* one shepherd."

ACTS 20:28 (SEE 1 PET. 5:1–3)

"Be on guard for yourselves and for all the flock, among which the Holy Spirit has made you overseers, to shepherd the church of God which He purchased with His own blood."

The metaphor of the flock of sheep as applied to the church is meant to highlight the vulnerability and dependence of the church on their Good Shepherd, Jesus Christ (see John 10:11, 14).

FAMILY/HOUSEHOLD

EPHESIANS 2:19

So then you are no longer strangers and aliens, but you are fellow citizens with the saints, and are of God's household.

1 PETER 4:17

For *it is* time for judgment to begin with the household of God; and if *it begins* with us first, what *will be* the outcome for those who do not obey the gospel of God?

The metaphors of the flock and of the family as applied to the church are meant to highlight the mutual love and care the members of the church are to have for one another.

BRIDE

EPHESIANS 5:23–27, 32

For the husband is the head of the wife, as Christ also is the head of the church, He Himself *being* the Savior of the body. [24] But as the church is subject to Christ, so also the wives *ought to be* to their husbands in everything.

> [25] Husbands, love your wives, just as Christ also loved the church and gave Himself up for her, [26] so that He might sanctify her, having cleansed her by the washing of water with the word, [27] that He might present to Himself the church in all her glory, having no spot or wrinkle or any such thing; but that she would be holy and blameless. . . .
> [32] This mystery is great; but I am speaking with reference to Christ and the church.

The metaphor of the bride as applied to the church is meant to highlight the love, devotion, and submission the church is to have for her bridegroom, Jesus Christ (see Eph. 5:22–24). This metaphor is also key to understanding the nature and purpose of the Rapture of the church (see **Rapture of the Church**).

BUILDING/TEMPLE

> **EPHESIANS 2:19–22**
>
> So then you are no longer strangers and aliens, but you are fellow citizens with the saints, and are of God's household, [20] having been built on the foundation of the apostles and prophets, Christ Jesus Himself being the corner *stone*, [21] in whom the whole building, being fitted together, is growing into a holy temple in the Lord, [22] in whom you also are being built together into a dwelling of God in the Spirit.

> **1 CORINTHIANS 3:9–11**
>
> For we are God's fellow workers; you are God's field, God's building. [10] According to the grace of God which was given to me, like a wise master builder I laid a foundation, and another is building on it. But each man must be careful how he builds on it. [11] For no man can lay a foundation other than the one which is laid, which is Jesus Christ.

> **2 CORINTHIANS 6:16**
>
> Or what agreement has the temple of God with idols? For we are the temple of the living God; just as God said,
> "I WILL DWELL IN THEM AND WALK AMONG THEM;
> AND I WILL BE THEIR GOD, AND THEY SHALL BE MY PEOPLE."

1 PETER 2:5
You also, as living stones, are being built up as a spiritual house for a holy priesthood, to offer up spiritual sacrifices acceptable to God through Jesus Christ.

The metaphor of the building and temple as applied to the church is meant to highlight the need for each member to "fit well" with other members, to edify and build up other members, and to align themselves with the cornerstone, Jesus Christ. As a temple collectively, the members are to keep themselves from defilement or anything that would tend to tarnish or despoil the internal purity and external testimony of the church.

BODY

The people are "members" of the body of Christ. This metaphor is unique in that it was never used of Israel in the Old Testament. It highlights the uniqueness of the church, which is not a nation but a body of people "from every nation and *all* tribes and peoples and tongues" (Rev. 7:9).

ROMANS 12:4–5
For just as we have many members in one body and all the members do not have the same function, [5] so we, who are many, are one body in Christ, and individually members one of another.

1 CORINTHIANS 12:12, 14, 18–20, 27
For even as the body is one and *yet* has many members, and all the members of the body, though they are many, are one body, so also is Christ. . . . [14] For the body is not one member, but many. . . . [18] But now God has placed the members, each one of them, in the body, just as He desired. [19] If they were all one member, where would the body be? [20] But now there are many members, but one body. . . . [27] Now you are Christ's body, and individually members of it.

This is the key metaphor of the church and emphasizes its uniqueness. The church is not an "organization" but an "organism." It functions well only when all members care for, show love toward, and live to serve the other members of the body.

CHRIST IS THE "HEAD" OF THE BODY

EPHESIANS 1:22
And He put all things in subjection under His feet, and gave Him as head over all things to the church.

EPHESIANS 4:15 (SEE COL. 2:18–19)
But speaking the truth in love, we are to grow up in all *aspects* into Him who is the head, *even* Christ.

Like a natural body, the church has many members but only one head— Jesus Christ. This means that all the members must remain in constant contact to the head, are to be guided by the head (who coordinates the movement of each member individually), and all are dependent on the head, naturally, for life.

The Responsibilities of Members

SERVING ONE ANOTHER

MATTHEW 23:11
"But the greatest among you shall be your servant."

1 CORINTHIANS 12:7
But to each one is given the manifestation of the Spirit for the common good.

SUBMISSION TO THE LEADERS

HEBREWS 13:7, 17
Remember those who led you, who spoke the word of God to you; and considering the result of their conduct, imitate their faith. . . .
[17] Obey your leaders and submit *to them*, for they keep watch over your souls as those who will give an account. Let them do this with joy and not with grief, for this would be unprofitable for you.

THE MARKS OF THE CHURCH

The marks of the church are the distinguishing and essential elements of the true church. Typically, theologians (especially of the Reformed churches) identified three such marks. The preaching of the Word of God, the regular practice of the ordinances (called by some "sacraments"), and the application of church discipline.[8]

Mark One: Discipline

MATTHEW 18:15–17

"If your brother sins, go and show him his fault in private; if he listens to you, you have won your brother. [16] But if he does not listen *to you*, take one or two more with you, so that BY THE MOUTH OF TWO OR THREE WITNESSES EVERY FACT MAY BE CONFIRMED. [17] If he refuses to listen to them, tell it to the church; and if he refuses to listen even to the church, let him be to you as a Gentile and a tax collector."

GALATIANS 6:1–2

Brethren, even if anyone is caught in any trespass, you who are spiritual, restore such a one in a spirit of gentleness; *each one* looking to yourself, so that you too will not be tempted. [2] Bear one another's burdens, and thereby fulfill the law of Christ.

Mark Two: The Ordinances of the Church

BAPTISM

MATTHEW 28:19

"Go therefore and make disciples of all the nations, baptizing them in the name of the Father and the Son and the Holy Spirit."

ACTS 2:37-38

Now when they heard *this*, they were pierced to the heart, and said to Peter and the rest of the apostles, "Brethren, what shall we do?" [38] Peter *said* to them, "Repent, and each of you be baptized in the name of Jesus

Christ for the forgiveness of your sins; and you will receive the gift of the Holy Spirit."

ACTS 8:36–38

As they went along the road they came to some water; and the eunuch said, "Look! Water! What prevents me from being baptized?" [37] [And Philip said, "If you believe with all your heart, you may." And he answered and said, "I believe that Jesus Christ is the Son of God."] [38] And he ordered the chariot to stop; and they both went down into the water, Philip as well as the eunuch, and he baptized him.

[Verse 37 is not in the best manuscripts, but the sense of that verse is surely the sense of the text and the event.]

ACTS 16:14–15A

A woman named Lydia, from the city of Thyatira, a seller of purple fabrics, a worshiper of God, was listening; and the Lord opened her heart to respond to the things spoken by Paul. [15] And when she and her household had been baptized, she urged us, saying, "If you have judged me to be faithful to the Lord, come into my house and stay."

ACTS 16:31–33

They said, "Believe in the Lord Jesus, and you will be saved, you and your household." [32] And they spoke the word of the Lord to him together with all who were in his house. [33] And he took them that *very* hour of the night and washed their wounds, and immediately he was baptized, he and all his *household*.

LORD'S SUPPER (BREAD AND CUP)

MATTHEW 26:26–28

While they were eating, Jesus took *some* bread, and after a blessing, He broke *it* and gave *it* to the disciples, and said, "Take, eat; this is My body." [27] And when He had taken a cup and given thanks, He gave *it* to them, saying, "Drink from it, all of you; [28] for this is My blood of the covenant, which is poured out for many for forgiveness of sins."

1 CORINTHIANS 11:23–25

For I received from the Lord that which I also delivered to you, that the Lord Jesus in the night in which He was betrayed took bread; [24] and when He had given thanks, He broke it and said, "This is My body, which is for you; do this in remembrance of Me." [25] In the same way *He took* the cup also after supper, saying, "This cup is the new covenant in My blood; do this, as often as you drink *it*, in remembrance of Me."

Mark Three: Teaching/Preaching

ACTS 2:42

They were continually devoting themselves to the apostles' teaching and to fellowship, to the breaking of bread and to prayer.

ACTS 5:42

And every day, in the temple and from house to house, they kept right on teaching and preaching Jesus *as* the Christ.

2 TIMOTHY 4:2 (SEE 1 TIM. 4:11)

Preach the word; be ready in season *and* out of season; reprove, rebuke, exhort, with great patience and instruction.

THE FUNCTIONS OF THE CHURCH

In addition to the marks of the church, the New Testament reveals certain essential functions of the church.

Overall Summary: Assembly

ACTS 2:42

They were continually devoting themselves to the apostles' teaching and to fellowship, to the breaking of bread and to prayer.

HEBREWS 10:25

Not forsaking our own assembling together, as is the habit of some, but encouraging *one another*; and all the more as you see the day drawing near.

A church, to *be* a church, to *function as* a church, must gather together to exhibit the marks of the church and to mutually engage in the functions of a church.

Evangelism

> **MATTHEW 28:19–20**
> "Go therefore and make disciples of all the nations, baptizing them in the name of the Father and the Son and the Holy Spirit, [20] teaching them to observe all that I commanded you; and lo, I am with you always, even to the end of the age."

Edification

> **EPHESIANS 4:15–16**
> But speaking the truth in love, we are to grow up in all *aspects* into Him who is the head, *even* Christ, [16] from whom the whole body, being fitted and held together by what every joint supplies, according to the proper working of each individual part, causes the growth of the body for the building up of itself in love.

Prayer

> **ACTS 4:31A**
> And when they had prayed . . .

> **ACTS 12:5, 12**
> So Peter was kept in the prison, but prayer for him was being made fervently by the church to God. . . .
> [12] And when he realized *this*, he went to the house of Mary, the mother of John who was also called Mark, where many were gathered together and were praying.

> **ACTS 13:3**
> Then, when they had fasted and prayed and laid their hands on them, they sent them away.

ACTS 16:25A

But about midnight Paul and Silas were praying and singing hymns of praise to God.

Worship/Singing

ACTS 16:25A

But about midnight Paul and Silas were praying and singing hymns of praise to God.

1 CORINTHIANS 14:26

What is *the outcome* then, brethren? When you assemble, each one has a psalm, has a teaching, has a revelation, has a tongue, has an interpretation. Let all things be done for edification.

EPHESIANS 5:19

Speaking to one another in psalms and hymns and spiritual songs, singing and making melody with your heart to the Lord.

COLOSSIANS 3:16

Let the word of Christ richly dwell within you, with all wisdom teaching and admonishing one another with psalms *and* hymns *and* spiritual songs, singing with thankfulness in your hearts to God.

Scripture Reading and Preaching the Word

1 TIMOTHY 4:13

Until I come, give attention to the *public* reading *of Scripture*, to exhortation and teaching.

2 TIMOTHY 4:2

Preach the word; be ready in season *and* out of season; reprove, rebuke, exhort, with great patience and instruction.

Giving

---

1 CORINTHIANS 16:1–2

Now concerning the collection for the saints, as I directed the churches of Galatia, so do you also. [2] On the first day of every week each one of you is to put aside and save, as he may prosper, so that no collections be made when I come.

2 CORINTHIANS 9:6–7

Now this *I say*, he who sows sparingly will also reap sparingly, and he who sows bountifully will also reap bountifully. [7] Each one *must do* just as he has purposed in his heart, not grudgingly or under compulsion, for God loves a cheerful giver.

The clear intention in these texts is that these functions are to take place in a regular, orderly, and consistent way with an identifiable group of people who assemble regularly to carry out these functions.

---

1. The notion that the church has replaced the nation of Israel in terms of the inheritance of the Old Testament covenant promises is called *supersessionism*. For a full refutation of supersessionism, see Michael J. Vlach, *Has the Church Replaced Israel?: A Theological Evaluation* (Nashville, TN: B&H Academic, 2010).

2. See S. Lewis Johnson Jr., "Paul and 'the Israel of God': An Exegetical and Eschatological Case-Study," in *Essays in Honor of J. Dwight Pentecost*, eds. Stanley D. Toussaint and Charles H. Dyer (Chicago: Moody Publishers, 1986), 181–96.

3. See Harold W. Hoehner, *Ephesians: An Exegetical Commentary* (Grand Rapids, MI: Baker Academic, 2002), 428–34.

4. Ibid., 439–41.

5. Ibid., 448.

6. MacArthur, *Titus*, 18.

7. Ibid., 27–28.

8. See Berkhof, *Systematic Theology*, 576–78.

CHAPTER 10

PROPHECY AND END TIMES

Eschatology

Eschatology is the study of "last things" (Greek *eschatos*, "last") or the study of biblical prophecy.

THE ORDER OF FUTURE EVENTS

Rapture of the Church

> **JOHN 14:1–4**
>
> "Do not let your heart be troubled; believe in God, believe also in Me. ² In My Father's house are many dwelling places; if it were not so, I would have told you; for I go to prepare a place for you. ³ If I go and prepare a place for you, I will come again and receive you to Myself, that where I am, *there* you may be also. ⁴ And you know the way where I am going."

On the evening that He was betrayed, Jesus gathered with His disciples in the upper room to celebrate the Passover (see Matt. 26:17–19; Mark 14:15). The hour of His passion was at hand—the hour when He "would depart out of this world to the Father" (see John 13:1). In order to prepare them for His departure, He delivered the so-called "Farewell Discourse"—John chapters 14, 15, 16. He knew ahead of time what these men would face (and how they would react) between the time of His arrest and His resurrection. So

He began this discourse with words of comfort and hope. He sought to allay their fears ("Do not let your heart be troubled") and to strengthen their faith in God and in Himself. And then He pointed them to a promise that was intended to assure them of their ultimate hope.

This promise was actually explained on the basis of a metaphor that would have been quite familiar to the disciples. When Jesus spoke of going to His Father's house, of preparing a dwelling place, and of returning to receive the disciples, He had in mind the wedding customs of that day. These customs can be seen in several places in the New Testament, for instance in the parable of the ten virgins in Matthew 25:1–12, where the virgins are waiting for the bridegroom to return for the bride. In that day a couple would first be "betrothed" to each other (e.g., the relationship of Joseph and Mary, see Matt. 1:18). This was something more than an engagement, it was a legal bonding; but it was less than a complete state of marital union. It was during this betrothal period that the bridegroom would prepare the home the couple would live in; typically, this would be in a part of his father's estate. During this time the bride would prepare herself for her husband. (This is the image Paul uses in Ephesians 5:27 in the comparison of Christ and the church to that of a man and wife. Only in this instance it is Christ preparing His bride—"that He might present to Himself the church in all her glory, having no spot or wrinkle or any such thing; but that she would be holy and blameless"—rather than the bride preparing herself.) After the bridegroom has prepared a place, he would return to the home of his betrothed and take her home to his house. At that time there would be a joyous celebration with food and drink (see John 2:1–10—the scene at the wedding at Cana).

This is the picture behind the promise Jesus is giving to the disciples. It is a promise that He will: (1) return, "come again" (Greek *palin erchomai*) and (2) receive or take them (Greek *paralēmpsomai*; from *paralambanō*; see this verb in Matthew 2:14 where Joseph "took the Child" Jesus to Egypt). The scene being imagined here is not that of Jesus returning *with* the redeemed to establish His kingdom (as in Rev. 19:11–15) but *for* His own, His bride to take them to Himself. It seems obvious that this receiving or taking would be to the place He had prepared, which would be where He would reside with them—bridegroom and bride. Since the church is compared to a bride (see Eph. 5:22–27; see 2 Cor. 11:2; Rev. 19:7) and Christ to a husband, this promise may be extended to the whole church, of which these disciples are representative. This is a picture of the Rapture of the church. In 1 Corinthians 15:50–52 Paul continues to use the bride/bridegroom metaphor and provide more details of this "blessed hope" (Titus 2:13).

> **1 CORINTHIANS 15:50–52**
>
> Now I say this, brethren, that flesh and blood cannot inherit the kingdom of God; nor does the perishable inherit the imperishable. [51] Behold, I tell you a mystery; we will not all sleep, but we will all be changed, [52] in a moment, in the twinkling of an eye, at the last trumpet; for the trumpet will sound, and the dead will be raised imperishable, and we will be changed.

> **1 THESSALONIANS 1:10**
>
> And to wait for His Son from heaven, whom He raised from the dead, *that is* Jesus, who rescues us from the wrath to come.

> **1 THESSALONIANS 4:13–18**
>
> But we do not want you to be uninformed, brethren, about those who are asleep, so that you will not grieve as do the rest who have no hope. [14] For if we believe that Jesus died and rose again, even so God will bring with Him those who have fallen asleep in Jesus. [15] For this we say to you by the word of the Lord, that we who are alive and remain until the coming of the Lord, will not precede those who have fallen asleep. [16] For the Lord Himself will descend from heaven with a shout, with the voice of *the* archangel and with the trumpet of God, and the dead in Christ will rise first. [17] Then we who are alive and remain will be caught up together with them in the clouds to meet the Lord in the air, and so we shall always be with the Lord. [18] Therefore comfort one another with these words.

Even though Paul was with the Thessalonians for a relatively short time, he taught them about the end time events and the coming of the Lord Jesus Christ.[1] In the interim between that ministry and the visit of Timothy (see 1 Thess. 3:2, 5) some of the believers had died and the church was enduring persecution. The first of these circumstances caused some to think their loved ones had missed the Lord's return for His bride, the Church (see John 14:1–3; Eph. 5:27). It should be noted that this question would only arise if Paul had taught the Thessalonians that the coming of the Lord was "imminent," that is, that it could happen at any moment. If Paul had taught them that the church would go through the tribulation, the death of some saints and the persecution they were experiencing would not be problematic but expected.

1 Thessalonians 4:13–18 is the main passage pertaining to the gathering of the saints—the supernatural event of the "catching away" or "rapture" of the church. It is important to note that Paul's purpose here was pastoral. It was meant to inform and comfort the brethren so that they "will not grieve" the loss of loved ones as the world grieves. They were to have hope. The ground of this hope is the death (securing atonement; see 1 Peter 2:21–25; Isa. 53) and resurrection (confirming that justification of Jesus; see Rom. 4:25) of Jesus. Paul assured them that those loved ones were only "asleep." This was a euphemism for death (used three times) that held out the promise of an awakening. Those believers who are "asleep in Jesus" were not lost and gone forever but they are "with the Lord" (see 2 Cor. 5:8). It is clear that Paul thought of the state of believers who have died as both "asleep" (this pertains to their bodies) and as being conscious in the presence of the Lord. This denies any thought of "soul sleep." Furthermore, this helps to explain how these deceased ones can both return with Him (1 Thess. 4:14) and also "rise first" (1 Thess. 4:16).

Next, Paul explains how the event of the "catching away" was to unfold; there will be a series of distinctive steps in 1 Thessalonians 4:15–17. He introduces the details of the sequence by affirming that his teaching is grounded in the teaching of Christ (see the comments on Matt. 24:36ff). The Thessalonians can be confident of what Paul teaches since this is "by the word of the Lord." (This may indicate some traditional teaching of Jesus not preserved in the gospel record or some direct revelation to Paul.) Paul then delivers the clearest teaching on the "rapture" of the church to be found in the New Testament—he deals with the persons involved, the plan of the event, and the point of his teaching. The "rapture" is so called based on the Latin text of this passage, which uses a form of the word *rapio* ("to seize," "to carry off violently"), which is used to translate the Greek term *harpazō* in verse 17. The persons involved are identified in two groups. First, there are those who are "asleep in Jesus" (1 Thess. 4:14), also identified as "the dead in Christ" (1 Thess. 4:16). That is, they are deceased believers. Also involved are living believers who are identified twice as "we who are alive and remain" (1 Thess. 4:15, 17). Paul has in mind all those who are New Testament believers, in Christ (1 Thess. 4:16), i.e., Christians, members of the church, both deceased and living. Paul is keen to make the point that the living church members are not given preferential treatment over the deceased. Indeed, Christ will bring the living souls of those who died in Him to be reunited with their resurrected bodies (see 1 Cor. 15:51–58)—none are lost.

Paul includes himself with those who are alive and remain (we); this indicates that Paul believed the rapture could occur in his lifetime—indeed, that it could occur at any time; for him it was an imminent possibility. Paul identifies the Lord as Jesus, Christ, and the Lord Himself as the agent performing this work; this is in contrast to the event described in Matthew 24:31 where, at the Second Coming, the angels will "gather together His elect"—thus, there are two distinct events associated with the *parousia*—the rapture and the second coming (or "revelation") of Christ.

The sequence of events associated with the rapture of believers will begin when "the Lord Himself" descends (1 Thess. 4:16; see Acts 1:11; John 14:1–3) from heaven. Then there will occur three distinct sounds: first "a shout" (like a military "command"), second, "the voice of the archangel" (the only archangel named in the Bible is Michael, see Dan. 12:1–3; Jude 9), and third, "the trumpet of God" (see 1 Cor. 15:52). The exact nature of these sounds is unclear, but apparently the purpose is to summon believers and signal that the blessed hope (see Titus 2:13) is about to be realized. Next, the souls of the "dead in Christ" are reunited with their resurrected bodies. At death, the believer's immaterial nature (his soul) goes into the presence of the Lord consciously and enjoys that presence (see Phil. 1:21, 23). But the Bible does not teach the immortality of the soul alone. It teaches the immortality *of the entire person*, body and soul. At the rapture of the Church, the soul of the believer will be joined once again to the Christian's resurrected body, and eternity will be experienced in this mode. Then, living believers will be "caught up" along with those resurrected saints. The nature of the event is indicated by the Greek term *harpazō* which means "to seize suddenly" or simply to "take away" (see on John 14:3 above). The term is used to describe a "taking by force," or "snatching away" (see Matt. 11:12; John 10:12; Acts 8:39). The location of the event is described as "in the clouds" and "in the air" (1 Thess. 4:17b; see Acts 1:9).

It has often been suggested that the Greek term *apantasis* ("to meet") has a "technical meaning" pertaining to a specific type of meeting—that of a delegation from a city with a visiting dignitary. However, the uses of this term in Matthew 25:6, 10 in the Parable of the Ten Virgins and in Acts 28:15 describing Paul's reception by the Christians in Rome do not support this supposed "technical meaning." Two metaphors have been proposed to describe the event. The first is that of a "visiting dignitary" wherein a group of city folk, officials and such, go out to greet an honored guest or conquering hero and return to the city. In this view, when Jesus comes the saints rise to greet Him and He returns with them to earth. The second metaphor is that of a bridegroom, coming to retrieve his bride. As such, this would be seen as the fulfillment of His promise in John 14:1–3 to come and retrieve His bride to take her to His Father's house where the wedding feast will complete the formal union of marriage (see Rev. 19:7–9). The first view imports a metaphor that is not found anywhere else to describe Christ's relationship with His church. The second view incorporates several other key texts (see John 14:1–3; Eph. 5:27; Rev. 19:7–9 see **Marriage Supper of the Lamb**) and provides a richer explanation of the event, using a recognized New Testament metaphor—Bride/church and Bridegroom/Christ.

The outcome of the event is a blessed promise—"so we shall always be with the Lord"—which is exactly what Jesus promised His disciples in John 14:1–3, which is the first text that revealed the promise of the rapture. Paul concluded with a message of comfort that was intended to give peace and hope to the church (see 1 Thess. 4:18).

EXCURSUS: Timing of the Rapture

The arguments that this event comes before the tribulation are: One, Paul has already promised the Thessalonians that Jesus "rescues us from the wrath to come" (1 Thess. 1:10); this is "wrath" that the believer will miss and the unbeliever will face (see 1 Thess. 2:16); this is best understood as the "wrath of the Lamb" (see Rev. 6:16)—the eschatological wrath that will come at the time of the Tribulation. Two, the Tribulation is the Seventieth Week of Daniel (see Dan. 9:24–27)—the time concerning Daniel's people and Jerusalem (Dan. 9:24a), the "time of Jacob's distress" (Jer. 30:7)—a time with a distinctly "Jewish character" as Jesus describes it in Matthew 24—a time of judgment on "the nations" of the earth and the "nation" of Israel, hence, the church's presence is not in keeping with the purpose of the tribulation (see **Tribulation**). Three, in 1 Thessalonians 4 and in other passages in the New Testament (e.g., Rom. 13:11–12; Titus 2:13; see James. 5:7, 8), it is clear that the apostle believed that he might be among those who would be "caught up," that is, he placed himself among those who were the "we who are alive and remain." He believed the return of the Lord was "imminent," that is, that it could happen at any time. Obviously, the signs, the "birth pangs" (see Matt. 24:8) which announce the beginning of the Tribulation, cannot come before the rapture if the rapture can happen "at any moment." Four, the event described in Matthew 24:29–31—the Second Coming (proper)—is not the same event as the one described in 1 Thessalonians 4:13–18. In 1 Thessalonians 4:13–18 it is the Lord Himself who comes to take His own to Himself (see 1 Thess. 4:16), however in Matthew 24:31 it is the task of elect angels to gather the elect. Also, based on other texts that describe the Second Coming (proper) (see Joel 2:12–16; Zech. 14:1–5; Rev. 19:11–21) there are significant differences between the two events. For instance, at the rapture He comes "in the air" (1 Thess. 4:17) but according to Zechariah 14:1–5 He comes all the way to the Mount of Olives. At the rapture the prospect is comfort (see 1 Thess. 4:18) and fellowship with the Lord, but at the Second Coming (proper) the prospect is judgment (see Matt. 24:36–41; Rev. 19:11–21).

> **REVELATION 3:10**
>
> "Because you have kept the word of My perseverance, I also will keep you from the hour of testing, that *hour* which is about to come upon the whole world, to test those who dwell on the earth."

The promise made by Christ to the church in Philadelphia may be taken as a promise to the church at large. It is a promise that the church will not go through the tribulation. This interpretation turns on identifying "the hour of testing" and the meaning of the phrase "keep you from."

While the term *hour* (Greek *horas*) may refer to an undefined period of time, here, "the hour of testing" is described in terms that indicate that it is a specific time, an exact time. It is a time yet future from the time of this letter ("is about to come"). It is not a local time but one that is coming "upon the whole world" and involving all "those who dwell on the earth." This would indicate that it is a worldwide event, not a localized persecution of the church in Philadelphia. It is a time of "testing" or trial (Greek *peirasmou*) and this testing is not for the church but is for and about the inhabitants of the earth. So what time or event or circumstance is in view here? The best answer is that this is the seven-year tribulation period (see Dan. 9:27; Matt. 24:9, 21).

What does Jesus mean by the expression "keep you from"? The term for *keep* (Greek *tereo*) is from the same root as the term *kept* (Greek *eteresas*) used twice already in this letter (see Rev. 3:8, 10). The Philadelphians have "kept My word," so He will "keep" them. Specifically, He says He will keep them *from* that hour. The Greek term "from" is the Greek preposition *ek* and is used more than 800 times in the New Testament in the sense of "from out of," or "out from."

Some interpreters suggest that the "out from" means simply "kept from" (the judgments and cataclysm of that period) in the sense of "kept through," but not subject to the judgments of, the tribulation. Others suggest that the church will go through part of the tribulation (perhaps suffer some as well) but the church will be "spared from" the "wrath-full" parts of the tribulation—"kept through the tribulation but 'spared from' God's wrath." But the

Greek expression *tereso ek* simply does not mean "kept through but from" nor "spared from." It means "kept out-from," or "away-from." This is a promise that the church will not go into, but be kept out of, the tribulation. While this promise does not speak directly of the Rapture, it does describe the result of or effect of the Rapture, namely, the church is not going to be in the tribulation.

Bema Seat Judgment

ROMANS 14:12
So then each one of us will give an account of himself to God.

1 CORINTHIANS 3:12–13
Now if any man builds on the foundation with gold, silver, precious stones, wood, hay, straw, [13] each man's work will become evident; for the day will show it because it is *to be* revealed with fire, and the fire itself will test the quality of each man's work.

2 CORINTHIANS 5:10
For we must all appear before the judgment seat of Christ, so that each one may be recompensed for his deeds in the body, according to what he has done, whether good or bad.

When Paul refers to the "judgment seat" (Greek *bema*), he likely has in mind an image taken from Greek Olympic style games. In those games the winners of the various contests would be presented at a raised platform (Greek *bema*) to receive their awards. Paul envisions such a scene to depict the time when Jesus will give rewards to Christians. This is not a judgment of salvation or eternal destiny because the ones being judged are Christians (who are assured of their salvation; see **Assurance and Perseverance**) and Paul includes himself ("So then each one of us") in this judgment. It is a judgment of their "deeds in the body" (i.e., in their own physical bodies) and as such it is a test of "the quality of each man's work" to determine if it is "good or bad," that is, of lasting value or is worthless and vain.

Marriage Supper of the Lamb

> **REVELATION 19:7–9**
>
> "Let us rejoice and be glad and give the glory to Him, for the marriage of the Lamb has come and His bride has made herself ready." [8] It was given to her to clothe herself in fine linen, bright *and* clean; for the fine linen is the righteous acts of the saints. [9] Then he said to me, "Write, 'Blessed are those who are invited to the marriage supper of the Lamb.'" And he said to me, "These are true words of God."

The Marriage Supper of the Lamb is the final phase of the experience of the Bride of Christ, the church. That experience began with a betrothal and promise (see John 14:1–3), continued through the time of preparation of the Bride (see Eph. 5:26–27), will come to the time of retrieval at the Rapture of the church (see 1 Thess. 4:13–18; see **Rapture of the Church**) and will culminate in this festive celebration of union.

Tribulation

The very terms used of the period of time known as "the tribulation" are indicative of the nature and purpose of the tribulation.

TERMS USED FOR THE TRIBULATION

The Time of Jacob's Distress

> **JEREMIAH 30:7**
>
> "Alas! for that day is great,
> There is none like it;
> And it is the time of Jacob's distress,
> But he will be saved from it."

This verse reveals that the tribulation is a time specifically for the nation of Israel. The name "Jacob" is a conventional way for Old Testament writers to refer to the nation of Israel (see Gen. 35:10; see Ps. 53:6; 78:5). It also reveals that it will be a time of "distress" and it will be unprecedented ("none like it"). "Designated here as 'the time of Jacob's trouble,' this period is shown to be characterized especially by trouble for Israel. The nature of the trouble is not identified in this verse, but its fact is made clear."[2]

The Day of the LORD

> **JOEL 2:1**
>
> Blow a trumpet in Zion,
> And sound an alarm on My holy mountain!
> Let all the inhabitants of the land tremble,
> For the day of the LORD is coming;
> Surely it is near.

> **1 THESSALONIANS 5:1–2**
>
> Now as to the times and the epochs, brethren, you have no need of anything to be written to you. ² For you yourselves know full well that the day of the Lord will come just like a thief in the night.

The theme of the Day of the Lord occurs repeatedly in both the Old and New Testaments. "It is mentioned explicitly nineteen times in the Old Testament (Isa. 2:12; 13:6, 9; Ezek. 13:5; 30:3; Joel 1:15; 2:1, 11, 31; 3:14; Amos 5:18 [2 times], 20; Obad. 15; Zeph. 1:7, 14 [2 times]; Zech. 14:1; Mal. 4:5) and four times in the New Testament see Acts 2:20; [1 Thess. 5:2], 2 Thess. 2:2; 2 Peter 3:10), and is alluded to in other passages (see Rev. 6:17; 16:14). It will be the time when God pours out His fury on the wicked; in fact, Scripture three times calls the Day of the Lord the 'day of vengeance' (Isa. 34:8; 61:2; 63:4)."[3]

The Great Tribulation

> **MATTHEW 24:21**
>
> "For then there will be a great tribulation, such as has not occurred since the beginning of the world until now, nor ever will."

The terms "great tribulation" (Greek *megalē thlipsis*) express the magnitude and anguish of the tribulation period. The term *tribulation* (Greek *thlipsis*) denotes "pressure," "affliction," "distress," and "trouble." In Matthew 24 it is clear that this trouble is to come on the nation and people of Israel ("those who are in Judea," Matt. 24:16; see Jer. 30:7). "The first purpose of the tribulation is to bring about the conversion of Israel, which will be accomplished through God's disciplinary dealing with His people Israel (Jer. 30:7; Ezek. 20:37; Dan. 12:1; Zech. 13:8–9). The second purpose of the tribulation is to judge unbelieving people and nations (Isa. 26:21; Jer. 25:32–33; 2 Thess. 2:12)."[4]

The Seventieth Week of Daniel

DANIEL 9:24–27

"Seventy weeks have been decreed for your people and your holy city, to finish the transgression, to make an end of sin, to make atonement for iniquity, to bring in everlasting righteousness, to seal up vision and prophecy and to anoint the most holy *place*. [25] So you are to know and discern *that* from the issuing of a decree to restore and rebuild Jerusalem until Messiah the Prince *there will be* seven weeks and sixty-two weeks; it will be built again, with plaza and moat, even in times of distress. [26] Then after the sixty-two weeks the Messiah will be cut off and have nothing, and the people of the prince who is to come will destroy the city and the sanctuary. And its end *will come* with a flood; even to the end there will be war; desolations are determined. [27] And he will make a firm covenant with the many for one week, but in the middle of the week he will put a stop to sacrifice and grain offering; and on the wing of abominations *will come* one who makes desolate, even until a complete destruction, one that is decreed, is poured out on the one who makes desolate."

It would be difficult to exaggerate the significance of this prophecy.[5] Many would argue that this is the key text not only for understanding key aspects regarding the person and work of the Messiah but for comprehending the whole of Yahweh's unfolding program for His chosen nation, Israel.

This prophecy is part of the series of prophetic texts in Daniel that outline the course of world history in his day and beyond. The dreams (see Dan. 2) and visions (see Dan. 7, 8, 10, et. al.) have to do with the unfolding program of God for *the nations* (the pagan nations and empires that are the main concern of "world history") and *the Nation*—Israel, the people of Daniel (9:24; 12:1), "Your people [who] are called by Your name" (9:19). After reading the book of Jeremiah, Daniel realized the time of the Nation's captivity would soon be at an end (see Dan. 9:2) and he wanted to know where his people (the Jews) fit into the larger future history of the nations. So Daniel prayed. In response to this prayer the angel Gabriel arrived to give Daniel "instruction" and "insight with understanding" (Dan. 9:21–22) about the future of the Nation. This is the prophecy of the seventy weeks in Daniel 9:24–27.

Three questions or issues arise from the very first line, "Seventy weeks have been decreed for your people and your holy city . . ." (Dan. 9:24a).

(1) What is the meaning of a "week"? The Hebrew term translated "weeks" here is *šābu'im* (lit. "sevens") and means "a unit of seven." It frequently means "a week"—as in "a unit of seven days." However, here it must mean a "week" of seven years. This means the time period (seventy weeks of seven years each) is a period of 490 years.

(2) What is the meaning of "have been decreed"? The Hebrew term *ḥatak*, has the basic notion of "to cut off" and from this "to decide, to determine," "to demarcate." The thought is that God demarcated 490 years for the outworking of God's purposes for the Nation of Israel.

(3) Who is being referred to by the designation "your people and your holy city"? This is a reference to Daniel's people—the Jewish people and to the city of Jerusalem.

Next comes a summary of the entire period of the seventy weeks. Gabriel reveals that six objectives would be accomplished over the course of these 70 weeks. These six objectives are listed in two groups of three.

The first objective is "to finish the transgression." The term to *finish* is the Hebrew term *kalah* "to bring to an end, to finish." In the form found here (Piel), it has an intensive nuance—"to finish completely." The term *transgression* is the Hebrew term *peša'* and refers to sin in an all-encompassing sense.

The second objective is "to make an end of sin." The Hebrew term 'to make an end" here (*hātēm*) has the idea of "to seal up" and the term for sin is actually a plural (*hatta'ōt*) and means "missing the mark."

The third objective is "to make atonement for iniquity." The Hebrew verb here is *kapēr*, "to cover" . . . [and] means "to atone, expiate." This is the principal Old Testament word for the idea of "atonement." While there may be some debate about the precise point to the first two objectives, there is no question that this third refers to the Messiah's atoning death for sin on the cross.

The fourth objective is "to bring in everlasting righteousness." The key term here is "everlasting" (Hebrew *'ōlāmîm*) and has the core meaning of "long duration" and can have the nuance of "continuous existence" (see Ps. 78:69 as of the earth; Ps. 148:3–6 as of the heavens). The term *righteousness* (Hebrew *ṣedeq*) denotes a state or quality of something that meets a "recognized standard of rightness" and in Scripture that standard is God Himself (see Isa. 45:24; Jer. 23:6; 33:16). Thus, the righteousness expected will be the manifestation the very holiness of God brought to fruition on the earth in judgment of all His enemies (see Isa. 13–23; Jer. 46–51 and Ezek. 25–32) and blessing for God's people (see Isa. 66); it will not be temporary or sporadic (as had been the case for the nation in its history of good and bad kings) but permanent.

The fifth objective is "to seal up vision and prophecy." The idea of "seal up" (Hebrew *ḥatōm*) is "to affix a seal" as on an official document to indicate a completed transaction (as on a deed, see Jer. 32:10, 11). Here the idea is that there will be a seal on this text of prophecy (see Dan. 12:4; see Isa. 8:16) to indicate that the prophecy was finished. In other words, when these (prophetic) objectives have been fulfilled, there will be a "seal affixed" to officially mark that fact.

The sixth objective is "to anoint the most holy place." The "most holy place" refers to the "holy of holies" in the tabernacle and temple (see Ex. 26:33). The idea of anointing would have been well known to anyone familiar with the rituals and services of the tabernacle (see Ex. 40:9; Lev. 8:10). The single clear implication of this objective is that there will be (as Ezekiel certainly indicates in Ezekiel chapters 38–40) a future millennial temple and a "holy of holies" to anoint.

In summary, it seems best to understand that the first three objectives were fulfilled in principle at Christ's first coming and that all six will be fulfilled completely for the Nation at the time of the return of the Messiah when He sets up the messianic kingdom.

Next, somewhat surprisingly, Gabriel reveals that the seventy weeks will be divided into three unequal portions. An initial seven weeks is followed by another sixty-two weeks (total of 69 weeks) that ends with "Messiah the Prince." Taking the term *weeks* as "weeks of years" (as noted above) yields a period of 49 years plus 434 years for a total of 483 years.

The title "Messiah (Hebrew *māšîaḥ*, 'anointed') the Prince" (Hebrew *nāgîd*, "leader, lead one") clearly refers to Jesus Christ, for the simple reason that no other historical figure fits the description and chronology. The chronology of the seventy weeks begins with the issuing of "a decree to rebuild and restore and rebuild Jerusalem" (*terminus ad quo*) and ends with the time of "Messiah the Prince" (*terminus ad quem*). That decree can be none other than that issued by Artaxerxes Longimanus, on March 5/4, 444 BC, which decree is referenced in Nehemiah 2:1–8. Calculating the years (483) and even days (173,880) from that event shows that the sixty-nine week period ends on March 29/30 (Nisan 10), AD 33, likely the very day of Jesus' triumphal entry (see Luke 19:28–40). The fact that Daniel 9:26 mentions the death of the Messiah (see below) supports this chronology.

Having established the timing of the sixty-nine weeks, Gabriel reveals the climactic events that will follow. The event indicated by the words "the Messiah will be cut off and have nothing" take place at an indistinct time *after*, that is, beyond the sixty-ninth week. Indeed, there is an undeniable pause (or gap) in the strict chronology of the prophecy to this point.

In Daniel 9:26 it is revealed that "the Messiah will be cut off." The Hebrew term here is *kārêt*, "to cut," and is often used to express the act of execution (e.g., Lev. 7:20; Ps. 37:9; Prov. 2:22). The expression "and have nothing" can be rendered "and have no one," that is, the Messiah will be deserted and alone at the time of the "cutting off." There can be no question that this refers to the crucifixion of Jesus—"He was despised and forsaken of men" (Isa. 53:3; see Mark 14:50).

Gabriel now turns to the period *after* the sixty-ninth week but before the seventieth week. The focus is on the city of Jerusalem and the temple. The phrase "the people of the prince to come" (lit. "people of the coming prince") requires very careful analysis. First, the "prince" here is not the same person as "Messiah the Prince" (Dan. 9:25), since Messiah the Prince has already come (and been cut off). The reference to "the prince" is not explained and thus indicates someone who is already familiar to Daniel (and the reader). Most likely this is the "little horn" of Daniel 7:8 (who is later identified as the beast or the Antichrist (see Dan. 7:21; Rev. 13).

However, it is not this prince who comes but "the people of the prince." The prince was identified in the prophecy of Daniel 7:7–8 as coming from the fourth great empire, which is none other than Rome. It was the armies of Rome that destroyed the city of Jerusalem and the sanctuary—the temple—in AD 70. The destruction was swift ("like a flood") and followed by years of war ("even to the end there will be war"). From that time on the Nation of Israel has continually experienced desolations ("desolations are determined"). Since this event happened more than forty years after the death of Jesus, there can likewise be little question that there is a gap of time between the end of the sixty-ninth week and the beginning of the seventieth week.

The divine agent Gabriel then turns Daniel's attention to the final, seventieth week. The prophecy reveals that the events in view will take place during "one week" and the most significant events will begin in the "middle of the week." The chronology revealed here corresponds to the timing Daniel noted in respect to the actions of the "little horn" of the fourth empire (see Dan. 7:25; see Dan. 12:7; see Rev. 12:14).

The key to understanding Gabriel's prophecy is the identity of "he" in Daniel 9:27. As noted, this cannot be "Messiah the Prince" (Dan. 9:25), as he was "cut off." Furthermore, Christ did not commit "the abomination of desolation," nor did Christ make a "firm covenant" with the people. Nothing in Christ's life corresponds to the timing or events indicated in this "one week." However, (as noted above) this chronology fits quite well with that of the "little horn" of chapter 7. And finally, the nearest antecedent (proper noun) of the personal pronoun "he" is found in verse 27, namely "the "prince who is to come." This is the Antichrist.

The Antichrist ("prince who is to come") makes "a firm covenant" of peace and security with the Nation during the first half of the seventieth week. But in the middle of the week he breaks that covenant. He will "put a stop to sacrifice and grain offering" and he will commit an act known as the "abomination of desolation," that is, there will be an "abomination" set up by "one who makes desolate." This is described in Daniel 11:31 and 12:11 (it is something "set up") and Revelation 13:14–15 (it is an "image of the beast," that is, of the Antichrist himself). In Matthew 24:15, Jesus refers to this despicable act as an event that was yet future. Since nothing like this happened in the destruction of Jerusalem by the Romans in AD 70, it seems best to understand that this entire week is still yet future. Jesus gave the title to this time when He referred to it as "a great tribulation."

The Seals, Trumpets, and Bowls / Judgments in the Tribulation

REVELATION 5:1
I saw in the right hand of Him who sat on the throne a book written inside and on the back, sealed up with seven seals.

REVELATION 6:1
Then I saw when the Lamb broke one of the seven seals, and I heard one of the four living creatures saying as with a voice of thunder, "Come."

REVELATION 8:6
And the seven angels who had the seven trumpets prepared themselves to sound them.

> **REVELATION 16:1**
>
> Then I heard a loud voice from the temple, saying to the seven angels, "Go and pour out on the earth the seven bowls of the wrath of God."

The series of judgments that span the entire seven years of the tribulation period describe unprecedented devastation on the earth. These judgments seem to unfold in this way: the first six seals (Rev. 6:1–17) cover a period from the onset of the tribulation into the second half of that period. The seventh seal (Rev. 8:1) unleashes the seven trumpet judgments (Rev. 8:6–11:19) and the seventh trumpet heralds the onset of the seven bowl judgments (Rev. 16:1–21). "The unfolding of the seven seals parallels our Lord's chronology of tribulation events found in His own message in Matthew 24."[6]

The Second Coming, Revelation, or Parousia of Christ

> **MATTHEW 24:30–31**
>
> "And then the sign of the Son of Man will appear in the sky, and then all the tribes of the earth will mourn, and they will see the SON OF MAN COMING ON THE CLOUDS OF THE SKY with power and great glory. [31] And He will send forth His angels with A GREAT TRUMPET and THEY WILL GATHER TOGETHER His elect from the four winds, from one end of the sky to the other."

> **REVELATION 19:11, 16**
>
> And I saw heaven opened, and behold, a white horse, and He who sat on it *is* called Faithful and True, and in righteousness He judges and wages war.... [16] And on His robe and on His thigh He has a name written, "KING OF KINGS, AND LORD OF LORDS."

The Millennial Kingdom

THE BASIS FOR THE MILLENNIAL KINGDOM: THE BIBLICAL COVENANTS

The true foundation for the doctrine of a future, thousand-year kingdom on the earth is to be found in the promises that Yahweh made to the nation of

Israel. Those promises are revealed in the biblical covenants He made with Abraham, David, and the nation (New Covenant) through Jeremiah.

The Abrahamic Covenant

> **GENESIS 12:1–3**
>
> Now the LORD said to Abram,
>> "Go forth from your country,
>> And from your relatives
>> And from your father's house,
>> To the land which I will show you;
>> ² And I will make you a great nation,
>> And I will bless you,
>> And make your name great;
>> And so you shall be a blessing;
>> ³ And I will bless those who bless you,
>> And the one who curses you I will curse.
>> And in you all the families of the earth will be blessed."

The promise Yahweh made to Abraham included the promise of a great name—a promise surely kept as the three great monotheistic religions of Judaism, Christianity, and Islam all honor Abraham's name and memory. It was also promised to Abraham that through him "all the families of the earth will be blessed." This has been fulfilled through his descendent Jesus Christ, the Messiah who is the savior of a people and "a great multitude which no one could count, from every nation and *all* tribes and peoples and tongues" (Rev. 7:9). Most significantly, in terms of the narrative of the Bible, the Lord promised, "I will make you a great nation." A nation requires three elements: *people, constitution,* and *land.* In effect, the (progressive and partial) fulfilling of the promise of "a great nation" is the story line of the Old Testament from Abraham to the time of David. The narrative in the second part of Genesis—up to and following the birth of Abraham's son Isaac, through the story of his grandson Jacob, through the story of his great-grandsons, the twelve sons of Jacob—is part one of the story of fulfillment regarding the *people* of the nation. Part two of that story picks up in Exodus and then moves to the fulfilling of the promise for the provision of a *constitution* through the giving of the Law, which is recorded in Exodus through Deuteronomy. The beginning of the (progressive and partial) fulfillment of the third element of a nation, the *land*, is found in the book of Joshua and continues through the book of Judges. It should be noted that these narratives of fulfillment are never meant to be final and complete. They are partial and look forward to an ultimate and greater fulfillment that only the progress of the story can reveal. Yet, Yahweh's repetition of "I will, I will, I will," speaks to the certainty of the ultimate fulfillment of this promise.

> **GENESIS 15:17–18A**
> It came about when the sun had set, that it was very dark, and behold, *there appeared* a smoking oven and a flaming torch which passed between these pieces. [18] On that day the LORD made a covenant with Abram, saying,
>> "To your descendants I have given this land."

> **GENESIS 17:2, 6–7**
>> "I will establish My covenant between Me and you,
>> And I will multiply you exceedingly."
> [6] "I will make you exceedingly fruitful, and I will make nations of you, and kings will come forth from you. [7] I will establish My covenant between Me and you and your descendants after you throughout their generations for an everlasting covenant, to be God to you and to your descendants after you."

As the promise for the first son who would be the harbinger of the fulfillment of a vast host of descendants was delayed, Abraham asked God for reassurance that these promises will be kept. Yahweh graciously provided Abraham with such a reassurance by making a covenant with him that especially reiterated the promise of the land. The picture of the covenant ceremony (see Gen. 15:9–11, 17) is typical of the covenants that were made between lords and vassals in the ancient Near East. Normally when such covenants were made and ratified, both parties would be required to pass between the pieces of the animals to pledge their fidelity. But in this setting Abraham was given a supernatural sleep ("terror *and* great darkness fell upon him," Gen. 15:12), and God alone passed between the pieces of slain animals in the form of "a smoking oven and a flaming torch." This action was surprising and significant. It meant that the covenant that was made did not obligate Abraham at all, but that all the obligations for the fulfillment of the covenant were taken on by God Himself. It was, from Abraham's perspective, an unconditional promise from God—it was all of grace. Furthermore, the very specificity of the dimensions of the land in verses 17 through 21 is an indication that the fulfillment of this land promise would be literal, physical land. That is, by naming the Canaanite tribes, and therefore the territories of those tribes, and by expressly designating the natural boundaries of the rivers, Yahweh was giving Abraham the precise dimensions of the promised land. Such precision and specificity argues strongly that Yahweh meant, and Abraham understood, that the promise would be fulfilled literally. Simply put, it would make no sense, in fact it would be misleading, to give this level of specificity to Abraham if ultimately the promise was intended to be fulfilled spiritually or figuratively. These exact dimensions of the land have never been completely fulfilled for the nation, leaving the ultimate fulfillment in the future.

The promises of Genesis 12 and 15 were reiterated on occasions of "covenant renewal" in subsequent narrative accounts, as in Genesis 17 (see Gen. 22:16–18; 26:2–5). In Genesis 17 Yahweh particularly emphasized that these covenant promises are "everlasting" (see 1 Chron. 16:16–17; Ps. 105:9–10). The term *everlasting* (Hebrew *'ôlām*) has the notion of "unending perpetuity." Jeremiah tied the perpetuity of God's covenant promises to the nation to the fixity of the motions of celestial bodies (see Jer. 31:35–36). God's promises to the nation are as certain and lasting as are the movements of the sun, moon, and stars that mark out days and seasons.

In summary, the covenant God made with Abraham was unilateral, unconditional, and everlasting. "The Scriptures clearly teach that this is an eternal covenant based on the gracious promises of God. There may be delays, postponements and chastisements, but an eternal covenant cannot, if God cannot deny Himself, be abrogated."[7]

The Davidic Covenant

> **2 SAMUEL 7:11B-13, 16 (SEE PS. 89)**
>
> """The LORD also declares to you that the LORD will make a house
> for you. ¹²When your days are complete and you lie down with your
> fathers, I will raise up your descendant after you, who will come forth
> from you, and I will establish his kingdom. ¹³He shall build a house for
> My name, and I will establish the throne of his kingdom forever. . . .
> ¹⁶Your house and your kingdom shall endure before Me forever; your
> throne shall be established forever."""

> **LUKE 1:32-33**
>
> "He will be great and will be called the Son of the Most High; and
> the Lord God will give Him the throne of His father David; ³³and
> He will reign over the house of Jacob forever, and His kingdom will
> have no end."

> **LUKE 1:69**
>
> "And has raised up a horn of salvation for us
> In the house of David His servant."

The covenant God made with David is based on, and is in effect an extension of, the Abrahamic Covenant. That covenant with the nation through Abraham had already included the prospect of a king for the nation. In Genesis 17:6 God promised Abraham that "kings will come forth from you." In Genesis 49:10 Jacob referred to a scepter for the tribe of Judah. Since a scepter is a symbol of royal authority, it is clear that Jacob anticipated that at some point there would be a king for the nation. When it was clear that God's choice for the kingship was not Saul but David (see 1 Sam. 16), and David had established his regency over the whole nation (see 2 Sam. 5), the stage was set for Yahweh to establish another covenant, a covenant with David. The establishment and outworking of this covenant in the nation's history would advance the biblical narrative.

Two major promises are given to David; the first was that David will have a "house" or dynasty. He was promised a "seed" (Hebrew *zar'ăkā*:

i.e. progeny), that is, "generations" or "descendants," who would perpetuate his royal line. This was fulfilled (progressively and partially) in the narrative of 1 and 2 Kings (see 1 and 2 Chron.). A significant feature of this promise is that it centers on one unique son of David. To this son the Yahweh says, "I will be a father to him and he will be a son to Me." The "son" that is in view in parts of this promise must be Solomon, for some of the provisions would apply only to a "son" who would need reproof and discipline. But in other parts of this promise the reference to "the son" must apply to a greater son of David who will come from David to establish an enduring, lasting kingdom. This king is the Messiah, Jesus Christ (see Luke 1:32–33; 69).

The second major promise is that this greater son would be given a throne. A "throne" is indicative of the "regency, rule" of this son of David. This throne would be everlasting: "I will establish the throne of his kingdom forever," "So I will establish his descendants forever, And his throne as the days of heaven." Here is another reason why the promises regarding David's son cannot have been fulfilled in Solomon for Solomon's throne did not last forever. The covenant promise made to David will be fulfilled in the millennial and everlasting kingdom of David's greater son, the Messiah, Jesus Christ.

The New Covenant

EZEKIEL 36:24–28

"For I will take you from the nations, gather you from all the lands and bring you into your own land. [25] Then I will sprinkle clean water on you, and you will be clean; I will cleanse you from all your filthiness and from all your idols. [26] Moreover, I will give you a new heart and put a new spirit within you; and I will remove the heart of stone from your flesh and give you a heart of flesh. [27] I will put My Spirit within you and cause you to walk in My statutes, and you will be careful to observe My ordinances. [28] You will live in the land that I gave to your forefathers; so you will be My people, and I will be your God."

JEREMIAH 31:27–28, 31–34

"Behold, days are coming," declares the LORD, "when I will sow the house of Israel and the house of Judah with the seed of man and with the seed of beast. [28] As I have watched over them to pluck up, to break down, to overthrow, to destroy and to bring disaster, so I will watch over them to build and to plant," declares the LORD. . . . [31] "Behold, days are coming," declares the LORD, "when I will make a new covenant with the house of Israel and with the house of Judah, [32] not like the covenant which I made with their fathers in the day I took them by the hand to bring them out of the land of Egypt, My covenant which they broke, although I was a husband to them," declares the LORD. [33] "But this is the covenant which I will make with the house of Israel after those days," declares the LORD, "I will put My law within them and on their heart I will write it; and I will be their God, and they shall be My people. [34] They will not teach again, each man his neighbor and each man his brother, saying, 'Know the LORD,' for they will all know Me, from the least of them to the greatest of them," declares the LORD, "for I will forgive their iniquity, and their sin I will remember no more."

ROMANS 11:26–27

And so all Israel shall be saved: as it is written,

"THE DELIVERER WILL COME FROM ZION,

HE WILL REMOVE UNGODLINESS FROM JACOB."

"THIS IS MY COVENANT WITH THEM,

WHEN I TAKE AWAY THEIR SINS."

Jeremiah 31 is the great chapter of the New Covenant. It speaks of a promise of salvation and forgiveness (esp. Jer. 31:31–34). But this promise is made to the nation of Israel ("the house of Israel and with the house of Judah") and is embedded in the promise of restoration and rebuilding of Jerusalem (see Jer. 31:1–5, 38–40). It seems the prophet expected the full fruition of this New Covenant to take place in a literal, rebuilt, and reinhabited Jerusalem. As with the other covenants, there was partial fulfillment of the New Covenant at Christ's first coming, when He brought about the promise of salvation and forgiveness through the cross. That part of the promise was extended in grace to Gentiles (see Rom. 11). But the ultimate fulfillment of this covenant will happen only when national Israel experiences that promise of salvation and forgiveness, and is restored, in faith, to the city of the promise—Jerusalem.

In summary, it is clear that the covenant promises to Abraham, David, and the nation (in the new covenant) are certain, unconditional, irrevocable (see Rom. 11:29), and everlasting in nature. Those promises of the nation, the people, the land, a throne, and a fully restored Jerusalem have never been completely fulfilled. Faith in those promises looks forward to a time when these promises will be literally and completely fulfilled, and that time will be the millennial kingdom.

EXCURSUS: Millennial Views

Typically, the several millennial views are labelled with reference to the second coming of the Lord Jesus Christ. Thus premillennialism (see previous section) holds that Christ returns before ("pre") the millennial kingdom, and postmillennialism holds that Christ returns after ("post") the millennial kingdom. The postmillennial view anticipates a long period of gradual improvement of the world (through gospel preaching and the influence of the Christian church and Christian civilization) after which Christ returns.

The other major view, amillennialism, holds that the kingdom is a spiritual kingdom. Some amillennial theologians say this began with the heavenly reign of Christ at the ascension, and thus there will be no (using the "a" in a negative way) distinct, earthly, and physical millennium as such. Amillennialism does not hold that the world will gradually improve but rather that the world, under the sway of Satan, will grow worse and worse until Christ returns to judge the world, Satan, and the lost. He will also come to vindicate believers and bring in the new heavens and earth.

While there are several arguments set forth by each view, the differences of these views can be reduced to one question: should the promises made in the biblical covenants (see **The Basis for the Millennial King-**

dom: The Biblical Covenants) be understood as being literally fulfilled or should they be understood as being spiritually or figuratively fulfilled?

In different ways, both amillennialism and postmillennialism hold that the promises in those biblical covenants are to be fulfilled spiritually. "Both views require extraordinary handling of the prophetic passages of Scripture, demanding that the interpreter allegorize or spiritualize the meaning of such texts, rather than employing the same historical and grammatical principles of interpretation we apply to the rest of Scripture."[8] Since the prophesies of Christ that were fulfilled in His first coming (see **Prophecies of the Messiah (Christ)**) were fulfilled literally, and since there was no indication at the time when those prophesies were first given that they were intended to be spiritually or figuratively fulfilled, it seems preferable to hold that the promises in those biblical covenants are to be fulfilled literally. Arguments that the church has inherited those promises in the place of national Israel (see **The Church Is Not Israel**) are unconvincing and require a spiritualizing, or figurative interpretation, of those promises. Only premillennialism expects a literal fulfillment of all of the promises of the biblical covenants. Thus, "if we simply interpret the prophetic passages with the same hermeneutical method we use for the rest of God's Word, premillennialism emerges naturally from the text. A simple, straightforward reading of Revelation 20 will reveal this; its plain ordinary meaning is simply a succinct statement of premillennialism."[9]

THE MILLENNIAL REIGN OF CHRIST

ISAIAH 11:1, 10
Then a shoot will spring from the stem of Jesse,
And a branch from his roots will bear fruit. . . .
[10] Then in that day
The nations will resort to the root of Jesse,
Who will stand as a signal for the peoples;
And His resting place will be glorious.

JEREMIAH 23:5–6

"Behold, *the* days are coming," declares the LORD,
"When I will raise up for David a righteous Branch;
And He will reign as king and act wisely
And do justice and righteousness in the land.
⁶ "In His days Judah will be saved,
And Israel will dwell securely;
And this is His name by which He will be called,
'The LORD our righteousness.'"

REVELATION 20:1–3

Then I saw an angel coming down from heaven, holding the key of the abyss and a great chain in his hand. ² And he laid hold of the dragon, the serpent of old, who is the devil and Satan, and bound him for a thousand years; ³ and he threw him into the abyss, and shut *it* and sealed *it* over him, so that he would not deceive the nations any longer, until the thousand years were completed; after these things he must be released for a short time.

The kingdom that will fulfill the covenant promises is the subject of large portions of the Old Testament and is not an insignificant theme in the New Testament. The king of this kingdom will be the Messiah, the greater son of David (see **The Davidic Covenant**)—the Lord Jesus Christ (see Luke 1:32–33, 69). He is called a "Branch" (*ṣemaḥ* and *nēṣer*), which is a messianic title. He will come from the line of David, confirming His right to this kingship. The conditions of this kingdom will be characterized by peace, security, abundance (see Isa. 11:1–10; Ezek. 32:13–15), justice, and righteousness. It will be a time when the world will thrive under the rule of the Messiah and without the opposition of Satan who will be bound for the duration.

This kingdom is yet future, it will be literally established on the earth with the king residing in Jerusalem (see **The Davidic Covenant**), and it will last for one thousand years. Although, the time of the millennium (lit. "one thousand") is given as a number only in this text, that number is mentioned six times in Revelation 20:1–7. Thus, it seems best to understand that the millennium is a specific time of one thousand years and not a long but indefinite stretch of time.

The Great White Throne Judgment

REVELATION 20:11-12

Then I saw a great white throne and Him who sat upon it, from whose presence earth and heaven fled away, and no place was found for them. [12] And I saw the dead, the great and the small, standing before the throne, and books were opened; and another book was opened, which is *the book* of life; and the dead were judged from the things which were written in the books, according to their deeds.

The "great white throne" is symbolic of the power and purity of the One who sits on it and passes judgment. This is the final judgment of the lost. The "dead, the great and the small" are all those whose names are "not found written in the book of life." The "book of life" is "the record of God's elect (see Dan. 12:1; Mal. 3:16; Luke 10:20; Phil. 4:3; Heb. 12:23) and all whose names are not recorded in it will be eternally damned."[10] This judgment that is passed on the lost is "according to their deeds," that is, it is according to their sinful deeds performed over the course of their lives. No lost persons will escape this judgment for all will be raised to face this judgment, even those who perished at sea and hence were not buried in the ground. "The blessed and holy participants in the first resurrection will not experience the second death ([Rev.] 20:6). But the rest of the dead, who did not participate in the first resurrection ([Rev.] 20:5), will face **the second death**, which is defined here as the **lake of fire**. Those who die in their sins in this present world of time and space will die a **second death** in eternity—they will be sentenced to the **lake of fire** forever."[11]

The New Heavens and New Earth

REVELATION 21:1-2, 10-11

Then I saw a new heaven and a new earth; for the first heaven and the first earth passed away, and there is no longer *any* sea. [2] And I saw the holy city, new Jerusalem, coming down out of heaven from God, made ready as a bride adorned for her husband. . . .
[10] And he carried me away in the Spirit to a great and high mountain, and

> showed me the holy city, Jerusalem, coming down out of heaven from God, [11] having the glory of God. Her brilliance was like a very costly stone, as a stone of crystal-clear jasper.

The "new heaven and a new earth" will be just that—a new planet and a new universe. When the purposes for this present heavens and earth are fulfilled, God will destroy this heavens and earth (see 2 Peter 3:7, 10). "When these have been destroyed, God will call into existence new heavens and new earth. In the eternal kingdom, therefore, these new heavens and earth are not simply a renovation of the old heavens and earth, but are, rather, the result of a definite act of creation. The word *new* (Greek *kainos*) denotes something that is fresh or new in quality but not something that is strange or uniquely different."[12] There will be a genuine connection to the present heavens and earth but the new heavens and the new earth will not be a mere renovation but a re-creation. "This destiny for which believers are headed is no fairy tale and will be as real as the current planet that humanity now inhabits."[13] The descriptions of the brilliance of the "new Jerusalem" are intended to be dazzling and indicative of its brilliance and purity. "Yet for all the beauty of this city, the best part is the presence of God and the Lamb, who are on the throne ([Rev.] 21:3; 22:3). God's servants will worship him and 'will see his face' with eternal, unbroken fellowship ([Rev.] 22:3–4)."[14]

PERSONAL ESCHATOLOGY

Death

The notion of death is not the *cessation* of existence so much as it is a *separation* in three senses.

BODILY DEATH

> **JAMES 2:26A**
> For just as the body without *the* spirit is dead.

The first separation is the spirit from the body at physical death. In this context James is making the argument that a living faith must demonstrate itself by works. He compares faith to a person's body and works to the person's spirit. This comparison assumes his readers will grant that a body is dead when a person's spirit has departed. Furthermore, James's comparison assumes the notion that a person's spirit lives on after the body dies.

> **ECCLESIASTES 12:7**
> Then the dust will return to the earth as it was, and the spirit will return to God who gave it.

When the author of Ecclesiastes refers to "the dust," he means a person's body. In Genesis 3:19b, in the curse laid on Adam by Yahweh, the man was told "For you are dust, And to dust you shall return." Adam's body had been formed from the dust, that is, the inanimate materials of the ground or earth (see Gen. 2:7). The statement "will return to the earth" speaks of the death and decay of a body. On the other hand, the spirit does not die and decay as does the body, but "returns to God." The spirit lives on and faces judgment (see Heb. 9:27) that leads to heaven or hell (see **Heaven** and **Hell**).

SPIRITUAL DEATH

> **EPHESIANS 2:1**
> And you were dead in your trespasses and sins.

> **COLOSSIANS 2:13**
> When you were dead in your transgressions and the uncircumcision of your flesh, He made you alive together with Him, having forgiven us all our transgressions.

The second separation is the separation of the sinner from God. This separation is indicated by expressions such as "dead in your trespasses and sins," and "dead in your transgressions." It is obvious that this does not refer to physical death, for in this death a person is still animated by and actively engaging in sin. The "death" here is an existence in a sphere or realm that is of "this [fallen] world" and under the sway of "the prince of the power of the air" (i.e., Satan; see Eph. 2:2). It is the realm in which, "the desires of the flesh and of the mind" are indulged and it is a realm under the wrath of God (see Eph. 2:3). It is a realm from which those who are by faith united to Christ are delivered by the death, burial, and resurrection of Christ (see Rom. 6:3–7). Those who are in Christ are now no longer dead in this sense but "alive together with Him" (see Col. 2:13; Eph. 2:5; Rom. 6:8–11).

ETERNAL DEATH

> **REVELATION 20:6**
> Blessed and holy is the one who has a part in the first resurrection; over these the second death has no power, but they will be priests of God and of Christ and will reign with Him for a thousand years.

> **2 THESSALONIANS 1:9**
> These will pay the penalty of eternal destruction, away from the presence of the Lord and from the glory of His power.

The third separation is the eternal separation of the unredeemed from God forever. In John 5:29 Jesus referred to two resurrections—one of life and one of judgment. Believers will experience the (first) resurrection of life and will not face "the second death," but unbelievers will experience the resurrection of judgment and they will face "the second death." This "second death" is the eternal conscious existence away "from the presence of God" in the lake of fire (see Rev. 20:14; 21:8; see **Hell**).

Hell

> **MATTHEW 8:11–12**
> "I say to you that many will come from east and west, and recline *at the table* with Abraham, Isaac and Jacob in the kingdom of heaven; [12] but the sons of the kingdom will be cast out into the outer darkness; in that place there will be weeping and gnashing of teeth."

MATTHEW 25:41

"Then He will also say to those on His left, 'Depart from Me, accursed ones, into the eternal fire which has been prepared for the devil and his angels.'"

MATTHEW 25:46

"These will go away into eternal punishment, but the righteous into eternal life."

MARK 9:47–48

"If your eye causes you to stumble, throw it out; it is better for you to enter the kingdom of God with one eye, than, having two eyes, to be cast into hell, [48] where THEIR WORM DOES NOT DIE, AND THE FIRE IS NOT QUENCHED."

REVELATION 20:14–15

Then death and Hades were thrown into the lake of fire. This is the second death, the lake of fire. [15] And if anyone's name was not found written in the book of life, he was thrown into the lake of fire.

The doctrine of hell, the eternal conscious punishment of the unsaved (see **The Great White Throne Judgment**) is not a pleasant notion to contemplate and it is offensive to many. Nevertheless, Scripture clearly teaches that hell exists and is the destiny of the devil (see Rev. 20:10), his demons (see Matt. 25:41) and the lost. Jesus referred to hell more than any other individual in the New Testament. The references to "eternal fire" and "eternal punishment" indicate that the destiny of the lost is as interminable for them as the "eternal life" is for the saved. Thus, the notion that hell is only temporary, or that the lost are ultimately annihilated (made to go out of existence) is not tenable for anyone who takes the Scriptures literally.

Heaven

Scripture repeatedly makes clear that heaven is a realm of unsurpassed joy, unfading glory, undiminished bliss, unlimited delights, and unending pleasures. . . . It will be perfect existence. We will have unbroken fellowship with all heaven's inhabitants. Life there will be devoid of any sorrows, cares, tears, fears, or pain.[15]

MATTHEW 5:12A

"Rejoice and be glad, for your reward in heaven is great."

MATTHEW 6:19–20

"Do not store up for yourselves treasures on earth, where moth and rust destroy, and where thieves break in and steal. [20] But store up for yourselves treasures in heaven, where neither moth nor rust destroys, and where thieves do not break in or steal."

LUKE 23:42–43

And he was saying, "Jesus, remember me when You come in Your kingdom!" [43] And He said to him, "Truly I say to you, today you shall be with Me in Paradise."

JOHN 14:2–4

"In My Father's house are many dwelling places; if it were not so, I would have told you; for I go to prepare a place for you. [3] If I go and prepare a place for you, I will come again and receive you to Myself, that where I am, *there* you may be also. [4] And you know the way where I am going."

HEBREWS 9:24 (SEE ISA. 25:8–12)

For Christ did not enter a holy place made with hands, a *mere* copy of the true one, but into heaven itself, now to appear in the presence of God for us.

REVELATION 21:4

"And He will wipe away every tear from their eyes; and there will no longer be *any* death; there will no longer be *any* mourning, or crying, or pain; the first things have passed away."

In Scripture heaven is depicted as a real place, a place where Jesus Christ is, and a place where believers will be with Him. It is called "Paradise" (Greek *Paradeisō*). This term evokes the restful and serene image of a garden or park, which is meant to convey the idea that heaven is a place of freedom from the stresses and struggles of earthly existence. It is a place with no sorrow, pain, or loss. Best of all, in heaven there is no sin because it is always and everywhere a holy place. Moreover, it is a place of "reward" (Greek *misthos*), or benefits and blessings, for those who have served faithfully and remain faithful to Christ.

---

1. The comments here are drawn from: Kevin D. Zuber, "1 Thessalonians," in *The Moody Bible Commentary*, eds. Michael Rydelnik and Michael Vanlaningham (Chicago: Moody Publishers, 2014), 1877–90.

2. Leon Wood, *The Bible and Future Events: An Introductory Survey of Last-Day Events* (Grand Rapids, MI: Zondervan, 1973), 134.

3. John MacArthur, *The MacArthur New Testament Commentary: I & 2 Thessalonians* (Chicago: Moody Publishers, 2002), 144.

4. Paul Enns, *The Moody Handbook of Theology* (Chicago: Moody Publishers, 2014), 423.

5. These comments are drawn from Kevin D. Zuber, "Daniel 9:24–27: When Will Messiah Come?," in Rydelnik and Blum, *Handbook of Messianic Prophecy*, 1139–52.

6. John MacArthur, *Because the Time Is Near* (Chicago: Moody Publishers, 2007), 125–26.

7. Charles C. Ryrie, *The Basis of the Premillennial Faith* (Neptune, NJ: Loizeaux Brothers, 1953), 53.

8. John F. MacArthur, *The Second Coming: Signs of Christ's Return and the End of the Age* (Wheaton, IL: Crossway Books, 1999), 24.

9. Ibid., 24.

10. John MacArthur, *The MacArthur New Testament Commentary: Revelation 12–22* (Chicago: Moody Publishers, 2000), 254.

11. Ibid., 256.

12. Benware, *Understanding End Times Prophecy*, 340. See W. E. Vine, *An Expository Dictionary of New Testament Words* (Old Tappan, NJ: Fleming H. Revell Company, 1940), 3:109.

13. MacArthur and Mayhue, *Biblical Doctrine*, 913.

14. Ibid.

15. John MacArthur, *The Glory of Heaven: The Truth About Heaven, Angels, and Eternal Life* (Wheaton, IL: Crossway, 2013), 84.

QUESTIONS AND PROMPTS
FOR FURTHER STUDY

QUESTIONS AND PROMPTS FOR PROLEGOMENA

1. Why is the knowledge of God important; how is it helpful; how is it satisfying?
2. Why is sound doctrine necessary and what are the values of sound doctrine?
3. What are the **Key Requirements for Doing Theology**?
4. How does a person's worldview affect his or her theology?

QUESTIONS AND PROMPTS FOR BIBLIOLOGY

1. What are the values and limitations of **General Revelation**?
2. Of the various forms of **Special Revelation** many are not operating today. Why were they used by God in the past?
3. How do **Jesus' Views of Inspiration** inform and support the doctrine of **Plenary Inspiration**?
4. Using the **Descriptions of Soundness and Truth of Scripture**, write a definition of Inerrancy.
5. Write a narrative (story) account of the process of **Canonicity**.

QUESTIONS AND PROMPTS FOR THEOLOGY PROPER

1. Does the Bible offer unbelievers "proofs for the existence of God"? Explain your answer.
2. How do the truths of the **Transcendence** and **Immanence** of God help us to understand what the Bible reveals about God's attributes?
3. Write a definition of God using the **Attributes of God**.
4. Using the **Names of God**, cite several ways these provide us with revelation about His nature and character.
5. Using the list of characteristics of the **Decree of God**, write a definition of the decree.

QUESTIONS AND PROMPTS FOR CHRISTOLOGY

1. What is the value or values of the **Prophecies of Christ** for understanding the **Person of Christ**?
2. What do **Christ's Teaching and Miracles** teach us about His person—Who He is? why He came?
3. Why is the **Name/Title—the Son of God** significant for each of those who used that Name/Title?
4. What is the significance of Jesus' own claims to deity?
5. What is the significance of the apostles' claims to Jesus' deity? Compare the significance of John's and Peter's claims (eyewitnesses of Jesus' ministry) to Paul's claims.
6. What is the significance of Jesus' humanity (with particular attention to how Scripture refers to His true humanity)?
7. What are the **Offices** of Christ and why do we need to know about those offices?
8. Using the terms under **His Death Described**, write a paragraph on what His death means.

QUESTIONS AND PROMPTS FOR PNEUMATOLOGY

1. Using the list of characteristics of personhood given, write a paragraph explaining the true **Personhood of the Holy Spirit**.
2. Using the list of assertions of deity given, write a paragraph explaining the deity of the Holy Spirit.
3. Using the list of attributes of deity given, write a paragraph explaining the deity of the Holy Spirit.
4. How do the items noted in the list of the works of deity given prove that the Spirit is God?
5. Describe the ministry of the Spirit in the Old Testament. How is that ministry unique compared to the ministry of the Spirit in the New Testament?

QUESTIONS AND PROMPTS FOR BIBLICAL ANTHROPOLOGY AND HAMARTIOLOGY

1. What are some implications from the Scripture teaching on the **Image of God** in man?
2. What was the nature of the events recorded in Genesis 3 (historical or fictional) and what are the implications of your answer?
3. What are the arguments for and ramifications of the doctrine of **Original Sin**?
4. What is the significance and what are the implications of the doctrine of **The Depravity and Inability of Man**?

QUESTIONS AND PROMPTS FOR SOTERIOLOGY

1. How does Scripture teach the doctrines of **Election and Predestination**?
2. Define and contrast the two views of **The Extent of Christ's Redemption**.
3. Using **The Elements of the Gospel** and information from the rest of the discussion of Soteriology, write a gospel presentation.
4. How do the **General Call** and **Effectual Call** relate?
5. What is regeneration and how does it fit in the *Ordo Salutis*?
6. Define and relate **Conversion**, **Repentance**, and **Faith**.
7. In one sentence give a complete definition of **Justification** and in one paragraph explain "Justification is . . ."
8. Explain the relationship of God's work and man's work in **Sanctification**.

QUESTIONS AND PROMPTS FOR ANGELOLOGY

1. What is the significance of the revelation concerning angels from Jesus' own references to them and their involvement in His life and ministry?
2. Why is it important to know that both **Satan** and **Demons** exist?
3. What do Isaiah 14 and Ezekiel 28 reveal about the **fall of Satan**? Explain your answer.

QUESTIONS AND PROMPTS FOR ECCLESIOLOGY

1. What is the definition and nature of the **local church**?
2. What is the definition and nature of the **universal church**?
3. What does the New Testament reveal about the order and polity of the church?
4. What do the metaphors of the church reveal about the **nature of the church**?
5. What are the arguments for the distinction between Israel and the church?
6. What are the **Marks of the Church** and the **Functions of the Church**, and how do they inform the practical life of the church?

QUESTIONS AND PROMPTS FOR ESCHATOLOGY

1. What is the overall order of **End Time Events**?
2. Using the scriptural terms for the **Tribulation**, describe the nature and events of that period.
3. What is the significance of the prophecy of the **Seventieth Week of Daniel**?
4. Explain why the biblical covenants virtually require a literal millennial kingdom.
5. What are the three senses of "death" in Scripture?

ACKNOWLEDGMENTS

The idea for this book occurred to me many years ago, but it took the prompting of Dr. Nathan Busenitz, academic dean at The Master's Seminary, for me to think seriously about actually producing something for publication. It was providential that just as Dr. Busenitz was prompting the faculty at TMS to consider publishing, I got a call from my friend and former Moody colleague, Dr. Bryan Litfin, acquisitions editor at Moody Publishers. He asked if I had any writing projects in mind. This book is the outcome of that idea, that prompting, and that inquiry. Bryan was especially helpful in refining the idea into something even better than my original idea, and I want to extend to him my sincere thanks for his patient encouragement and diligence in getting the project completed.

I also want to thank Kevin Mungons, developmental editor, for his expert editorial work and advice, as well as the entire editorial and production staff at Moody Publishers. It was a joy to work with Kevin, a true professional; however, all deficiencies in this work are mine alone.

I want to acknowledge the students I have had the privilege to teach, and the saints in the churches I have been honored to shepherd over the years. Many of the expositional comments in this book were originally conceived and articulated while preparing lectures and sermons.

Of course, I want to give my sincere thanks to Dr. John MacArthur for writing the very gracious foreword. The footnotes in this book provide just a fleeting glimpse of the tremendous influence that Dr. MacArthur's preaching and writing have had on my teaching, my ministry, and my Christian life. It is an immense privilege to be teaching on the campus of the church and at the school where Dr. MacArthur has served for so many years.

Finally, I want to thank my wife, Diane, for her faithful love and support for more than forty-eight years. And thanks to my sons, David and Christopher, for their encouragement and love.

This book is dedicated to my mother who went to be with the Lord in May of 2020.

BIBLIOGRAPHY

Allison, Gregg R. *Historical Theology: An Introduction to Christian Doctrine.* Grand Rapids, MI: Zondervan, 2011.

Anselm. *Proslogion.* Translated by Thomas Williams. Indianapolis, IN: Hackett Publishing Company, 1995.

Bahnsen, Greg L. *Always Ready: Directions for Defending the Faith.* Edited by Robert R. Booth. Nacogdoches, TX: Covenant Media Press, 1996.

———. *Van Til's Apologetic: Readings and Analysis.* Phillipsburg, NJ: P&R Publishing, 1998.

Bavinck, Herman. *Reformed Dogmatics: Holy Spirit, Church, and New Creation.* Edited by John Bolt. Translated by John Vriend. 4 vols. Grand Rapids, MI: Baker Academic, 2006.

Benware, Paul N. *Understanding End Times Prophecy: A Comprehensive Approach.* Chicago: Moody Publishers, 2006.

Berkhof, Louis. *The History of Christian Doctrines.* 1937. Reprint, Grand Rapids, MI: Baker Book House, 1975.

———. *Systematic Theology.* 4th ed. Grand Rapids, MI: William B. Eerdmans Publishing Company, 1939.

Boice, James Montgomery. *The Gospel of Matthew.* 4 vols. Grand Rapids, MI: Baker Books, 2001.

Bradshaw, T. "Process Theology." In *New Dictionary of Theology: Historical and Systematic,* edited by Martin Davie, Tim Grass, Stephen R. Holmes, John McDowell and T. A. Noble, 707–9. Downers Grove, IL: InterVarsity Press, 2016.

Bray, Gerald. *God Is Love: A Biblical and Systematic Theology.* Wheaton, IL: Crossway, 2012.

Bretherton, L. "Blasphemy." In *New Dictionary of Theology: Historical and Systematic,* edited by Martin Davie, Tim Grass, Stephen R. Holmes, John McDowell and T. A. Noble, 125. Downers Grove, IL: InterVarsity Press, 2016.

Calvin, John. *Institutes of the Christian Religion.* Edited by John T. McNeill. Translated by Ford Lewis Battles. 2 vols. 1559. Reprint, Louisville: Westminster John Knox Press, 1960.

Charnock, Stephen. *Discourses upon the Existence and Attributes of God.* 2 vols. 1853. Reprint, Grand Rapids, MI: Baker Books, 1979.

Chou, Abner. "'Did God Really Say?'—Hermeneutics and History in Genesis 3." In *What Happened in the Garden: The Reality and Ramifications of the Creation and Fall of Man,* edited by Abner Chou, 19–46. Grand Rapids, MI: Kregel Academic, 2016.

Culver, Robert Duncan. *Systematic Theology: Biblical and Historical.* Fearn, Scotland: Mentor, 2005.

Dabney, Robert Lewis. *Systematic Theology.* 1871. Reprint, Edinburgh: Banner of Truth, 1985.

Davie, Martin, Tim Grass, Stephen R. Holmes, John McDowell, and T. A. Noble, eds. *New Dictionary of Theology: Historical and Systematic.* Downers Grove, IL: InterVarsity Press, 2016.

Davis, Leo Donald. *The First Seven Ecumenical Councils (325–787): Their History and Theology.* Collegeville, MN: The Liturgical Press, 1983.

Demarest, Bruce. *The Cross and Salvation: The Doctrine of Salvation.* Wheaton, IL: Crossway Books, 1997.

Dickason, C. Fred. *Angels: Elect and Evil.* Chicago: Moody Publishers, 1995.

Dolezal, James E. *All That Is in God: Evangelical Theology and the Challenge of Classical Christian Theism.* Grand Rapids, MI: Reformation Heritage Books, 2017.

Elwell, Walter A., ed. *Evangelical Dictionary of Theology.* 2nd ed. Grand Rapids, MI: Baker Academic, 2001.

Enns, Paul. *The Moody Handbook of Theology.* Chicago: Moody Publishers, 2014.

Erickson, Millard J. *Christian Theology.* Grand Rapids, MI: Baker Academic, 1986.

———. *The Concise Dictionary of Christian Theology.* Rev. ed. Wheaton, IL: Crossway, 2001.

Eveson, Philip H. *The Great Exchange: Justification by Faith Alone.* Leominster, UK: Day One Publications, 1996.

Fee, Gordon D. *The First Epistle to the Corinthians.* Grand Rapids, MI: William B. Eerdmans Publishing Company, 1987.

———. *Pauline Christology: An Exegetical-Theological Study.* Peabody, MA: Hendrickson Publishers, 2007.

————. *Paul's Letter to the Philippians.* Grand Rapids, MI: William B. Eerdmans Publishing Company, 1995.

Feinberg, John S. *No One Like Him: The Doctrine of God.* Wheaton, IL: Crossway, 2001.

Feinberg, Paul D. "Bible, Inerrancy and Infallibility of." In *Evangelical Dictionary of Theology,* edited by Walter A. Elwell, 2nd ed. Grand Rapids, MI: Baker Academic, 2001.

Finkbeiner, David. "Built Upon the Truth: Biblical Authority Yesterday and Today." In *Foundational Faith: Unchangeable Truth for an Ever-Changing World,* edited by John Koessler, 47–80. Chicago: Moody Publishers, 2003.

Frame, John M. *Apologetics to the Glory of God: An Introduction.* Phillipsburg, NJ: P&R Publishing, 1994.

————. *Systematic Theology: An Introduction to Christian Belief.* Phillipsburg, NJ: P&R Publishing, 2013.

Grudem, Wayne. *Systematic Theology: An Introduction to Biblical Doctrine.* Grand Rapids, MI: Zondervan, 1994.

Harris, R. Laird, Gleason L. Archer Jr., and Bruce K. Waltke, eds. *Theological Wordbook of the Old Testament.* 2 vols. Chicago: Moody Publishers, 1980.

Hodge, Charles. *Systematic Theology.* 3 vols. 1871–1873. Reprint, Grand Rapids, MI: William B. Eerdmans Publishing Company, 1975.

Hoekema, Anthony A. *Saved by Grace.* Grand Rapids, MI: William B. Eerdmans Publishing Company, 1989.

Hoehner, Harold W. *Ephesians: An Exegetical Commentary.* Grand Rapids, MI: Baker Academic, 2002.

Hoffecker, W. Andrew, ed. *Revolutions in Worldview: Understanding the Flow of Western Thought.* Phillipsburg, NJ: P&R Publishing, 2007.

Jeffery, Steve, Michael Ovey, and Andrew Sach. *Pierced for Our Transgressions: Rediscovering the Glory of Penal Substitution.* Wheaton, IL: Crossway, 2007.

Johnson Jr., S. Lewis. "Paul and 'the Israel of God': An Exegetical and Eschatological Case-Study." In *Essays in Honor of J. Dwight Pentecost,* edited by Stanley D. Toussaint and Charles H. Dyer, 181–196. Chicago: Moody Publishers, 1986.

Kaiser, Walter C. "The Baptism in the Holy Spirit as the Promise of the Father: A Reformed Perspective." In *Perspectives on Spirit Baptism: Five Views,* edited by

Chad Owen Brand, 15–46. Nashville, TN: B&H Books, 2004.

Kent Jr., Homer A. *The Epistle to the Hebrews: A Commentary.* Winona Lake, IN: BMH Books, 1972.

Köstenberger, Andreas J. "What Does it Mean to Be Filled with the Spirit? A Biblical Investigation." *Journal of the Evangelical Theological Society* (June 1997): 229–240.

Lewis, Gordon R., and Bruce A. Demarest. *Integrative Theology.* 3 vols. Grand Rapids, MI: Zondervan, 1987.

MacArthur, John. *The Battle for the Beginning: Creation, Evolution, and the Bible.* Rev. ed. Nashville, TN: Thomas Nelson, 2005.

———. *Because the Time Is Near.* Chicago: Moody Publishers, 2007.

———. *The Glory of Heaven: The Truth About Heaven, Angels, and Eternal Life.* Wheaton, IL: Crossway, 2013.

———. *The Gospel According to the Apostles: The Role of Works in the Life of Faith.* Nashville, TN: Thomas Nelson, 2000.

———. *The Gospel According to Jesus: What Is Authentic Faith?* Rev. ed. Grand Rapids, MI: Zondervan, 2008.

———. *The MacArthur New Testament Commentary: 1 & 2 Thessalonians.* Chicago: Moody Publishers 2002.

———. *The MacArthur New Testament Commentary: James.* Chicago: Moody Publishers, 1998.

———. *The MacArthur New Testament Commentary: Matthew 1–7.* Chicago: Moody Publishers, 1985.

———. *The MacArthur New Testament Commentary: Matthew 8–15.* Chicago: Moody Publishers, 1987.

———. *The MacArthur New Testament Commentary: Matthew 16–23.* Chicago: Moody Publishers, 1988.

———. *The MacArthur New Testament Commentary: Revelation 12–22.* Chicago: Moody Publishers, 2000.

———. *The MacArthur New Testament Commentary: Romans 1–8.* Chicago: Moody Publishers, 1991.

———. *The MacArthur New Testament Commentary: Titus.* Chicago: Moody Publishers, 1996.

———. *None Other: Discovering the God of the Bible.* Orlando, FL: Reformation Trust Publishing, 2017.

———. *The Second Coming: Signs of Christ's Return and the End of the Age.* Wheaton, IL: Crossway, 1999.

MacArthur, John and Richard Mayhue, eds. *Biblical Doctrine: A Systematic Summary of Bible Truth.* Wheaton, IL: Crossway, 2017.

Martin, Alfred and John Martin. *Isaiah: The Glory of the Messiah.* Chicago: Moody Publishers, 1983.

McCready, Douglas. *He Came Down from Heaven: The Preexistence of Christ and the Christian Faith.* Downers Grove, IL: InterVarsity Press, 2005.

McKnight, Scot. *The Letter to the Colossians.* Grand Rapids, MI: William B. Eerdmans Publishing Company, 2018.

Moo, Douglas J. *The Epistle to the Romans.* Grand Rapids, MI: Willian B. Eerdmans Publishing Company, 1996.

———. *The Letters to the Colossians and to Philemon.* Grand Rapids, MI: William B. Eerdmans Publishing Company, 2008.

Morris, Leon. *The Apostolic Preaching of the Cross.* 3rd ed. Grand Rapids, MI: William B. Eerdmans Publishing Company, 1965.

———. *The Atonement: Its Meaning and Significance.* Downers Grove, IL: InterVarsity Press, 1983.

———. *The Epistle to the Romans.* Grand Rapids, MI: Willian B. Eerdmans Publishing Company, 1988.

Mounce, William D. ed. *Mounce's Complete Expository Dictionary of Old and New Testament Words.* Grand Rapids, MI: Zondervan, 2006.

Murray, John. *Collected Writings of John Murray.* 4 vols. Edinburgh: Banner of Truth, 1977.

———. *Redemption Accomplished and Applied.* 1955. Reprint, Grand Rapids, MI: William B. Eerdmans Publishing Company, 2015.

O'Brien, Peter T. *The Epistle to the Philippians.* Grand Rapids, MI: William B. Eerdmans Publishing Company, 1991.

Oswalt, John. *The Bible Among the Myths: Unique Revelation or Just Ancient Literature?* Grand Rapids, MI: Zondervan, 2009.

Ovey, M. "Ascension [and Heavenly Session of Christ]." In *New Dictionary of Theology: Historical and Systematic*, edited by Martin Davie, Tim Grass, Stephen R. Holmes, John McDowell and T. A. Noble, 66–68. Downers Grove, IL: InterVarsity Press, 2016.

Philips, W. Gary, William E. Brown, and John Stonestreet. *Making Sense of Your World: A Biblical Worldview*. Salem, WI: Sheffield Publishing Company, 2008.

Pink, Arthur W. *The Attributes of God*. 1920. Reprint, Grand Rapids, MI: Guardian, 1975.

Reymond, Robert L. *A New Systematic Theology of the Christian Faith*. Nashville, TN: Thomas Nelson, 1998.

Rydelnik, Michael, and Edwin Blum, eds. *The Moody Handbook of Messianic Prophecy: Studies and Expositions of the Messiah in the Old Testament*. Chicago: Moody Publishers, 2019.

Rydelnik, Michael, and Michael Vanlaningham, eds. *The Moody Bible Commentary*. Chicago: Moody Publishers, 2014.

Ryrie, Charles C. *Basic Theology: A Popular Systematic Guide to Understanding Biblical Truth*. Chicago: Moody Publishers, 1999.

———. *The Basis of the Premillennial Faith*. Neptune, NJ: Loizeaux Brothers, 1953.

Schreiner, Thomas R. "Penal Substitution View." In *The Nature of the Atonement: Four Views*, edited by James Beilby and Paul R. Eddy, 67–116. Downers Grove, IL: InterVarsity Press, 2006.

Shedd, William G. T. *Dogmatic Theology*. 3 vols. 1888. Reprint, Minneapolis: Klock & Klock Christian Publishers, 1979.

Steele, David N., Curtis C. Thomas, and S. Lance Quinn. *The Five Points of Calvinism: Defined, Defended, and Documented*. Phillipsburg, NJ: P&R Publishing, 2004.

Stein, Robert H. *Jesus the Messiah: A Survey of the Life of Christ*. Downers Grove, IL: InterVarsity Press, 1996.

Stigers, Harold G. *A Commentary on Genesis*. Grand Rapids, MI: Zondervan, 1976.

Thiessen, Henry Clarence. *Lectures in Systematic Theology*. Grand Rapids, MI: William B. Eerdmans Publishing Company, 1979.

Tozer, A. W. *The Knowledge of the Holy*. New York: Harper & Brothers, 1961.

Van Til, Cornelius. *Defense of the Faith*. 3rd ed. Philadelphia: P&R Publishing, 1967.

Vine, W. E. *An Expository Dictionary of New Testament Words*. Vol. 3. Old Tappan, NJ: Fleming H. Revell Company, 1940.

Vlach, Michael J. *Has the Church Replaced Israel?: A Theological Evaluation*. Nashville: B&H Academic, 2010.

Wallace, Daniel B. *Granville Sharp's Canon and Its Kin: Semantics and Significance*. New York: Peter Lang Publishing, 2009.

Walvoord, John F. *The Holy Spirit*. Grand Rapids, MI: Zondervan, 1966.

Warfield, Benjamin B. *Biblical and Theological Studies*. Edited by Samuel G. Craig. 1952. Reprint, Philadelphia: P&R Publishing, 1968.

Whitcomb, John C. *The Early Earth: An Introduction to Biblical Creationism*. Grand Rapids, MI: Baker Book House, 1986.

Williamson, G. I. *The Westminster Shorter Catechism*. Phillipsburg, NJ: P&R Publishing, 1970.

Wood, Leon. *The Bible and Future Events: An Introductory Survey of Last-Day Events*. Grand Rapids, MI: Zondervan, 1973.

SCRIPTURE INDEX

SUBJECT INDEX

DIG DEEP INTO THE
WHOLE NEW TESTAMENT!

MACARTHUR NEW TESTAMENT COMMENTARY SERIES

The set includes:

Matthew (4 volumes)
Mark (2 volumes)
Luke (4 volumes)
John (2 volumes)
Acts (2 volumes)
Romans (2 volumes)
1 Corinthians
2 Corinthians

Galatians
Ephesians
Philippians
Colossians & Philemon
1 & 2 Thessalonians
1 Timothy
2 Timothy
Titus

Hebrews
James
1 Peter
2 Peter and Jude
1–3 John
Revelation (2 volumes)
Index

MOODY
Publishers®

From the Word to Life®

This bestselling 34-volume hardcover commentary set features verse-by-verse interpretation and rich application of God's Word. Easy to understand, yet rich in scholarly background.

978-0-8024-1347-5 | also available as an eBook

STUDY THE BIBLE WITH PROFESSORS
FROM MOODY BIBLE INSTITUTE

MOODY
Publishers®

From the Word to Life®

Study the Bible with a team of 30 Moody Bible Institute professors. This in-depth, user-friendly, one-volume commentary will help you better understand and apply God's Word to all of life. Additional study helps include maps, charts, bibliographies for further reading, and a subject and Scripture index.

978-0-8024-2867-7 | also available as an eBook

LOVING GOD MEANS LOVING HIS WORD.

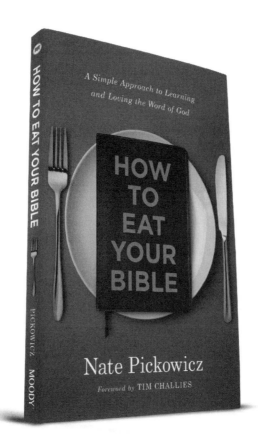

How to Eat Your Bible offers an entry point into Scripture that will help you cultivate an appetite for lifelong study of God's Word. Find practical guidance for overcoming the hurdles that have kept you from making Bible study a regular part of your life.

978-0-8024-2039-8 | also available as eBook and audiobook

THERE IS NO GREATER PURSUIT THAN TO KNOW CHRIST MORE FULLY AND TO LOVE HIM MORE DEEPLY.

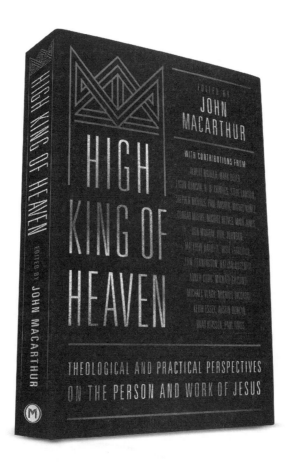